GOVERNING HYBRID ORGANISATIONS

Intuitively, organisations can easily be categorised as 'public' or 'private'. However, this book questions such a black and white dichotomy between public and private, and seeks a deeper understanding of hybrid organisations. These organisations can be found at micro, meso and macro levels of societal activity, consisting of networks between companies, public agencies and other entities. The line between these two realms is increasingly blurred – giving rise to hybrid organisations.

Governing Hybrid Organisations presents an engaging discussion around hybrid organisations, highlighting them as important and fascinating examples of modern institutional diversity. Chapters examine the changing landscape of service delivery and the nature and governance of hybrid organisations, using international examples and cases from different service contexts. The authors put forward a clear analytical framework for understanding hybrid governance, looking at strategy and performance management.

This text will be valuable for students of public management, public administration, business management and organisational studies, and will also be illuminating for practising managers.

Jan-Erik Johanson is Professor of Administrative Science at the Faculty of Management, University of Tampere, Finland, and the Director of the research group on Administrative Science.

Jarmo Vakkuri is Professor of Local Public Economics at the Faculty of Management, University of Tampere, Finland, and the Director of the research group on Public Financial Management.

"Increasingly, the scholarly and practitioner communities recognize the organizational and social significance of hybrid organizations and processes of 'hybridity.' But theory and research have not kept pace with the rapid development of hybrids. Not until now. The authors provide a big step forward in our understanding of the causes, workings and implications of hybrid organizations. Their work is deeply informed by contemporary organization theory but also goes beyond it with a penetrating analysis of the social meaning of these new myth-breaking organizations. The book should be of interest to anyone interested in hybrid organizations . . . or organizations, period."

– **Barry Bozeman, Director**, *Center for Organization Research and Design, Arizona State University, USA*

"Hybrid organisations flourish everywhere. For government agencies, hybridising with private businesses can enrich the capacities of government but also add extra layers of complexity. In this book, Johanson and Vakkuri offer a nuanced interpretation of the governance of hybrids. If you are interested in hybrid organisations, read this book."

– **Irvine Lapsley**, *Professor of Accounting Emeritus, University of Edinburgh, UK*

GOVERNING HYBRID ORGANISATIONS

Exploring Diversity of Institutional Life

Jan-Erik Johanson and Jarmo Vakkuri

LONDON AND NEW YORK

First published 2018
by Routledge
2 Park Square, Milton Park, Abingdon, Oxon OX14 4RN

and by Routledge
711 Third Avenue, New York, NY 10017

Routledge is an imprint of the Taylor & Francis Group, an informa business

© 2018 Jan-Erik Johanson and Jarmo Vakkuri

The right of Jan-Erik Johanson and Jarmo Vakkuri to be identified as authors of this work has been asserted by them in accordance with sections 77 and 78 of the Copyright, Designs and Patents Act 1988.

All rights reserved. No part of this book may be reprinted or reproduced or utilised in any form or by any electronic, mechanical, or other means, now known or hereafter invented, including photocopying and recording, or in any information storage or retrieval system, without permission in writing from the publishers.

Trademark notice: Product or corporate names may be trademarks or registered trademarks, and are used only for identification and explanation without intent to infringe.

British Library Cataloguing-in-Publication Data
A catalogue record for this book is available from the British Library

Library of Congress Cataloging-in-Publication Data
Names: Johanson, Jan-Erik, author. | Vakkuri, Jarmo, author.
Title: Governing hybrid organisations / Jan-Erik Johanson and Jarmo Vakkuri.
Description: Abingdon, Oxon ; New York, NY : Routledge, 2018. | Includes bibliographical references and index.
Identifiers: LCCN 2017012184 | ISBN 9781138655812 (hardback) | ISBN 9781138655829 (pbk.) | ISBN 9781315622293 (ebook)
Subjects: LCSH: Public-private sector cooperation—Management.
Classification: LCC HD3871 .J64 2018 | DDC 658/.046—dc23
LC record available at https://lccn.loc.gov/2017012184

ISBN: 978-1-138-65581-2 (hbk)
ISBN: 978-1-138-65582-9 (pbk)
ISBN: 978-1-315-62229-3 (ebk)

Typeset in Bembo
by Apex CoVantage, LLC

CONTENTS

List of figures vii
List of tables viii
Preface ix
Acknowledgements x

1 Monsters on the run: introduction to governing hybrid organisations 1

Characteristics of hybrids 2
Tricky problems of governance arising 4
Strategy formation: adaptation and change 8
Performance measurement: value creation through profit seeking and evaluation 10
The organisation of this book 12

2 Why do monsters exist? Public, private, and hybrid organisations in perspective 15

Hybrid governance over time 17
The public and private in organisational reasoning 22
Valuation of activities in society 27
Working towards public and private interests 37
Hybrids and hybridity in the context of government reforms 39

3 How to tame monsters: hybridity and its variants 43

Is there more than meets the eye? Hybridity as levels of societal activities 44
Levels of hybridity 45
Meso as a constitutive level of analysis 51

vi Contents

Public policy considerations	57
Hybrids as singular, dyadic, and multilateral structures	59
Making sense of public-private distinctions: the world of classifications	67
The beauty of simplification in distinguishing public from private	76

4 Setting the path for monsters: how do hybrids explore their strategic options and objectives?   **79**

Public agencies and hybrids	81
State-owned enterprises	82
Social enterprises	84
Analytic dimensions	85
Strategic design mode	88
Strategic scanning mode	94
Strategic governance mode	98
Strategy formation in business, public, and hybrid contexts	103

5 Tracing the footprints of monsters: the performative orientation of organisations   **106**

Performance, performativity, and quantification of performance	106
Polysemic performance	109
Performance measurement in private enterprises: in search of relevance	110
Public sector performance: problems and origins of value	112
Performance measurement problems in hybrid organisations	116
A comparison of performance dimensions in three contexts of institutional action	117
Measurement principles applied to hybrid settings	121

6 Chartering the terrain of monsters: exploring strategy-performance interfaces in hybrid activities   **139**

Case illustrations revisited: hybridity through its contexts	140
Strategy-performance constellations in hybrid activities	142
Why and how do hybrids justify their actions? Strategy-performance interfaces as a problem in the justification of hybrid activities	150
Legitimisation through strategy	152
Legitimisation through performance	155

7 Are they monsters after all? Understanding the governance of hybrid organisations   **158**

Where have we come?	158
Governing hybrid organisations revisited	161

References	*169*
Index	*185*

FIGURES

1.1	Exploring hybrid organisations	8
2.1	Four basic types of goods	31
3.1	Analytic perspectives on hybrid governance	44
3.2	Hybridity as singular, dyadic, and triadic structure	59
3.3	Hierarchical classification of institutional units in the System of National Accounts	72
4.1	Three modes of strategy formation	87
5.1	Performance measurement as part of social structures	108
5.2	Elements of economic measurement	122
6.1	Strategy-performance link in hybrid activities	143

TABLES

2.1	Main features in the orders of worth	34
3.1	A hierarchical classification of institutional units in the System of National Accounts	71
4.1	Three modes of strategy formation	87
4.2	Private enterprises, public agencies, and hybrid organisations in the strategic context	104
5.1	Private enterprises, public agencies, and hybrid organisations in the performance context	118
5.2	Performance measurement problems and questions in hybrid organisations: the case of universities	137

PREFACE

Our journey to the world of hybrid organisations has been extremely joyful. As researchers and teachers, our interest in governance, organising, and organisations already had a long history. In this book, we wanted to explore institutional settings that conduct important societal tasks and have significant value for people. However, we were also interested in hybrid organisations because they are highly complicated, and in terms of their activities, they are often incongruent with our previous systems of thinking, research, and institutional practice. For us, hybridity represents a fascinating laboratory of the institutional world where things do not always add up and make sense. What we have learnt, though, is that this is often more associated with our own limitations and understanding of institutional diversity than with hybrid organisations and governance as such. Here, 'our' naturally refers to ourselves as authors, but also to the wider community of research scholars and experts.

One important driver of our book project has been simple intellectual and scientific curiosity. This curiosity has guided us to discuss hybrids and hybridity as a state in between private and public organisations and institutional action. There is something mysteriously intriguing in the messiness and ambiguity of hybrid organisations that facilitated our curiosity during the project. It has also been rewarding to discover that there is actually a plethora of things and topics to explore about hybridity. We have been able to practice our simple method of wondering by asking: Why do we observe such a clear delineation between public and private, how do human beings deal with something that cannot neatly be located in existing institutional categories, and what can we learn from all that to make the institutional world slightly more understandable, sensible, and organised?

ACKNOWLEDGEMENTS

In scientific efforts, you are often able to resort to the guidance of others. We have had the great pleasure of wondering about the organisational world together with several colleagues and research groups in different settings of academia. Furthermore, it has been a privilege for us to collaborate for years with varying types of organisations, decision-makers, and practitioners by discussing problems regarding organising, performances, and strategies in the divergent settings of institutional life.

Several research projects have contributed to this book. These include the Nodehealth project, funded by TEKES (the Finnish Funding Agency for Innovation); the Evaluecreation project funded by TEKES; a project on power in pension policy, funded by the Academy of Finland; ambiguities in public policy making, funded by the Academy of Finland; a European Union Cost program on local public sector reforms (LocRef); and publicly funded services and research on the interface of the public and private sector funded by the University of Tampere.

We have presented papers and ideas, and we have chaired and co-chaired sessions in several academic forums that include the European Group of Public Administration (EGPA), International Research Society for Public Management (IRSPM), European Institute for Advanced Studies in Management (EIASM) workshops, European Group of Organization Studies (EGOS), and Transatlantic Dialogue (TAD). We wish to thank all our colleagues for contributing their valuable insights and for the time that they have invested in the process of wondering with us. Particularly, we want to thank the members and organisers of the Special Interest Group on Accounting and Accountability of the IRSPM organisation. Furthermore, the authors have been involved with several special issues in academic journals, some of which have been complementary to this book. We would like to mention the special issue of *Public Money & Management* titled 'Performance Measurement of Hybrid Organizations.'

Our background is the Northern European tradition and culture. It is, and it should be, something that readers notice. Scientific research is reflected and shaped by the institutional and cultural environment where the scholars come from. However, it has been our conscious intention to address hybridity as a global phenomenon. In fact, the many faces of hybridity are represented in different national contexts and in different continents. We are greatly indebted to our colleagues and students in Asian countries, particularly in Vietnam and China.

We also are grateful to several scholars and individuals for important discussions and scientific debates on hybrid organisations. These include Roland Almqvist, Binh Do Thi Thanh, Päivi Husman, Giuseppe Grossi, Graeme Hodge, Ileana Steccolini, Åge Johnsen, Paul Joyce, James G. March, Christoph Reichard, Matti Skoog, Ville-Pekka Sorsa, Anna Thomasson, Jari Vuori, and Guangjian Xu.

In addition, we would like to extend our gratitude to the Faculty of Management at the University of Tampere. We have enjoyed and benefited from the pleasant research spirit among our faculty. As we are a community of more than 200 people and a learning forum for thousands of students, it is impossible to give personalised thanks. This is why we say thank you to the whole community.

Last, but of course not least, we want to thank our families (Marjo, Julia, and Olivia Vakkuri as well as Eikka, Iina, Rami Johanson, and Laura Tuominen) for their love and understanding.

1
MONSTERS ON THE RUN

Introduction to governing hybrid organisations

This book is about hybrid forms of governance and hybridity in social life. We are particularly interested in the hybridity of organisational and institutional systems, which are used to fulfil some important functions and activities in society that have important value to citizens. On a fundamental level, a sustainable environment is a precondition for human existence. People need to commute from place A to place B. People have ambitions to educate themselves, and societies wish to maintain a sufficient level of health for their citizens. Economic activities and transactions are built upon the premise of undisturbed energy supply. There is no one definite way these necessities should be organised. This book discusses the forms, processes, and mechanisms of organising such activities from a specific viewpoint.

Hybridity is an ambiguous concept. It is very easy to see hybridity everywhere. For us, hybridity refers to an impure existence in between pure types. More specifically, we are interested in the intersection and boundaries between the private and public sector forms of organisations. This is why we discuss hybridity through hybrid forms of governance and hybrid organisations. The problem in naming and categorising objects is that our thought processes imprison us. We lose our ability to think differently. With respect to pursuing important societal goals, it is sometimes difficult to disentangle public organisations and activities from private efforts.

One reason for black-and-white dichotomies of public and private organisations is the normative stance of discussions. The distinction may be indicative of opinions concerning how public and private organisations should be, not how they actually are. People presume social life to include certain properties and virtues that are pertinent to specific modes of organisations, spheres of influence, and institutional actions. It is possible to render this argumentation without actually acknowledging the particulars of organisational action and activities. These arguments are often prescriptions, not descriptions (Van der Wal et al. 2008). One important and intellectually powerful example is the distinction between two syndromes offered by Jane Jacobs: the guardian moral syndrome and the commercial moral syndrome. The guardian moral syndrome refers, to some extent, to obsolete virtues of government activities that respect hierarchy, adhere to traditions, treasure honour, and show fortitude. The commercial moral syndrome is associated with ideal-type morals and the ethics of business activities that evade the use of force and instead encourage competition, efficiency, initiative, and collaboration. Both of these syndromes are necessary to run modern societies. Interestingly enough, a dialogue between Kate and Jasper in Jacobs's book (Jacobs 1992) offers a provocative policy recommendation of not mixing these two completely separate and unrelated domains of social activities. This is because mixing these two syndromes creates new and unexperienced types of moral abysses, functional perversions, corruption, and dysfunctional modes of organisations that are sources of institutional impurity. Jacobs calls these mixed forms monstrous hybrids, which either compromise the neutrality of government or distort the efficiency of business operations.

Our view of hybridity and hybrid organisations is a more sympathetic one. Hybrid organisations resemble a labradoodle, which is a cross-breed between a golden retriever and a poodle. It is enormously cute and causes very little allergies, but it may suffer from genetic illnesses and behavioural problems, and it lacks institutional recognition from all-breed purebred dog registries. Hybrid organisations struggle with similar problems. Not only do they mix features of pure types, but they are also poorly understood and understudied, and they are regulated haphazardly. In a more formal tone, this book raises the need for a more comprehensive understanding of hybrid activities and organisations, not as if they are residuals of public and private but as if they have an institutional space of their own (Skelcher and Smith 2015). We should then be able to relate hybrid activities and contexts to something that also, in a more general fashion, epitomises institutional action in society. For us, as students of public administration, it is comfortable to do this by using two concepts of purposive institutional action: strategy and performance. Broadly speaking, this book treats strategy as a system for exploring goals, performance, and the future as mechanisms for understanding and demonstrating past achievements and accountabilities. In both cases, we are dealing with the important and fundamental aspects of the institutional actions of governments, business firms, and nonprofits.

Characteristics of hybrids

Hybridity refers to ambiguous types of social organising. It is possible to discuss hybridity as a demarcation from the original 'pure' public and private species. Within the context of administration, impurity can take place within public and private activity or between them. Discrepancies between politics and administration within government produce hybridity similar to the organisational forms created by the friction between the ownership and control of private enterprises. The focus of our book is the relationship between public administration and business activity, the aim of 'doing well by doing good' (Kreps and Monin 2011). We seek understanding on hybridity not merely as demarcation or deviation but rather as an 'Archimedean point' where 'a robust theoretical platform can be introduced from which it is possible to develop, test, and analyse different models of hybridity' (Skelcher and Smith 2015, 444).

Within studies of business organisations, many scholars have criticised the dichotomous view of markets and hierarchies (e.g. Powell 1990). Critical remarks and speculations have sought to understand social activities as a continuum-like system in which discrete market transactions are located at one end and highly centralised hierarchical forms are located at the other. Descriptively speaking, in real life, intermediate forms of organising resemble something from both extremes, as is the case, for instance, with hybrid forms of organising (Powell 1987; Bartlett et al. 1994). In the context of sociology, economic sociology, and institutional economics, hybridity has clearly posed a dilemma to scholars and the conceptual systems and frameworks scholars use. For example, Ménard (2004) discusses hybrids as a 'collection of weirdos' that needs to be systematically theorised further, and, if not, cases of hybridity should be returned to analytical discussions in which the traditional market-hierarchy dichotomy can be used.

Looking at hybrids from the perspective of public administration research, we refer to institutional settings in which corporations with both public and private owners may operate according to public interest or activity, or in which private (for-profit or nonprofit) firms increasingly take care of public service provisions. In practice, hybrid forms of governance may thus assume many forms: government-owned corporations, public-private partnerships (PPPs), social enterprises, commissions, public procurement, purchaser-provider models, and contracting out. More specifically, the notion of hybridity can be considered to cover the following:

1 **Mixed ownership**. Consider the current forms of organising important societal functions, such as energy delivery and supply and the infrastructure in different countries of the world. These societal functions are often organised as state-owned enterprises (SOEs) that aim to combine the politically driven goals of modern nation states while exploiting business logics and operating on global financial markets (Thynne 2011). In many cases, public ownership is also seen as a solution to grievances among customer groups (Hansmann 1996). Mixed ownership can be seen as another form of hybrid arrangement, which is seen in entities aiming to combine the best of both worlds between public and private actors. This is why societies, especially government systems, have thought it important to control these combinations through ownership.

2 **Goal incongruence and competing institutional logics**. Think about institutions that aim to balance the logic of profit seeking vis-à-vis the logic of societal effectiveness. While these organisations – in terms of ownership – may quite often be purely private firms, their activities are shaped by different forms of ambiguity and ambivalence. They should be able to employ different but parallel institutional logics. They should be able to provide financial value

for their shareholders but also social impacts on society and citizens. Consider health care firms operating in the area of outsourced health care services, where the impetus is to use business logics while supplementing or replacing the public provision of health care. Alternatively, consider social enterprises, the objective of which is to 'do well by doing good,' where 'good' refers to legitimate social aims, and 'well' is understood as being profitable (Reay and Hinings 2009; Kreps and Monin 2011; Pache and Santos 2013; Ebrahim et al. 2014).

3 **Multiplicity of funding arrangements**. Think about modern megaprojects such as the International Space Station, the Beijing–Shanghai High-Speed Railway, the Airbus A380 aircraft, or the Channel Tunnel connecting the UK and continental Europe. These projects not only take time and massive amounts of financial and intellectual resources but also institutional collaboration between public and private actors. These arrangements may include private investors and financiers as well as taxpayers who all have different interests and stakes in a project and its arrangement. Despite all the complexities in the valuation and measurement of the returns and paybacks of such activities, all parties are necessary to make these projects possible (Greve and Hodge 2007).

4 **Public and private forms of financial and social control**. There can be different types of control systems applied to systems of service delivery. In general, forms of control may include, for instance, the regulatory control of markets, professional self- (or clan-) control, and customer-driven market control within a single system of service delivery (Power 1997; Kickert 2001; Jordana and Levi-Faur 2004; Kelly 2005). In fact, it is difficult to distinguish public forms of control from private ones. Instead, modern control systems are defined by the simultaneity of different dimensions of control. Private business firms are controlled by public institutions, whereas public agencies may be controlled by private firms operating in the markets of public sector audits (Vakkuri et al. 2006). Instead of having a public vs. private mentality, it is probably more important to understand whether control is exercised by an external or internal party. In hybrid settings, we argue, forms of control are usually mixed. These organisations and arrangements are influenced by multiple pressures of control from both inside and outside forces.

Tricky problems of governance arising

The issues of ownership, institutional logics, funding, and control provide a broad framework for hybrid activity situated in between market competition and politics within government. In our thinking, hybridity is a space in between governments and markets that is populated by hybrid organisations, compilations of organisations, industries, and systems which seek the simultaneous advancement of public policy goals and business aims with the use of both public and private resources. With such a definition, hybridity covers research objects such as PPPs, nonprofits, SOEs, universities, hospitals, and health policy systems.

Hybrid activities and organisations are not easy objects of governance. It is complicated to understand what drives and facilitates hybrid action, what kinds of institutional processes produce hybrid forms of governance in society, and how hybrid organisations can be governed and controlled. Consider the tricky questions that the task of governance confronts:

1. **How should we understand the space in between public and private?** In a public-private interface, hybridity can take a variety of forms. First, hybrids can be entities with a particular organisational form. Second, hybrids appear as governance structures. Third, hybrids represent relationships among actors in a network. The following discussion of hybrid organisations as entities, governance structures, and compilations of relationships is based on a very simple separation. The hybrid as entity is an approach that takes hybrids as singular beings. Most notably, hybrid entities refer to a specific type of organisational forms and structures that combine one way or another the features of purely public and private organisational forms. The governance structures perspective views hybrids as arrangements that efficiently solve the cost of business interactions, and the relational view sees hybrids as part of social structures and networks. One possibility is to see hybrids as a meso-level construct which is disentangled from the idiosyncrasies of singular micro forms of organisations but distinct from highly abstract macro forms of the aggregation of wholes, such as countries, industries, or national economies. Real-life developments and theoretical advancement suggest that organisations themselves are in the flux of transformation. 'Organisation' refers not only to a single entity regulated by a single manager or single authority structure within private enterprise or government hierarchy; it also refers to pairwise interaction patterns and to multiparty alliances among a number of organisations representing various public, private, and mixed organisational forms.

2. **What kind of empirical categorisations are used to classify hybridity?** One of the main reasons to study hybridity is related to the existing ideas and mental models of public and private spheres. Deviations from the deeply-rooted distinction between government activity and business endeavours are a nuisance for heuristic simplifications. In this sense, hybridity poses a threat to the image of how societies are constructed. The dichotomy of the public and private sectors is in itself a fragile distinction which is upheld by existing measurement and calculation systems and theoretical assumptions of the nature of public and private goods. This distinction makes it difficult to include additional categories in existing classifications. Hybrids appear as conceptual waste which does not have a proper place in existing measurement categories. Furthermore, private producers to a large extent take care of many of the duties previously performed by public agencies. Likewise, within private enterprises, some practices (such as corporate social responsibility policies) emphasise the nature of the firm as part of their environing societies. There is, however, no need to overestimate the purposiveness in populating the grey area between

the public and private spheres. Many of the developments in the increasing of the space in between existing categories result from ad hoc solutions to administrative problems rather than planned change. Uncertainty is a powerful mechanism that instigates processes of choice and imitation. Inadequate understandings of decision-making environments, ambiguous processes of setting goals and objectives, and loose links between means and ends in making choices contribute to different variations of uncertainties that institutional actors aim to alleviate (DiMaggio and Powell 1983; Powell and DiMaggio 1991). Societal actors need to learn to 'muddle through' in different institutional environments. Quite often, traditional trial and error will do (Lindblom 1959).

3 **How do hybrid organisations legitimate their activities?** Any organisation needs support for its actions. In the case of hybrid organisations, there is a genuine institutional deficit of approval. Hybrids need to acquire support for their existence from multiple sources, but there are hardly any universal principles for acquiring approval from multiple audiences. Institutional structures of industrialised societies give a different role not only to public and private activity but also to the nature of action between existing categories. Both government-assisted solutions and market-enabled hybrid solutions exist, but, in the developing world in particular, hybrid activity might represent the only viable option in organising large-scale economic activity. The position of hybrids is not only embedded in societal institutions; it is also temporally bound.

Ideal public bureaucracy typically emphasises control and reporting relationships in the vertical line between managers and subordinates, which does not take the needs of the citizens as its first priority. Within government ranks, the existence of powerful professional groups and the distinction between elected politicians and appointed officials are some features which do not always respect straightforward vertical accountability structures. There is no need to belittle the bureaucratic nature of private enterprises, which aim at avoiding market anomalies by constituting top-down-oriented management structures not relaxed by democratic political debate or professional allegiances. Within hybrid settings, accountability structures are inherently ambiguous. In a hybrid context, the distinction between responsibility to shareholders of a typical stock-hold company and responsibility to electoral constituencies in political systems cannot be easily made. The mixing of politics and markets within the same administrative structures might be a problem for an external observer trying to apply existing principles of accountability to hybrid activities. From the viewpoint of hybrid activity, the ambiguity of accountability opens up possibilities to evade obligating responsibilities and exploit dual commitments to the public and private spheres.

4 **How are hybrid activities valued in society?** The distinction between profit seeking and evaluation is relevant in separating the achievements of private and public activities. One option is to see public value creation as a broader category of value generation than profit seeking with private enterprises (Moore 1995). In this respect, effectiveness and legitimation considerations in hybrid activities

come to the fore in the public sphere. However, the distinction between financial value in terms of calculable currencies and value as important aspects of human life is not as clear as it seems. The discussion of worth is not only a language game which combines financial and social values; it also puts forward that these values are two sides of the same coin. The valuation of finances is dependent upon the values we hold dear in our lives (Stark 2009). The principles of valuation can contradict one another, and, within the hybrid context, the valuation of performance relates to multiple and possibly conflicting perspectives. Yet another option is to see hybridity in terms of classic economic theory and thus as falling between public and private goods. With our collection of case illustrations of hybrid activities, we aim to provide extensive understanding of different mechanisms of value creation among hybrid activities. The level of ambiguity in demonstrating, measuring, and creating value may vary in different contexts of hybrid organisations.

Governing hybrid organisations entails problems at different levels. We are not able to fully grasp the intrinsic characteristics of hybridity and hybrid organisations. Thus, we face dilemmas of understanding, categorising, and naming institutional activities. In a sense, we see monsters on the run among organisational populations because we are not exactly certain what they are and look like, and how we should understand and classify them. One intention of this book is to contribute to such understanding in the context of societal systems. Regardless of conceptual and intellectual ambiguity in understanding hybridity in social action, it is our deliberate choice to place hybrid governance as the focus of our examination (see Figure 1.1). Furthermore, we are interested in the purposive nature of hybrid activities and organisations. Notions of hybridity based on normative strength, actor identity, value commitments, and environmental turbulence focus on two important aspects of institutional action: strategy formation and performance measurement.

The importance of strategy-performance interfaces orients our examination to the goal-oriented productive activities of hybrids. The performance aspect emphasises the productive nature of hybrid activity in manufacturing and service production. Thus, the advocacy or the leisure activities of hybrid organisations are not prominent in the analysis. The orientations of strategy and performance help us understand two important and powerful, albeit simple, questions about any purposive social action. First, with strategic orientation, we ask *how the objectives of purposive institutional action are created and instigated* (March 1988a; March and Olsen 1999). The notion of objectives may assume different forms depending on the context. Some contexts may include more incongruence and ambiguity than others. Second, with performative orientation, we ask *how the achievements of purposive institutional action are demonstrated*. How do institutions and decision-makers in different policy contexts legitimise their use of intellectual and financial resources? The performative aspect is required to hold decision-makers accountable in different settings of policy making (Allen 2012). Again, demonstrating achievements and performance

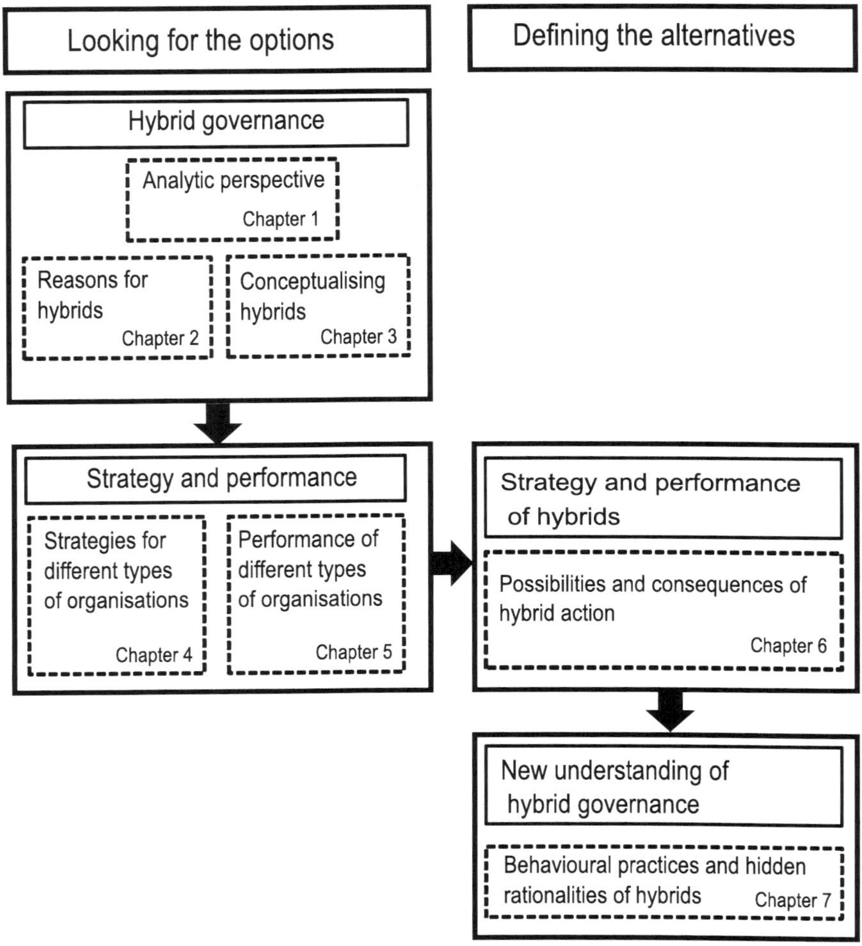

8 Monsters on the run

FIGURE 1.1 Exploring hybrid organisations

yields distinct forms and systems. The previous literature has raised several problems for hybrid activities (Hodges 2012).

Strategy formation: adaptation and change

Public organisations face not only the influence of global developments but also the influence of local political and administrative constellations. Many changes in public administrations have emphasised the goal-oriented action of public organisations and the importance of showing value for the money of public actions. These reforms have meant more decision-making power for public managers, more imitation of private enterprise activities, more careful evaluation of public action, and the adoption of customer choice. At the same time, governments have been emptied in the sense that private enterprises now take care of many public sector duties. Often, this has not meant the decrease of public sector duties but the emergence of nongovernmental quasi-public organisations in addition to new and more complicated regulations to oversee outsourced practices. It is somewhat paradoxical that the increase in private sector practice fundamentally alters possibilities for change. In a sense, any public organisation is the bearer of the combined powers of the state, which holds absolute and unrestricted power in that it stands above all other associations and groups in society (Heywood 2002) and is capable of achieving change in the environment of an organisation according to the decisions of political decision-makers. Private enterprises, in contrast, are fundamentally geared to cater to the investments of shareholders through successful adaptation to market competition. Change in the environment of an organisation cannot be the key goal of private enterprise. There are, however, connecting themes of strategic design, internal strategic scanning, and strategic governance within strategy literature which can be applied to public, private, and hybrid organisations alike (Johanson 2009):

- *Strategic design.* The fundamental assumption of strategic design is that organisations can face future circumstances with current understanding. While it is obvious that strategy by its very nature incorporates planning, the strategic design mode relies heavily on predetermination. The future can be programmed in advance (Mintzberg 1994). The strategic design approach tends to emphasise an environment's opportunities and threats. The anticipation of future events and the subsequent programming of actions is in its essence a very practical task that does not separate actions between types of organisations. In the public sector, strategic management is often equated with strategic planning (Bryson 1995; Poister et al. 2010). The difference in the sectoral alignment of the public, private, and hybrid spheres lies in the projected goals of planning and programming exercises. Public interests serving the demands of constituencies are different from private interests serving the interests of shareholders. Hybrids must often serve these dual commitments at the same time.
- *Strategic scanning.* The success of organisations is not directly evident in their adaptation to their environment; rather, success is found in the unique resource combinations of organisations. An important compilation of ideas is a resource-based view of a firm (Barney 1991; Barney et al. 2001). A resource-based view argues that industries make little sense in financial terms, as differences in performance are often greater within than between industries (Rumelt 1991). Finding the internal strength of an organisation is one side of the coin. The other side is the fact that, if the environment is fundamentally unpredictable, preoccupation with scanning the environment appears to be a waste of resources. The important feature of strategic scanning is that it directs attention to strengths and weaknesses rather than to the environment's opportunities and threats, which the strategic design mode espouses. Within business organisations, the inimitability of the use of resources and capabilities is important in

hiding unique features from rivals. In the hybrid context, the possible existence of profit motives makes secrecy a valued practice, whereas within public organisations there are hardly any reasons to not share best practices and newly found internal innovations with other public bodies.
- *Strategic governance.* The third mode of strategy formation, strategic governance, is emerging from, on the one hand, the increased interdependence of the world at the global as well as national and local levels (Kersbergen and Waarden 2004), and, on the other hand, the developments in sharing knowledge and duties across the borders of organisations (Dyer and Singh 1998). The strategic governance framework brings forth the combination of internal strengths and environmental opportunities. Networks play an important role in connecting levels of governance and organisations together in different network management structures (Provan and Kenis 2008) and a variety of research subjects (Borgatti and Foster 2003). The economic exchanges of business environments are embedded in social networks (Granovetter 1985), and networks are part of the interplay between public agencies within government circles (Johanson 2014). The challenge of network formation in public, private, and hybrid contexts is similar. The emergence of mutual benefits through the sharing of duties requires the relaxation of control over one's own actions, which can be difficult due to business secrecy, democratic control, or fear of the capture of one's own resources.

Performance measurement: value creation through profit seeking and evaluation

For actors legitimising decisions, it is imperative to convince and demonstrate to relevant audiences and stakeholders what the actors have done and achieved and whether these achievements are in congruence with intentions, objectives, or other forms of predesigned principles of performativity. Sometimes business enterprises may willingly deviate from the profit-making principle to serve social goals because shareholders may assume that this contributes to their legitimacy. The lack of market price information in several public sector activities makes it difficult to evaluate the impact and attribution of government interventions and public services and creates a need to evaluate the effectiveness of public activities. Such assessments are highly dependent upon the visibility and measurability of outputs and outcomes. Of course, it would be naïve to maintain that contradictions in performative measurement are only applicable to hybrid activities. Indeed, it is widely acknowledged that no single performance conception is unambiguous or free from contrasting interpretations and uses. As this book discusses, both business operations and public sector activities are difficult targets for performance evaluations.

The straightforward distinction between a profit-maximising private enterprise and an effectiveness-driven public organisation is deceptively simple. The common feature of these concepts is that they aim to measure the ultimate value of private and public action, not only the efficiency of operational processes. While differences in profit making vis-à-vis effectiveness may be one way to delineate the boundaries between a private enterprise and a public agency, the efficiency of operations is naturally a mutual concern for both public and private organisations. Although efficiency criteria might vary significantly in different contexts of institutional action, decision-makers are interested in the procedural optimalities of operations. In fact, with the absence of more detailed information on outcomes of institutional action, efficiencies may serve as reasonable surrogates for making important choices for the future (Vakkuri 2010). It is easier for public agencies and private firms to prove their efficiencies and procedural optimalities than the effects of their services on users, citizens, and society at large.

In general, three modes of economic rationalities are relevant in understanding performance in public, private, and hybrid contexts.

- *Economy*: This is associated with the classic principle of means-ends parsimony, the Occam's Razor of economic thinking. Due to the finiteness of financial resources, the minimisation of economic means in achieving desired ends is considered a virtue in institutional life (Simon 1979a; Hood 1995). Doing more with less constitutes an important prerequisite for evaluating and demonstrating institutional intelligence. If we compare this principle across the three institutional contexts of public, private, and hybrid, we may see different interpretations of the same general principle. However, the philosophy of parsimony applies: Actors are interested in searching for structures, technologies, and procedural solutions that would require minimum costs for delivering services, manufacturing products, or providing common goods.
- *Efficiency*: In their operations, organisations look for optimal relationships between the inputs that they utilise and the outputs that they deliver. What is 'optimal' may be found with respect to given standards or other organisations, peers, or benchmarks. Koopmans (1977) talks about efficiency as the optimality of input-output relationships. In business firms, optimality may be associated with technical efficiencies with an emphasis on the rationality of transforming inputs – for example, labour, capital, and infrastructure – into outputs and goods that are sold on the market, or it may be associated with optimalities that are dependent on the size and volume of the business operations (Charnes et al. 1994). In the public sector, the notion of efficiency also relates to the fair and equal distribution of outputs and outcomes in given contexts. In hybrid activities, efficiency rationales should be able to follow both principles simultaneously. It is no wonder that, in hybrid contexts, certain services may appear inefficient when evaluated separately from other parts of the service provision system.
- *Effectiveness*: It is important to discern the extent to which public agencies and policies have achieved their goals and objectives, as well as the extent to which these policies have accrued to expected and unexpected, intended and unintended, consequences of policy action. Effectiveness, as we understand it in our book, is first and foremost about value creation (Moore 1995). For institutional

survival, business firms need to create value for two important stakeholders: customers and owners. Value creation for customers is an important condition to succeed in the marketplace. The public sector intends to create value for society, taxpayers, and the public. Legitimacy largely influences and shapes this process. Democratic societies, with an emphasis on the openness and transparency of public policy and administration systems, have important difficulties in pursuing desired impacts without simultaneously paying considerable attention to the appropriateness of the process. Hybrid activities incorporate a combination of the two abovementioned mechanisms of value creation, which makes them a complicated venue for understanding, valuing, and demonstrating effectiveness.

The organisation of this book

As human beings, we are bound by our understanding of reality. Understanding hybrid governance is no exception. It would be possible to assume that there is one perspective on hybridity – as it is – and another perspective as we attempt to know and understand hybridity. Our intention is to talk about hybridity both as a construction of academic, intellectual, theoretical, and conceptual systems and as a practical world of institutions, limitations, and ambiguities that are associated with hybridity and hybrid governance.

The idea of this book follows the metaphor of monstrous hybrids (Jacobs 1992). We have adopted this illuminating metaphor to epitomise prevailing and prominent thinking in which hybridity and hybrid organisations meet several criteria to be considered monsters. The idea of monstrous hybrids leads us to ask the following questions:

- Why do monsters exist, and why do we call them monsters? Why do we see hybrids in the institutional landscape? (Chapter 2)
- How do we tame monsters? Could we find some novel ways to conceptualise and categorise hybridity in social life? (Chapter 3)
- How do we know what the monsters aim at? Why and how do hybrids explore their strategic options and objectives? (Chapter 4)
- How do we trace the footprints of monsters? How do hybrids demonstrate and legitimise their performances and accountabilities? (Chapter 5)
- How do we charter the terrain occupied by monsters? How do we understand the links between strategies and performances in hybrid contexts? (Chapter 6)
- Are they monsters after all? What did we learn from our encounter with monstrous hybrids? Do hybrids make more sense than previously thought, and can we find some hidden rationalities as to why they exist and why they behave as they do? (Chapter 7)

As we indicated earlier, our approach to hybridity is fairly sympathetic. For us, this book is an intellectual journey to institutional richness in which many things appear to still be unknown, sometimes poorly understood and scrutinised, and in which it is sometimes too easy to see hybrids as monsters or as other forms of institutional weirdos. By the same token, we observe that this reasoning does not explain many governance problems that may be due to mechanisms of hybridity. Therefore, we fail to locate some of the so-called monsters among institutional populations. By being scientifically humble and by using a traditional method of scientific doubt and reasoning, we are wondering whether either of the positions are completely true. Perhaps we are all in the process of understanding our approach to hybridity in a more general fashion.

We organise the discussion as follows. The introductory chapter portrays the framework for the examination of hybrids and details the nature of hybridity, modes of strategy formation, and regimes of performance measurement applicable in public, private, and hybrid contexts. Chapter 2 illustrates hybridity within public and private governance as well as its origins and the difficulties of conceptualising hybrid activities as temporal and socially embedded activity. Chapter 3 deals with the alternative theoretical ways of categorising hybrid activity according to the number of actors and according to the different levels of analysis. This chapter also includes an examination of how real-life categorisation of economic activity is able to take into account the existence of hybrid activities. Chapter 4 expounds the strategy formation of public, private, and hybrid organisations, and Chapter 5 details corresponding performance measurement regimes. Chapter 6 combines strategy formation and performance measurement in the hybrid context in two respects: (1) as an avenue for combining performances with the strategic goals of a hybrid organisation, and (2) as macro consequences of hybrid activity in societies. Chapter 7 not only puts forward a summation of previous chapters but also comments on the global aspect of hybrid activities' future developments.

This book contains a number of case descriptions about hybrid arrangements performing practical duties in building infrastructure, supplying energy, providing health care, advancing environmental sustainability, educating students, creating innovations, arranging global air travel, and organising old-age financial security. The case of the *publicani* in the ancient Roman Republic holds a special position in our inquiry, as it represents a point of departure for thinking differently about existing categories. The cases originate from a number of geographical areas in North America, Europe, and Asia, not only in the developed world but also in developing countries. Many of the cases have universal appeal in dealing with the basic aspects of organising a society, and many of them share a global reach. Illustrative case examples cannot provide empirical evidence for testing the viability of hybrid arrangements, but they do point out the significance of society as an important feature surrounding hybrid activities.

The literature covered in this book presents a number of perspectives in economics, sociology, and organisation theory. We have tried not to hide the application of such diverse literature, but at the same time we have tried to emphasise the substantive relevance of the various theoretical backgrounds for the purposes of understanding hybrid organisations. The applied nature of our perspective makes the employment of diverse literature easier. The origin of our thoughts comes from public administration literature, which is able to accommodate ideas from a number of different perspectives. At times, we have toned down internal debates within specific literature to make it easier for the reader to follow the storyline. For those educated in specific areas of expertise, our referencing directs the reader to relevant literary sources and debates.

2
WHY DO MONSTERS EXIST?
Public, private, and hybrid organisations in perspective

The following classification of animals, which is said to have appeared in the Chinese encyclopaedia *Celestial Emporium of Benevolent Knowledge*, illustrates the difficulty of finding order in the natural world:

> Animals are divided into (a) those that belong to the Emperor, (b) embalmed ones, (c) those that are trained, (d) suckling pigs, (e) mermaids, (f) fabulous ones, (g) stray dogs, (h) those that are included in this classification, (i) those that tremble as if they were mad, (j) innumerable ones, (k) those drawn with a very fine camel's hair brush, (l) others, (m) those that have just broken a flower vase, (n) those that resemble flies from a distance.
>
> *(Borges 1966, 108)*

A classification is a spatial, temporal, or spatio-temporal segmentation of the world. First, in an ideal situation, classification follows consistent and unique classificatory principles. A genealogical map of one's family tree or a classification of flora and fauna according to their predominant features, as well as the evolution of such features, illustrates classifications that enable us to attach every individual being to their representative categories. In such instances, categorisation proceeds with relatively consistent principles, such as family descendance, the evolution of species, or the capacity to breed. Second, in an ideal case, categories are mutually exclusive, and they can be separated from one another. Third, an ideal system of classification is complete in the sense that it should cover all the beings under the categorisation, which refers to the idea that if a new and unknown species appears, the categorisation should be able to incorporate it (Bowker and Star 2000).

It is evident that there is something very strange about Borges's classification of animals, as it appears to follow a haphazard compilation of different classificatory principles, such as appearance, activity, and ownership. Many animals could be classified into multiple categories, and even though the system is exhaustive because of its notion of 'others,' it is remarkably ambiguous.

The idea that the institutional world can be neatly divided into two types, private and public, is lucrative. It breeds the contemporary discourse of social life. Such a distinction has historically contributed to the establishment, design, and organisation of different societal systems. In many societies, the distinction has been associated with legal and regulatory systems (public and private law), systems of national registration, bookkeeping and economics (private and public economy), and the political systems of market economies. This black-and-white reasoning appears to make sense in many regards.

But why do monstrous hybrids exist? This chapter explores hybrids and hybridity from the viewpoint of previous research. Our main ambition is to discuss some of the complications regarding the distinctions between public and private. We are not searching for an exhaustive introduction. We are fully aware of the abundance of such research literature (Bozeman 1987; Powell 1990; Moore 1995; Williamson 1999a; Morrell 2009; Bozeman and Moulton 2011; Bozeman 2013). Instead, our intention is to compile different research traditions and discussion streams with a simple question: Why is the distinction between public and private so complicated in research and in intellectual thinking?

We approach this question by debating three important elements. First, the notions of public and private are shaped and defined by conceptual and linguistic conventions. We are particularly interested in the beauty of simplification in social choice and political decision-making by exploring the institutional, political, and cognitive underpinnings of the distinction between public and private. From many perspectives, the distinction is not a problem. Rather, it is perceived to be a solution to the problem of understanding societal actions, institutions, and organisations (March 1978). Such a solution is urgently required by the modern apparatus of decision-making. The system of academic research is one important element in that apparatus. By increasing levels of specialisation and sophistication, the apparatus may become more conceptually nuanced but also more diversified. We address a few important streams of research discussion from organisation studies, economics, sociology, and public administration to discuss and illustrate complicated distinctions between public and private. Second, history is an important element. We discuss the distinction between public and private with an emphasis on an historical approach to institutional organising and hybridity. The concepts, structures, and governance of public, private, and hybrid activities evolve over time, which obfuscates distinctions between organisational modes (Padgett and Powell 2012). Do we have the same monsters that the Romans had? Third, it is also the case that the modern politico-administrative system produces hybridity. The political imperative of using the markets has shaped the ways in which government systems work and how the public and private interact. However, as we propose, instead of pure markets we see different forms of hybridity emerging.

To discuss the complexities of public and private distinctions in academic research, we emphasise the following areas in particular. We are interested in the complexities of distinctions between public and private in the study of organisational life. In essence, the valuation of social and economic actions depends on the worth we attach to them. Furthermore, we discuss the delineation between public and private goods. We explore briefly the research debate on public and private interests and end the chapter by discussing hybridisation as a consequence of government reforms.

Hybrid governance over time

What defines public and private is temporally bound. One can argue that hybrids have existed for ages. Indeed, it is possible to use the conventional phrase that 'already the ancient Romans' had hybrid arrangements. Hybrid arrangements in the Roman Republic have been explored in previous research interested in institutional change and institutional forms in ancient structures of power, ancient social relationships, and ancient decision-making (Badian 1983).

The Roman Republic used several forms of collaborative governance between public and private action. Some of us know the term 'publicans,' which refers to actors – 'entrepreneurs' – who were in the business of conducting outsourced public activities directed by the Romans. Publicans (or *publicani*) in ancient Rome formed rudimentary private enterprises responsible for many public duties: the collection of excise duties, public contracting for supplies, the maintenance of public spaces, and contracts for public building projects (Badian 1983). Publicans were probably best known for their activity in collecting taxes, which made them extremely unpopular in the Roman provinces. The Roman Republic extensively employed the system that has sometimes been called 'tax farming.' This system was widely used until the seventeenth century in many countries, such as Egypt, Greece, and England (Allen 2012).

CASE 2.1 *SOCIETAS PUBLICANORUM* AND *PUBLICANI* IN THE ROMAN REPUBLIC

The legacy of the Roman Republic continues to provide inspiration for the operation of modern governments, as the empire first witnessed the challenges associated with the management of large territorial areas and populations in a more or less sustainable fashion. The era of the Roman Republic began with the overthrowing of the kings around 500 BC and ended with the beginning of the imperial rule of the Caesars in 27 BC. During the republican era, civil service, which was the size of modern middle-sized city governments, dealt with organising public policy for nearly thirty million people under the rule of the Roman Republic. The solution for the day-to-day operation of public administration was the extensive use of private contracting in the implementation of public policies. The earliest accounts of contracting describe contracts for feeding sacred hens, which were honoured for warning the citizens of Rome of approaching enemies, on the hill of Capitolium in Rome in 390 BC (Badian 1983).

Private organisations, *societas publicanorum*, and their managers, the *publicani*, took care of most public duties, such as constructing public buildings, supplying equipment for the army, operating mines, and, most importantly, collecting taxes. The societies participated in tenders for public duties. Those who offered the lowest price won construction deals, and those who guaranteed the highest amount of collected taxes for the senate succeeded in tax collection tenders. The management structure of the societies represented a core-periphery structure with a relatively small permanent management structure and a large short-term operative workforce, which could be adjusted according to successes and losses in consecutive competitive tenders. The *societas publicanorum* were probably the first type of limited liability shareholder-owned companies. Interestingly enough, a legal structure for limiting liability in purely private business activity did not exist at the time. To limit personal liability, which could lead to slavery and the confiscation of all personal property, early entrepreneurs invented the practice of common slave ownership, in which a jointly owned slave served as chief executive officer of the enterprise. As slaves were 'things' responsible for only their own cost, they liberated the owners of their personal liabilities (Malmendier 2009).

In the Roman Republic, the distinction between politics and business was clear-cut. Senators could not take part in the management of the *societas publicanorum* or other business activities, but they could be shareholders of the companies. Likewise, private contractors could not enter seats in the senate. Consequently, the *publicani*, as the most influential group in the order of the knights, became part of the power-balancing mechanism of ancient Rome. Tax farming deals in newly acquired eastern provinces in Asia Minor proved to be a highly lucrative source of income for the companies, which placed *publicani* in competitive positions with the appointed local governors of the provinces. Also, the exclusion of the *publicani* from the senate opened up positions for them in the special courts, allowing them to weigh the limits and practices of government power (Badian 1983; Silver 2007).

The actions of the *publicani* were fiercely criticised. They were accused of insurance fraud in delivering goods during the Punic wars, of excessive greed when collecting taxes in the provinces, of exceptionally crude conduct towards slave labour working in the mines, and of fraudulent practices in trying to get rid of unprofitable public contracts. However, surviving literary sources are mainly based on accounts of senators, who were in a competitive position with the *publicani*. Still, the overall operation of the private contractors seems to have supplied satisfactory results for the management of the republic. The degradation of the role of private contracting coincided with the beginning of the rule of the emperors, during which the oligarchic power of the senate had to give way for the autocratic rule of the Caesars, and a more centralised public civil service system replaced private contractors in implementing the most important parts of public policy. However, the order of the knights, to which the *publicani* belonged, formed the backbone of the population from which civil servants were recruited. Throughout history, the *publicani*, or, more precisely, their local henchmen, were probably best known from their minor local tax collecting duties in Roman provinces during the imperial era (Badian 1983).

Why is it important to understand the notion of hybridity in history? Societies of different times have invented multiple forms of organising important functions and service delivery. Inventions have reflected interpretations of what we nowadays call 'public' and 'private.' Thus, public, private, and hybrid as notions and concepts evolve over time. There may be economic rationalities that are less time dependent and that help explain why some societal functions are more likely to be organised in the public and private sectors. We know of the case of clear public goods, which includes problems of excludability and significant externalities, when it makes sense to use government actions to contribute to justified provisions of goods in society. We have some institutional codes for delineating public vis-à-vis private.

However, many of these concepts evolve over time not only due to the fairly young history of such conceptual systems but also because societies have changed significantly (Morrell 2009). The idea of 'externalities' may have been perceived differently in the Middle Ages or before the era of nation states (Allen 2012). The sphere of influence was different, which made it difficult to actually define a public good or the public that a good was supposed to serve. Furthermore, we know that many of those principles were subject to contrasting interpretations. In principle, government intervention may be useful and feasible, but in terms of institutional and policy practice, the outcomes of such interventions may be drastically different from what was expected in the first place. Efficient intentions turn into something else. This should not be any news to scholars and experts in public policy, as it has an important bearing on the notion of hybrids.

Quite naturally, ideas, ideals, and ideologies between public and private forms of action travel back and forth. One may observe double movement. The maturation of welfare states has meant that public services no longer expand as they did in developed countries post–World War II. The aging of the population puts an extra burden on existing public services, and, at the same time, many countries struggle with slow economic growth. The situation in the developing world is quite different: the education of young populations, the construction of infrastructure, and the building up of industrial bases demands the attention of developing societies. Some of the changes, such as globalisation or climate change, affect societies all over the world, but the influence of these changes depends on local policies and cultures, which are likely to channel the same demands – even environmental ones – differently in local conditions.

The influential idea of an economy-society interface originated in the ideas of Karl Polanyi (1944), who argued that the development of the market economy did not advance without institutional backup but instead required conscious and deliberate planning in order to emerge. In the early phases of capitalism, societies were all but prepared to confront the consequences of the market economy, which was witnessed in the poverty and squalor of eighteenth-century Britain. According to Polanyi, there were several reasons for the negative consequences of the development of the market economy. First, capitalism disentangled or disembedded markets from social relationships, which meant that the production and accumulation of wealth did not have to pay respect to the survival of the workforce. Second, the British government and societal institutions were unprepared to confront the market economy's devastating effect on society. As a contrast to these harmful consequences, the delay in the growth of capitalism meant that societies were better equipped to accommodate the development of the markets by instituting safeguards to protect labour through instruments such as social security, trade unions, and labour protection laws in continental Europe. The double movement between market development and government response signifies the constant interaction among markets, governments, and civil society. Recently, the financial crisis of 2008 has raised opinions that current changes in market economies may even include the seeds of their own destruction due to uncontrollable and destructive features of the financial sector (e.g. Streeck 2014).

The double movement signifies the consecutive development of the market economy and the institutional response to tackle its negative consequences on the population. The most important analytical conclusion for the purposes at hand is that economy, society, and government are not totally separate; instead, they are in constant interaction with one another. The double movement between economy and society has had a tremendous influence on the functioning of both public and private organisations. Most importantly, the reciprocal interaction between markets and governments has altered the population of organisations to the extent that there is an ever-widening grey area of arrangements that do not coincide well with a straightforward separation between public and private spheres. For one thing, the functioning of the markets necessitates governments' constant vigilance in order to make sure that markets follow the rules of competition (economic regulation) and do not harm citizens (social regulation). A discussion of regulatory states clearly shows the expansion of regulatory institutions alongside the growth of globalised market trade (Moran 2002). Governments have not only deregulated industries; they have also outsourced many public duties to private operators and tried to imitate market arrangements.

In addition, the development of public administration was related to the separation of politics from the public administration in the executive part of government. The early formulation of this development stated that politics define goals, which are then implemented by civil servants in individual cases. The birth of the discipline of public administration was initiated by the intellectual and practical separation of politics from administration. In the first half of the twentieth century, the political administrative dichotomy was combined with the search for a universal administrative principle, such as the suitable number of subordinates for managers or the optimal number of hierarchical levels for an organisation. Disillusionment with the formulation of universal principles for the practice of administration led to the distinction between interests and facts, the former being the sphere for political decision-makers and the latter for civil servants (Simon and Barnard 1947). Later, an idea emerged in the 1960s that separated politics and administration on the basis of an energy/balance model in which politicians provide the necessary energy for change, which is balanced by the stabilising effect for continuity of public administration. Some closure within the administration-politics dichotomy was reached by the 1980s when a pure hybrid model of government was put forward. Politics and administration were becoming hybridised, which meant there would be no need to separate political decision-making from the formulation and implementation of goals (Aberbach et al. 1981). Discussion on the division between politics and administration has not faded away (Lee and Raadschelders 2008). Even if we accepted a hybrid government, it would be problematic for the accountability of politicians if administrators were in fact responsible for decisions.

Similar developments are present in private enterprise. The separation of control from ownership in the emergence of large market enterprises has been both an intellectual and practical problem when discussing private firms. The alignment of interests between owners and managers is not an easy task. The objectives of owners and managers may contradict one another, and, even if they share mutual interest, managers enjoy the advantage of knowledge over owners, which makes it difficult for owners to control them. Moreover, managers might be risk-averse due to the fear of losing their jobs. The methods for reaching an alignment between principals and agents are externally motivated in the principal-agent perspective. Principals may control their agents through direct supervision, and they may offer financial incentives for agents to take more risk and to put more effort in their work. This theoretical scheme has been applied to settle the relationships between corporate management (agent) and shareholders (principal) of companies (Eisenhardt 1989). There are also possibilities for relying on the internal motivation of managers to serve the goals of the owners. Managers can see their organisation and employees as extensions of their own selves which need constant nurturing and care (Davis et al. 1997). In a sense, the development in the analysis of private firms is orthogonally opposite to the development in the analysis of public administration. The mixture of ownership and control as witnessed in the ownership and manager roles of entrepreneurs represents hybridity, which had to be abandoned along with the growing scale of operations within large conglomerates.

There is a discussion in agency theory about the optimal ownership structure. Following this thought, the ownership issue points to the idea that those suffering the most from not owning an enterprise would be the most likely owners. The deviation from the standard stock-hold company limited by shares can be fruitful for the goal-attainment of the organisation. Consequently, producer and consumer cooperatives, mutual enterprises, and nonprofits are context-specific solutions to the ownership issue. For instance, public ownership of local energy utilities makes sense due to the ability of the public owner to solve possible grievances between households and industrial consumers who have different demands for the use of energy (Hansmann 1996).

This book does not intend to present the institutional history of hybrid arrangements. However, we broadly acknowledge the extremely significant role of institutional development and change, not only in the multifaceted interaction between public and private sectors over time but also in the theoretical and conceptual systems that we use to describe public, private, and hybrid forms of governance in society. We argue that some of the analytical and conceptual ambiguity of hybrid arrangements originates from the fairly brief history of academic research on hybrids and hybridity. This may also partly explain the black-and-white dichotomous characterisations of public and private forms of action, which academic research and business and policy practice reflect.

The public and private in organisational reasoning

The distinction between public and private has facilitated a vibrant academic debate in different fields of research, including the organisational research field. The study of organisational life seems to be a forum that encapsulates much of the discussion regarding different value propositions, assumptions of institutional and individual behaviour, and forms of organising societal activities and functions. As we live in a world of organisations (Simon 1991), the distinction between public and private as distilled through organisational action is an emblematic representation of our current way of life.

For our book, an interesting approach in the organisational research discussion is the way in which researchers argue about and legitimise the borderline between public and private organisations. Furthermore, it is fascinating how the state in between is conceptualized and illustrated. Let us consider the classic thinking by Herbert Simon (Simon 1998). In the article based on his presentation at the American Society for Public Administration conference in 1997, Simon framed the distinction as a complicated and ambiguous relationship. He argues that although the distinction constitutes an important frame to think about organisations in modern societies, the boundary between public and private is actually fluid. Simon (1998, 9) writes:

> As some of my examples make obvious, there is no sharp line between public and private organizations. We usually use ownership and control as the defin-

ing criteria, but ownership does not always imply control, as is seen in the case of corporations that have no dominant stockholders.

Simon uses as examples state highway departments that contract their activities to engineering firms, postal services that use private airlines and trucking firms to conduct the carrying assignment, and private firms that are controlled by governments and public bodies from outside. For Simon, the notions of public and private industries are not simple or univocal. Instead, in different points in time societies search for a proper balance between public and private, and the dynamics of institutional evolution is partly about shifts in those balances.

Simon's characterisations can be seen as intelligible reflections on, and to some extent reactions to, research and policy discourse on why it would make sense to organise some societal activities through private firms and others through public bureaucracies. He appears to argue in favour of an organising solution that is less black-and-white and dichotomous and more contextual, contingent on the specific needs and requirements of societies and nations. Perhaps the boundaries between the public and private as well as between organisations and markets are more vivid in ideal-type constructions of different research traditions and public policy reform agendas than in the actual lives of individuals, organisations, and societies (Simon 1991).

But what about the empirical comparisons between public and private organisations? Van der Wal et al. (2008) present a very good argument that recognises the obvious lack of empirical descriptive studies regarding similarities and differences between public and private organisations. Their study addresses those distinctions through perceived value systems in public and private organisations in the Netherlands. For the researchers, the basic question is whether it makes sense to distinguish two different value systems, one for private organisations and the other for public organisations. How can we answer this question by asking managers? It is always difficult to discern value propositions by asking the respondents how they perceive the values, which often renders these types of empirical comparisons as just another form of prescriptions – empirically constituted prescriptions of how the values ought to be. In the study, the managers answered survey questions about both 'should be' values and 'actual' values (Van der Wal et al. 2008). Therefore, their answers may be limited in the extent to which they characterise how values are actually appreciated and implemented in organisational practice.

However, it is important to raise two issues that Van der Wal et al. (2008) eloquently discuss in their study and that also provide important perspectives for understanding the complicated distinction between the public and private in organisational reasoning. First, there seem to be both similarities and differences between public and private organisations using conceptual value systems. There appear to be two somewhat distinct value systems specific to these types of organisations. For instance, impartiality (i.e. being unbiased towards different stakeholders) seems to be an extremely important value in public sector contexts, but not so much in business environments. Furthermore, while profitability (i.e. acting towards financial or other similar gains) and innovativeness (i.e. acting to invent new products or policies) are considered some of the most important values in business firms, they are missing in the list of values of public agencies.

Second, there are important values that seem to be common to both forms of organisations. Let us consider two examples: efficiency (i.e. using minimal means to achieve desired ends) and accountability (i.e. justifying consciously one's actions to relevant stakeholders or accountors). Efficiency, as Van der Wal et al. (2008) succinctly argue, is a misunderstood concept. That concept is frequently linked to New Public Management (NPM) reforms in government with the assumption that efficiency has entered the vocabulary of public policy due to NPM or other similar policy reforms. A common belief is that governments apply the efficiency principle because public organisations are being transformed into business firms. This idea clearly omits the fact that efficiency has been one of the cornerstones of classic public administration discussion and that the problem of efficiency has been to consider different ways to allocate and organise scarce means to achieve politically justified ends (Simon and Barnard 1947). As Van der Wal et al. (2008) contend, efficiency is both an instrumental and moral value. Using taxpayers' resources with an attempt to mitigate the absence of waste is also a moral imperative. Therefore, it is no surprise that efficiency is one of the unifying concepts and values of organisations. Moreover, resembling a classic form of responsibility, accountability has served as a common value for both public and private organisations. The principle is general – somebody is accountable to someone else – yet the institutional variants may be complex (Mayston 1993; Schillemans 2011). Nevertheless, the general principle applies.

Obviously, there are different ways to tackle the complicated distinction between public and private organisations. One approach is to discuss limitations in the black-and-white dichotomous distinction and provide extensions as residuals and different types of elaborations and triptychs (Powell 1990; Skelcher and Smith 2015). Another option is the attempt to reshape the perceived relationships between the public and private in organisational settings. One of the influential researchers in this area is Barry Bozeman (Bozeman 1987; Bozeman and Moulton 2011; Bozeman 2013), especially because of his idea of 'publicness' in organisations. Bozeman (2013, 176) argues that, instead of representing the public and private as dichotomous categorisations, we should see them as dimensions, because 'much can be learned by knowing the particular mix of political and economic authority in organizations.'

Bozeman's argument makes the reader aware of the significant potential for reshaping and relocating the public and private in the context of organisational life. Bozeman's (1987) book *All Organizations Are Public* represents the distinction between public and private as ambiguous and associated with the blurring of societal sectors. Bozeman makes a powerful argument in terms of relocating the roles of the public and private. Perhaps the most persuasive and enduring argument is that organisations are actually more public than many people think. As many private business corporations are influenced by different forms and systems of regulation, or their business is significantly dependent upon government contracts, organisations may incorporate different characteristics of publicness, and the logic explaining their actions may be shaped by the intersection of economic and political authority (Bozeman 1987; Bozeman and Moulton 2011). Bozeman's idea of the publicness grid is based on the relationship between political and economic authority. The grid aims to locate different entity forms according to the axis of the two types of authority. In some respects, this results in fairly conventional groupings of different organisations. One extreme deals with a 'private firm controlled by the owners', whereas the other represents a 'government agency that is funded using taxes' (Bozeman 1987, 95). There are also several organisational entities in between.

Bozeman relies on the concept of authority when arguing that 'all organizations are public because political authority affects some of the behavior and processes of all organizations' (Bozeman 1987, 83). Therefore, 'public' is associated with the extent to which an organisation is subject to political authority. Due to this extent, some organisations may be more public with regard to some of their activities and processes than others. This reasoning places significant emphasis on the concept of authority, as political authority drives public organisations, while market authority drives private organisations. If we think of authority using Lindblom's (1977) idea of some people permitting somebody else to make decisions for them, it is easy to follow Bozeman's reasoning that publicness is a dimension. It is quite likely that this is contingent on the nature of the decisions and on the following fundamental questions: Who are the people? Who is this 'somebody else'?

Bozeman is not actually very clear on the concept of authority. For instance, in discussing the concept of economic authority, he refers to property rights theory, which would relate privateness to ownership and particularly to complexities in exchanging property rights in society. Therefore, as there are lots of organisational entities that are partly owned by governments and partly owned by private investors or firms, it is easy to characterise ownership as a dimension of privateness. In fact, Bozeman (1987) also talks about hybrid organisations that are partly private and partly public. He names government-sponsored enterprises (GSE) and multi-organisation enterprises (MOE) as examples. Bozeman also defines a private organisation as an organisation that is constrained or enabled by market-based action, which causes some problems in defining the 'somebody else.' If a private organisation is constrained or enabled by economic authority, indicating that a person gives permission for market-based action to make decisions for her, we may have a problem in understanding what that (market-based action) actually is. All in all, it is fairly easy to see in the logic of Bozeman's argument that we are dealing with a multidimensional notion of publicness.

George Boyne (2002) provides another approach, which discusses management differences in public and private organisations. Boyne questions the widely acknowledged and presumed uniqueness of public organisations in terms of organisational characteristics. He talks about unwarranted assumptions (and arguments) regarding differences and similarities between public and private organisations. Boyne asks if there is actually a significant difference between the public and private in organisational settings.

Why is this question important? It is important because the vast number of public policy reforms during the last thirty to thirty-five years has originated from the doctrine of adopting and transferring organisational and managerial practices from the private to the public sector (Hood 1991). The strong opposition to this policy trend has emphasised the uniqueness of public organisations. Different types of claims and arguments have been made for this purpose. By using a meta-analytical approach and previous studies, Boyne (2002) distinguishes four variables according to which the distinction between public and private organisations is usually investigated:

- Publicness vis-à-vis environmental conditions
- Publicness vis-à-vis goal setting in organisations
- Publicness vis-à-vis organisational structuring
- Publicness vis-à-vis managerial values in organisations

Interestingly enough, irrespective of several assumptions regarding the uniqueness and differences of public and private organisations, there does not seem to be solid, warranted empirical evidence of such differences. With his approach, Boyne is able to corroborate only three out of thirteen hypotheses characterising the four dimensions of publicness. Therefore, Boyne argues that either the differences are more diluted than we might expect or there is actually not enough research-based evidence to demonstrate de facto differences between public and private organisations. The latter argument would indicate that we actually do not know enough about the possible differences. One policy implication could be that we should not be too hesitant to adopt business management to reform public organisations. Given the fact that there are no striking differences, there should be no significant risks in transforming public organisations into more private and business-oriented organisations.

Quite naturally, there are several issues to be carefully considered. Perhaps we should look before we leap. Let us consider three perspectives. First, as Boyne (2002) succinctly argues, there may not be empirical evidence of all the differences between public and private organisations, but the ironic twist is that there is actually no solid body of empirical knowledge on the successes and failures of applying management artefacts and strategies in private organisations. In other words, the question of transferring management practices from the private to the public sector thus loses relevance. If we are interested in empirical proof, we do not actually know whether these practices work in private organisations, let alone whether they would work after the dissemination process to public agencies. Second, in accordance with the above, the process of dissemination is not a black box. It is widely acknowledged that, as management artefacts and systems are adopted and transferred from one context to another, they are revised, reshaped, and transformed. Therefore, lean management and a balanced scorecard are not the same in different contexts. Organisations modify artefacts to meet local needs and conditions (Vakkuri 2010; Orlikowski 2000; Orlikowski 2002). Third, it is important to understand that Boyne's argument, albeit extremely interesting, is based on a metatheoretical approach. It is a reflection of the existing conventional assumptions of the research field and research discussions in academic journals. If we accept the argument that there is a lot more to do in understanding the similarities and differences between public and private organisations, and even more to do in comprehending the space in between public and private organisations, we may easily conclude that the traditional research perspective is not the optimal antecedent for the future (Ritzer 1993).

Valuation of activities in society

Valuation of economic and social action in society is by no means a straightforward task. It is dependent upon the perspective we take on social and economic activities. Within economic thought, financial value, types of economic transactions, and goods are the central objects of examination. In contrast, within sociological thought, the perspective on valuation extends to the examination of social activities and to debates on the social side of value creation. The following discussion of the nature of public goods and justification theory bears direct relevance on the examination of hybrids. On the one hand, in the discussion of public goods, there are types of goods which do not coincide fully with either public or private properties or which may include private and public properties simultaneously. In a sense, to be exact, many goods are hybrid goods. On the other hand, justification theory identifies several orders of worth which consist of a number of dimensions which provide consistent principles for the valuation of social and economic actions. Hybridity in justification theory appears in the controversies of the principles originating from the different orders of worth. In other words, we are dealing with two different approaches to valuation, one originating from the ambiguous characteristics of goods and the other originating from complexities between different social mechanisms of worth. Let us discuss both of these next.

One important task of societies and market economies is to provide citizens with goods and services they need and prefer (Lane 1993). People need to commute, they wish to stay healthy, and they are interested in educating themselves. There is wide-ranging research regarding the most efficient means for providing important goods for citizens and also the most intelligible means for controlling the bads that citizens and societies wish to avoid.

In the research literature, one important starting point for discussing the distinction between private and public goods is Paul Samuelson's (1954) article. Samuelson defines public goods as 'collective consumption goods' where 'each individual's consumption of such a good leads to no subtraction from any other individual's consumption of that good' (1954, 387). Hudson and Jones (2005) refer to two implications of Samuelson's definition. First, there is no rivalry in the consumption of a good, meaning that a person consuming a good does not limit others in their consumption of the same good. Second is nonprice exclusiveness – it is not possible to exclude some groups of people from consuming the good if the same good has been made available to other groups of people. These types of goods usually include properties of (positive) externalities; that is, the marginal costs of producing additional amounts of such a good can be very small, and the benefits may spread to a large number of people. In terms of the allocation of public goods, there may be other properties, such as the free-rider problem. People may not be willing to contribute to the finance of public goods. If they know (or believe) that others contribute, they may be willing to enjoy the benefits without investing any of their own resources. The classic problem, accordingly, is how these types of goods should be provided and with what types of resources. This logic has been interpreted as a source for public policy intervention (Lane 1993).

However, by no means has Samuelson's initial argument been adopted as an unambiguous starting point. In his critical response, Margolis (1955) asks whether purely public goods could be found at all, and, if they could be found, to what extent the provision and allocation of such goods should reflect Samuelson's ideologically laden framework. The basic idea may apply to lighthouses and national defense, but what about other goods and services in society? What would be the actual proportion of purely private and public goods? Interestingly enough, Hudson and Jones (2005) refer to different levels of 'publicness' in goods and services. They contend that only very few things in society can be classified as purely public or private goods. Instead, we should think about goods as having a blend of public and private characteristics. Furthermore, Hudson and Jones go on to question the notion of public goods and private goods by asking who defines them. It is obvious that there are no lawlike theoretical or conceptual principles stating the distinction between public and private goods in society. Rather, we may think that there is some theoretical-conceptual basis for the distinctions, the abundance of practical institutional solutions in different societal systems of the world, and the comprehensive interaction between theoretical conceptualisations and practical solutions. Researchers conceptualising the distinctions are obviously influenced by the empirics of the public-private distinctions they see, and the empirics of policy solutions are significantly influenced by schools of thought, zeitgeists, thinkers, and researchers in the field. Reciprocity between the two approaches helps us understand actual institutional and policy practice (Ostrom 2010).

CASE 2.2 THE CONSTRUCTION AND OPERATION OF CHINA'S HIGHWAY NETWORK THROUGH THE COLLABORATION OF PUBLIC AND PRIVATE ACTION

The maintenance of the infrastructure of societies epitomises the collaborative role of public and private action. Thus, in the literature, infrastructure has been one of the common examples of hybrid forms of governance. China is no exception in this respect. In China, highways are classified into five categories: expressways, Class I highways, Class II highways, Class III highways, and Class IV highways. The classifications are based on the technical grading of highways, which has an impact on the highways' toll systems.

In China, interaction between the public and private sector stems from a fairly traditional division of interests. While public interest is associated with road maintenance, enhancing the smooth flow of highways and improving general social welfare, the interest of private companies is collaborating with the public sector, earning profits from these arrangements, and creating new future opportunities for their businesses (Xu and Wu 2015). This interaction, if understood through the outputs of the collaborative arrangements, has been successful. Before 1988, there were no highways in mainland China. At the end of 2013, the total mileage of expressways amounted to 104,400 kilometres. The interaction resulted in several hybrid entities; that is, highway companies. There are twenty-three publicly listed highway companies, nineteen of which are also listed in the Shanghai and the Schenzen Stock Exchange.

In the Chinese context, such hybrid forms of governance are frequently called public-private partnerships (PPPs). These are assumed to serve several purposes (Xu and Wu 2015). Firstly, they aim at balancing the increasing needs of infrastructure with the limited financial resources of government. Giving an opportunity for highway companies to earn profits from tolls enables new highway construction to meet the needs of rapid urbanisation and traffic congestion. Secondly, in China, PPP arrangements are interestingly enough seen as an efficient instrument to provide public goods. In terms of resource mobilisation, they may be a more effective way to organise infrastructure than classic budget allocation. Thirdly, expressways are understood as club goods, indicating that there may be different pricing mechanisms involved. There are mixed criteria for performance, as fees may contribute not only to financing infrastructure but also to reducing congestion (at a certain level of road users).

It is not easy to achieve a balance between the different interests of public and private actors in the area of highway construction in China. To some extent, deregulation may be required, but regulation and reregulation may also be necessary. There is a need to control the appropriate levels of tolls and fees (which tend to rise), as there is more emphasis on shareholders' value. Moreover, for many Chinese local governments, expressways have become cash cows, an instrument to deal with budget deficits. Nevertheless, the apparent benefits of PPP arrangements have been noted. These include, for instance, more effective management of infrastructure operations to some extent (Xu and Wu 2015).

Morrell (2009) introduces interesting approaches to the discussion of public goods. It is extremely complicated to classify public goods as satisfying the criteria of nonexcludability and nonrivalry. It may be so that almost any good is nonexcludable and nonrivalrous, but only to some degree. Thus, different goods involve different levels of publicness. Morrell (2009) discusses goods that one would associate with the public domain. For Morrell, this is primarily a heuristic device for understanding the provision of goods that includes the notion of shared benefits. It is important to realise the cultural and historical foundations of the notion of 'goods.' Calhoun (1998) discusses the idea of public goods as a social and cultural project in which too much emphasis has been placed on 'good' and not enough emphasis has been placed on 'public.' Therefore, according to Calhoun, we need to ask *which* public and *whose* good (Calhoun 1998). The political and societal process of defining these is not, and should not be, free from conflicts. Instead, the very notion of a 'public good' is contested. Mansbridge (1998) talks about such a cultural-historical project by presenting the strong dichotomy between public and private goods as products of historical development in the Middle Ages. In those times, theologians described the conflict between the kings seeking their private goods (*bonum privatum*) and those pursuing the common good (*bonum commune*) (Mansbridge 1998).

Traditional research concerning the allocation and provision of goods has produced different typologies reflecting ambiguities in the idealised public-private distinction. One example is from Lane (1993), who introduces a cross tabulation of goods according to the two conventional criteria of goods. For Lane, public goods satisfy both the criteria of nonrivalry and nonexcludability. Two people can enjoy these goods simultaneously without the goods losing any of their utility, and the two people do not have to pay for using the service. Classic examples are clean water and clean air. Common pool goods satisfy the criteria of nonexcludability but not nonrivalry. In other words, it may be impossible to exclude users from using the service through price mechanisms, but the consumption of the good is not defined by jointness. The supply of the good can be depleted, but users are not restricted in their use of the good. Consider different types of natural resources. Although the provision of natural resources is indeed finite in modern society, utilising natural resources is beneficial to all. For this reason, the allocation and provision of common goods are usually referred to as a tragedy of the commons (Ostrom 1990). A private good satisfies both the criteria of excludability and rivalry. Driving your car costs you some money, but when you pay for it, you can drive your car, and no one else can do that at the same time. Finally, a toll good (Buchanan 1965) satisfies the criteria of excludability but is nonrivalrous. Joining a club is not usually possible for all, but once you have become a member of the club, you are entitled to enjoy the benefits of the membership even without contributing to those within the club. Consider membership in the European Union, in which the allocation and provision of club goods facilitate numerous political discussions about free-riders, and consider also the relationships between the membership fees and benefits of the European Union. (On 'merit goods,' see Musgrave 1959.)

Ostrom (1990; 2010) revises Samuelson's original notion of public goods by reconceptualising the 'rivalry of consumption' with the 'subtractability of use.' Furthermore, her idea adds dimensionality to typologies of public and private goods. Also, for Ostrom, it is difficult to talk about purely public and private goods. Instead, the question is frequently more about conceptual variants of goods.

Ostrom (2010) makes an important observation when contemplating the characteristics of goods and bads in society and the consequent forms of institutional rules, arrangements, and activities. It is important to understand the interaction between the theory and practice of policy design. Theoretical black-and-white discussions on public and private forms of organising, together with 'Leviathan' or 'privatisation' as policy solutions, as abstract as they usually are, constitute an intellectually powerful apparatus for understanding the policy practice of societies. However, often more than a coherent and consistent set of theories, this discussion provides rhetorically powerful metaphors for policy design that are based on an idealised understanding of institutions and institutional behaviour. They may even be 'institution-free' (Ostrom 1990). In arguments for public sector intervention, there is no specific analysis of how that intervention should be constituted and organised, or of what types of limits regulatory interventions should have. Moreover, arguments favouring private property rights do not capture how this set of rights should be compiled or how the various characteristics of goods should be quantified and evaluated. Metaphors about the public and private have important powers as ideal-type notions.

To elucidate this diversity of organising and goods, Ostrom (2010) defines different types of goods that reflect less dichotomous presumptions about the properties of goods. These four general types of goods entail several subcategories of goods that may have distinct relevance in different institutional settings and that also vary with respect to different institutional attributes (see Figure 2.1).

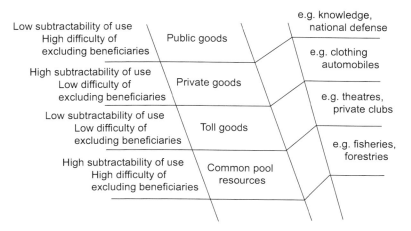

FIGURE 2.1 Four basic types of goods

Adapted from Ostrom (1990, 24).

It would be tempting to assume that hybridity of goods would coalesce with hybridity in forms of organising societal functions and activities. In other words, there would be a traditional and fairly strict distinction between public and private goods, which also would imply that there is a fairly clear-cut divide between the public and private sectors as well as public and private organisations. This does not make too much sense for two reasons. First, irrespective of its analytical rigour and eloquence, Samuelson's (1954) original definition of a public good is indeed very general, as the subsequent research discussion succinctly demonstrates. The definition cannot be used as a consistent starting point to explore institutional systems and structures of society or the interfaces between public and private forms of organising (Marquand 2004). Rather, we should think about the extent of publicness or privateness in the context of organising and providing goods in society. Second, as an analogous frame of reasoning, the idea of hybrid goods would be associated with goods that lie in the continuum between the extremes of public and private goods. Therefore, hybrid goods would require hybrid forms of governance and organising. In the context of our book, that would be a highly constraining argument. Hybrid forms of governance are not restricted to the provision of goods that can be classified as hybrid goods. In fact, several classic public goods (acknowledging the limitations of the definition) are governed through hybrid forms of action. Consider national defense, for which most activities, ranging from the purchasing and provision of military equipment to actual forms of organising military operations, can be and are conducted through public-private collaboration. Using Allen's (2012) historical examples of how 'internal markets' in the English army had a considerable impact on the organising activities of the armed forces between the thirteenth and nineteenth centuries, we are invited to look for tiny distinctions between public and private forms of action. As Allen (2012) argues, using markets and purchasing command positions within the army would probably be considered somewhat strange in modern society, but in the premodern period that was used as an important instrument to hire army commanders.

Theoretical advancement in new economic sociology, new institutionalism, and the theory of justification increases our understanding of how hybrids can be studied, even though the distinction between public and private activity is seldom the subject matter of sociological inquiry (Powell 1990; Powell 1987). New economic sociology and new institutionalism have grown from discussion in the US. Justification theory represents European endeavours in comprehending the nature of economic activity.

Some of the developments in the US influenced the formation of economic sociology. In the 1970s, sociologists critiqued the emphasis on the constraints on agency provided by values and norms in society in contrast to the voluntary internal motives in guiding actions. Consequently, the argument of new economic sociology was that there is a need to see economic activity as a socially embedded activity connected to the social relationships between individuals and groups. On the one hand, new economic sociology aimed to see society as culturally constrained action and economy as embedded in social activities. The subject matter of such an analysis lies in the examination of social networks in market transactions. Social networks contain both binding and liberating aspects in their constitutions. Social networks offer opportunities for action constrained by the social obligation imposed by cultural norms for uniformity. At the same time, these networks constrain market transactions through the building of trust and expectations of reciprocity in the evolution of social networks (Granovetter 1985). In this sense, social networks are a bridge connecting economy and society together, as they appear as a constitutive aspect in both of these realms. New institutional theory was not alien to developments in social network theory. Some of the network ideas are included in the constitution of relevant research agendas, but the fundamental escape of new institutionalism from the examination of rule-following behaviour was analysing cognitive and unconscious elements in economic activity (DiMaggio and Powell 1991).

The legacy of economic sociology in the US enabled the analysis of market activities by emphasising aspects of social embeddedness and taken-for-granted beliefs in the formation of economic activities, but it did not try to connect value formation in economic transactions and the generation of cultural values in the realm of society. It is deceptively simple to argue that economic value and cultural value are two sides of the same coin because they represent worth in its different appearances. In other words, what we perceive as valuable depends on the ways in which we assign value and worth to activities in society. These activities are not restricted by distinctions of economic and social activities; rather, they represent distinct and often incommensurable yardsticks for the valuation of actions (Stark 2009).

The economics of convention takes a different stand in overcoming the separation between social and economic interactions. This analysis is explicitly situated in French culture and society, but the examination seems also to have wider appeal in other societies. Boltanski and Thévenot (2006) argue that morality is an integral part of the valuation of both the economic and social realms of activity. To put it otherwise, there is no distinction between the economy and moral economy, as all economies include moral justifications. Justifications of activities may differ, but what is considered valuable is justified in one way or the other. Values are not juxtaposed as different categories. Instead, the orders of worth constitute both of these aspects. The aim is to examine 'operations that people carry out when they want to show their disagreement without resorting to violence, and the ways they construct, display, and conclude more or less lasting agreements' (Boltanski and Thévenot 2006, 25). The basic question is how to reach a legitimate agreement without resorting to violence when multiple and often contradictory logics are simultaneously at play.

There are two levels of examination in the analysis of worth: Polities are part of the higher level and worlds are part of the lower level. Polities are derived from classical texts in political philosophy, whereas worlds are extracted from management guides dealing with the operation of private firms. A polity may refer to an overall system of politics, but it also has a link to the city and, consequently, the democratic orientation of communities with a definite geographical location.

Polities define principles that can be applied in disputes in everyday life. There is a principle of common humanity, which enables the reference to shared aspirations of all humanity. In practice, people find themselves in different positions (conditions) in a community, which requires coordination to integrate the interests involved in these positions. A scale of values is needed to justify different and possibly unequal positions without discrediting the principle of the common good. First, advancement to superior positions requires a type of cost-benefit analysis. Investments in attaining the benefits of superior positions can be assessed in terms of the sacrifice required to achieve these conditions. Second, increased happiness related to the achievement of superior positions should benefit the community as a whole. In other words, increased happiness should add something to the common good (Callinicos 2006). Further, the hierarchical ordering of society cannot be legitimated solely in terms of acquired power and aspirations for domination; instead, it can be justified in terms of the greater good provided by principles in six major polities.

The difference between polities and worlds is similar to the difference between grammar and conversation. Grammar defines the way in which conversation can take place, but actual discussion proceeds with particular individuals in specific instances (Boltanski and Thévenot 1999). Irrespective of the level of abstraction, both polities and worlds are empirical concepts which may vary in different societies. Consequently, the project world and the green world are later additions to existing categories in view of empirical developments. In the following, there is a short description of the six original worlds (see Table 2.1).

In the world of inspiration, worth originates from contact with an external source. Artistic expression serves as an example. Imagination, not paying attention to the opinions of others, and creating something that does not conform to existing rules are denominators in valuating this world. In a domestic world, people's worth depends on a hierarchy of trust based on a chain of personal dependencies. Position in one's family lineage, such as the positions of fathers and sons, puts family members in a specific order in relation to one another. Likewise, such dependencies

TABLE 2.1 Main features in the orders of worth

Order of worth	Main features
Inspired world	Creativity, passion, emotion
Domestic world	Reputation, trustworthiness, authority
World of fame	Popularity, media, vogue, trends
Civic world	Collective welfare, equality, rules, and regulations
Market world	Price, competition, short-term
Industrial world	Technical efficiency, engineering, long-term
Green world	Environmental friendliness, sustainability, future generations
Project world	Connectivity, flexibility, social capital, networks

Adapted from Boltanski and Thévenot (2006), Thévenot et al. (2000), and Boltanski et al. (2005).

arise outside family contexts, for instance, between those who recommend someone to a specific post and those who are recommended. In a world of renown or fame, worth is a result of other people's opinions. Celebrities, or men and women in the public eye, are those who are worthy in the world of fame. Of course, being a celebrity necessitates the recognition of others, which in turn requires effort in making oneself known to those others. In the civic world, civic worth does not respect the personal dependencies of domestic worth or the opinions of others in the world of fame. People are valuable to the extent that they are part of some larger unity representing the general good. Relevant objects of the civic world are not individuals but rather their collective representations, such as federations or unions, which gain their worth by being able to mobilise collective action. In a market world, worth is related to one's ability to gather wealth in the interaction between buyers and sellers in competitive markets without respect to one's personal attachments or emotional dependencies. In the industrial world, worth is based on efficiency, which deals with managing the future with the aid of planning and professional expertise and the use of statistics, graphs, and scenarios (Boltanski and Thévenot 1999).

In this thinking, action needs to be justified in critical moments. In such instances, agents move from personal convenience to collective convention. The conventions are defined in two terms: (1) history objectified in 'things' such as structures, laws, and regulations (externalisation), and (2) history objectified in 'bodies' such as dispositions (bodily and mental schemata) which make up habits (internalisation). The existence of different polities and worlds for the evaluation of worth gives grounds for disputes. There can be two types of controversies: those internal to the specific world and those originating from using principles from different worlds. A reality test is a relevant procedure in solving grievances within a single world. For instance, a dispute over the fame of a celebrity does not only concern the personal opinions of the individuals involved. Fame can also be assessed in terms of records sold, books translated, or name recognition among the general public as recorded by Internet search engines. Disputes might take a more serious turn when the use of an alternative world is used as a basis for arguments. In this case, two reality tests are simultaneously in play. The dispute might end through the acceptance of one world and one reality test as points of reference. It is also possible for discussants to reach a compromise in mixing the principles of alternative worlds. Yet another variant of a solution is ending the dispute by forgetting the controversy without making any agreement (Jagd 2007).

Blood donation is a good illustration of the possible grievances between the one donating blood and the one interpreting the action. A person might give blood for the sake of the common good and humanity (the civic world) or for the sake of opportunistic motives to acquire money (the market world). It is possible for the ideas of the actor donating blood and the ideas of the interpreter judging the action to coincide with respect to two possible worlds. In such cases, blood donation could be interpreted as sympathetic (both interpreter and actor perceive the action as belonging to the civic world) or as realistic (both actor and interpreter see the action as belonging to the market world). In critical situations, interpretations originate from different worlds. An actor donating blood out of self-interest (the market world) can be judged as greedy by the interpreter (the civic world). Alternatively, an actor might have nothing but altruistic motives (the civic world), but the interpreter judges him or her as naïve in doing so (the market world) (Jagd 2007).

The delegation of worlds does not provide a clear distinction between public and private spheres of institutional life, nor does it acknowledge hybridity as a separate venue for orders of worth. In fact, there are two worlds related to markets (the industrial and market worlds) and one world (the civic world) that covers some aspect of government activity. The orders of worth enable focus on the value orientation of public and private strategies, which in purely formal terms do not differ much from one another. Analysis of the environment, long-term trajectories, and hierarchical implementation procedures – from general objectives to the most detailed standard operation procedures – reminds us of the industrial world. However, in terms of evaluation, public and private spheres are distinct from one another. The profit motive provides a point of reference for economy and efficiency considerations in private enterprises. Within the public domain, civic virtues emphasise collective rather than private particularistic interests. Collective values often evade exact measurement, and public activities benefit serving not only customers but also citizens at large, often with no or nominal cost to the recipient of the service (Moore 1995).

An examination of the orders of worth is relevant in explaining some of the tensions within strategy modes identified in Chapter 1. The strategic scanning approach underlines the importance of novel and unique resource combinations in the strategy-formation process, which does not follow any predefined rules and evades rational calculation. It makes very little difference whether the resources are physical or human or whether they appear in the form of learnt and changing capabilities. Innovation and creativeness serve as modes of evaluation of such goal-oriented action, which cannot be sorted out in advance. Building up novel uncharted resource combinations certainly demands ingenuity, creativity, and passion as described by the inspired world, but the importance of emotion and passion in developing new ideas is difficult to maintain within permanent organisations. Within the perspective of strategic governance, contact with actors in the environment is of key interest. Two worlds are relevant here: the domestic world, in which hierarchy and tradition functions as criteria for the evaluation of possible contacts, and the project world, which is based on flexible, nonpermanent relationships between individuals and organisations alike.

How would hybrid organisations be situated in the orders of worth? First, hybrids do not enjoy the position of objectified history in laws and regulations nor in our mental schemata of organised activity. This makes hybrids vulnerable to disputes when faced with ambiguous situations. In a more fundamental tone, the existence of hybrids can be questioned. Second, hybrids, which reside between public and private activity by their nature, incorporate different orders of worth. This arrangement can cause disputes; for instance, why should we contract public duties to providers when this might compromise some equal citizenship rights?

Third, the dual nature of hybrid organisations combines public and private goals as well as criteria for evaluation. Multiple points of reference give ample opportunities for grievances. For instance, why build PPPs instead of relying on private enterprises or public agencies? The problem of valuation gives grounds for criticising such activities based on the lack of civic virtues by giving too much importance to the markets and also on the basis of markets and industries by not giving total control to the economic actors.

Working towards public and private interests

Distinctions between the public and private spheres may cover goods that are provided in society. These distinctions may cover organisations and entities that are regulated, controlled, and managed through public-private distinctions. In addition, the distinction between public and private may stem from an ancient idea of public and private interests, in which societal activities may be assumed to be different because of the extent to which the activities serve individual and private interests or public or common interests (Morrell and Harrington-Buhay 2012).

Not surprisingly, there are no common uniform definitions – or operationalisations of definitions – of public and private interests. For instance, Denhardt and Denhardt (2007) compare problems conceptualising public interest with problems conceptualising love. Both of these concepts yield different meanings to different people. They are not stable over time; conceptualisations are used for whatever political purpose at different times and in different places. Conceptualisations also motivate human action and behaviour by giving mental frames for intellectual thinking. Finally, it is not common to use concepts together with exact operationalisations and measurements. Denhardt and Denhardt (2007, 68) conclude by acknowledging the fluidity of public interest, but they use the concept to understand public service provision: 'We acknowledge that the public interest is ambiguous and fluid at the same time that we advocate for its centrality to democratic governance.'

Denhardt and Denhardt (2007) conceptualise public interests in the context of normative positions, indicating that discussion on public interest is not about description but instead stems from a prescriptive-normative stance. Furthermore, one can have an abolitionist position by denying the relevance of the concept of public interest as such. It is also possible to have a political process perspective on public interest, maintaining that public interests may be identified only in the framework of policy implementation. Finally, the notion of public interest may be based on shared values in contradiction with selfish, individualistic values (Cochran 1974; Jorgensen and Bozeman 2007).

Previous research discussion has not been too apt in dealing with the interdependence of public and private interests. In their critical analysis regarding the scope of organisational research, Mahoney et al. (2009, 1036–1037) propose three major areas of development. First, Mahoney et al. are not satisfied with how institutional settings merging public and private interests are actually addressed. Instead of asking 'when and how do private interests aggregate to a common interest,' researchers should be interested in institutions and organisations 'that simultaneously reflect public and private interests.' Mahoney et al. (2009) make suggestions for how theoretical developments can provide substantial contributions to understanding the space in between public and private forms of action. These suggestions include, for instance, strategic management theories, transaction cost theory, property rights theory, and agency theories. Second, the interests of private institutions are often embedded in the interests of public policies. Private institutions may be initiators, instruments, and even objectives of public policy governance. Thus, Mahoney et al. (2009) adopt a policy-specific approach by associating public-private interaction with certain fields of policy areas. They discuss the US example of subprime loans and the subsequent financial crisis in 2008–09, during which Goldman Sachs took on an important role as a policy instrument in contributing to more stable financial markets. Goldman Sachs did so under the supervision and coordination of the US Federal Reserve. Third, Mahoney et al. (2009) have an interesting exploration of the significance of the Limited Liability Corporation as an institutional form. This institution may have created a baseline for investigating private institutions and their links to public policies. This is a problem, because economic and social activities organised through this institutional form cover only a tiny fraction of all social and commercial activities in the world. Moreover, it is fair to say that these corporations may operate in areas with important links to public interests. Therefore, it may be the case that organisational researchers, as well as other researchers in the field, may have focused on a politically important and powerful form of institution but at the expense of understanding what is in fact happening in the world of organisational and institutional activities (Mahoney et al. 2009).

The classic problem regarding public interest addressed by Mahoney et al. (2009), and also intelligibly discussed by Cochran (1974), is the assumption of how private interests transform into public ones. If you assume that public interest can only be seen as an aggregation or a sum of individual private interests (Cochran also talks about private goods), conceptual problems may arise. The concept of 'public' does not exist without explicit reference to such an aggregation procedure. However, if you assume that there can be shared values, communities, or even publics, it is easier to adopt a public interest approach to societal or political discussion. In this formulation, you assume that public interest is more than the sum of individual private interests in society.

One important characteristic of the distinction between public and private interests is the dichotomy of the individual and the collective (Ostrom 1990). While certain activities may serve individual interests, they may not be beneficial to the collective as a whole. Or, political activities conducted through appropriate and legitimate democratic processes may always be beneficial to some groups of people or individuals but detrimental to other groups or individuals. Special emphasis on the distinction between the public and private in the context of interests is what individuals or collectives aim to pursue in society. The notion of 'interest' is indeed problematic, contextual, and full of contrasting interpretations and value propositions. By no means is the 'public' part easier in this respect. We may be misled if we do not deal with multiple publics. Morrell and Harrington-Buhay question the monolithic notion of public interest by asking to what extent and in what ways interests vary among different publics. These may vary significantly in different settings of societies and democracies across the world and in different institutional contexts of public policy and public service delivery (Morrell and Harrington-Buhay 2012).

In one sense, the distinction between public and private interests may be easier to create if we hold the assumption of the individual-collective dichotomy. Then, starting from the assumption that an individual is the focus of analysis, we may assume that anything else different from the individual is public or common. We have the possibility for such a distinctive rationale in the context of interests but not in the context of organisations or goods, which are more intangible and which have boundaries in the focus of analysis vis-à-vis environments that are more blurred and shaped by interaction and reciprocity.

However, this is not to argue that the conception of an individual is clear. In the research literature, there is wide discussion on the trajectories of individuals changing into customers, consumers, and the like. Subsequently, the distinction between public and private interest is not always easy, because the distinction is contingent upon what is meant by 'private': Is it an individual, citizen, customer, or something else? This has an important impact on the ways in which the behaviour of individuals is understood. The notion of 'customer' is based on the idea of voluntary transactions. Defined as a citizen, the individual may be forced to contribute to services that she does not want and that in fact she may find objectionable (Kelly 2005). There are significant differences in implications as to how private interests may or may not add up to, or coalesce with, public interests. Consequently, what is private may be understood and conceptualised in several ways.

Hybrids and hybridity in the context of government reforms

Perhaps we would not be students of public administration unless we had at least something to say about the link between hybrids and the modernisation of government activities. Although we contend that it may be the case that public administration research sometimes pays too much attention to the reformative aspect of public sector activities, we think it is important to link these two aspects with each other. In other words, how should we understand hybrids in the context of public sector reforms? Do we see hybrids as results of public sector reform agendas, or do we observe that public sector reforms have been instigated (intentionally or unintentionally) with hybrids in mind? Are we talking about hybrids by design or by default?

It is no news anymore that, at least in several OECD countries, the public sector has been considered inadequate, inefficient, and ineffective for several decades (Hood 1991; Hood and Dixon 2015). This is the lesson we have learnt from New Public Management (NPM) theory. Since NPM probably does not fit into the classic formulation of a theory and is more a loose, empirically based collection of reform policies throughout the OECD countries, NPM discourse tells us something about the ways in which the reformative perspective of government has been perceived in different parts of the world. Reforming governments has been the zeitgeist for a long time.

Usually, it is not only important to understand the actual impacts of how government systems have evolved but also the political, ideological, and managerial intentions these institutional development processes have been based on (March and Heath 1994). Just consider the classic argument that actors may have rational intentions, but the outcomes of such intentions are always only boundedly rational. One intention in government reforms, which is in fact an extremely influential one, has been the idea of mixing governments with markets. This assumption has been adopted from several areas of economics and political science. It maintains that, if you introduce competitive dynamics into government systems, you will see efficiency gains and more variation in public services (Lancaster 1979). Hypothetically, the public sector would then spend less and spend more wisely.

However, institutional life is usually much more complicated than that. In fact, you could argue that, if you seriously try to mix government with markets, you get hybrids. As it is not possible to introduce a pure market mechanism in the context of business firms and business hierarchies, it is even more complicated to do so in the context of public hierarchies that operate with multiple rationalities, identities, and preferences of institutional action (Ouchi 1979; Ebrahim et al. 2014).

Nevertheless, this is the belief system that has formed the basis of government reforms in OECD countries for several decades. Concepts such as 'market-type mechanisms' (Pollitt 2001), 'quasi-market models' (Le Grand and Bartlett 1993), and 'neo-liberal waves of public sector reforms' (Vedung 2010) have become the everyday vocabulary of public sector reforms. Such public policy reform initiatives have included, for instance, the following instruments:

1   **Vouchers**. This is known as a system in which, instead of allocating public budgets and funding to service-providing organisations, funds are allocated to the users of the service. This allocation (i.e. vouchers) entitles the user to utilise her voice when making choices between service providers. This is assumed to facilitate competitive dynamics between service providers. The idea has been widely used in public sector reforms in different contexts, such as elderly care and other parts of social care and health care. Vouchers for school education have been propagated by influential thinkers of market reforms, especially by Milton Friedman (1997, 343), who considers vouchers not as an end as such but rather as a transitionary stage from a government to a market system. It is obvious that voucher systems rely on institutional logics that are different from systems in which publicly financed and controlled hierarchies educate children and students. Voucher systems aim to transform the traditional design by giving students (and/or their parents) more of a voice when selecting schools or other types of service providers. Furthermore, at the systemic level, in policy discus-

sion voucher systems are assumed to contribute to higher levels of variation, both in terms of volume and service quality (Lancaster 1979).
2   **Contracting out**. This system is based on an assumption that public service provision is fundamentally a 'make or buy' decision (Williamson 1999a). The shift from make to buy has been noticeable, which has magnified the uses of contractual arrangements and schemes in government service provision. The buy decision may have implicated new types of internal quasi-markets (a purchaser-provider split) or externalised public service provision to outside parties, organisations, and providers (Vining and Globerman 1999). Contracting out thus reflects the policy rationale that, for the sake of efficiency and improved performance, it would be sensible to impose a credible threat to the in-house operations of a city or other contexts of government organisations. Moreover, the shift may be seen as an attempt to replace hierarchical in-house control with indirect forms of control through peer pressure, competitive dynamics, and markets (Vedung 2010).
3   **Privatisation**. At the macro level of society, an extreme form of indirect control is privatisation, in which control is actually delegated to private economic agents. The conscious choice of selling government assets or state-owned enterprises (SOEs) to private agents has become one of the most influential policy tools for enabling market-based allocation mechanisms. However, time span is important to bear in mind, as different types of pendulum shifts may be observed in privatisation schemes around the world (Megginson and Netter 2001). Two issues should be considered in the context of our book. First, throughout the world, privatisation has often concentrated on specific sectors of society that provide important goods for society and incorporate both public and private characteristics of goods. These goods include, for example, energy, transportation, and telecommunications (Nelson 2005). Therefore, it is no wonder that different countries have adopted distinct policy pathways and trajectories to pursue the privatisation of assets. Some countries may have used a transformative approach by applying comprehensive privatisation programmes, whereas some countries have chosen more incremental paths by which government agencies have been turned into government enterprises. Afterward, these agencies have been turned into SOEs or other types of government-owned companies and then sold to private investors. Second, in many countries, the hybridity of activities does not vanish through privatisation. Privatisation may have provided a boost to innovative business industries or put an end to ideologically laden discussions of owning resources in a society (Friedman 1997), but it has not been able to evade the hybridity of goods or the hybridity of parallel institutional logics.
4   **Public–private partnerships (PPPs)**. The impetus to mix governments with markets has created an industry of new forms of interaction between public and private sectors. PPPs have become one of the magic concepts, or umbrella concepts (Pollitt and Hupe 2011), that depict such institutional interactions. According to Hodge and Greve (2009), PPPs may assume several dif-

ferent forms and thus create families of conceptual positions. PPPs can include the following:

- institutional collaboration for coproduction and risk sharing
- infrastructure contracts with sophisticated financial arrangements (e.g. private finance initiatives in the UK)
- networks of public policy
- more general community development
- urban renewal programmes and projects

(Hodge and Greve 2009, 33)

As Hodge and Greve (2009) succinctly argue, the concept of PPPs includes different levels of interaction between public and private sectors. Sometimes the use of the word 'partnership' may provide leeway to use a concept that is less politically delicate than, for instance, 'privatisation' or 'contracting out.' However, the same notion may include stricter institutional arrangements in which funding arrangements are defined by national legislations and regulations.

In the context of public policy reforms, what do we know about the impacts of proposed and realised reforms? It is not actually clear whether and to what extent these market-type reform initiatives have contributed to intended outcomes. Hood and Dixon (2015) intelligibly argue that this is partly due to insufficient evidence of the economic impacts of public sector reforms. In other words, if you make the sensible assumption that demonstrating impacts of market-type reforms in government should be based on some kind of scientific evidence, not on beliefs, the case is actually very unclear. Due to limitations in the particular intertemporal comparability of performance information, Hood and Dixon (2015) find it complicated to demonstrate the ultimate outcomes and value of performance management reforms in the context of the UK.

However, institutionally speaking, we think it is evident that the process of mixing governments with markets in public sector reform agendas has created new hybrids and new types of hybrid arrangements (Koppell 2005). The reformative attempt to mix pure types of hierarchies and markets has not accounted for what was expected in the first place: more cost efficiency, more variation, and more customer orientation in the public sector. We do see some of those impacts, but in more detail we see institutional structures and organisations, the performance of which is even more difficult to demonstrate than before (Hodges 2012). Therefore, the epistemological problem is that we actually do not know.

3
HOW TO TAME MONSTERS
Hybridity and its variants

The aim of this chapter is to broaden the view of hybridity in social activities, contexts, and organisations. It is our contention that the dichotomous perspective of public and private action has constrained our understanding regarding what hybrids and hybridity actually involve. This is not to state that we cannot comprehend the cognitive rationales of the distinctions between public and private. However, it is the strict prima facie assumption of the clear-cut public and private sector delineation that prevents us from seeing institutional life in all its richness. Hybridity, we contend, is one aspect in exploring such richness. For us, it is erroneous to see such an exploration process as creating monstrous hybrids, institutional weirdos, or an increase in theoretical complexity for its own sake.

Our process of enhancing understanding of the public, the private, and the hybrid is divided into several elements. We discuss hybridity at different levels of social and economic action. Furthermore, we combine levels of hybridity with some traditional discussions in social theory associated with social structures. Finally, this chapter concludes by discussing hybrid structures and activities as institutional, political, and cognitive practices in the context of uncertainty avoidance. We study ideals of administrative pragmatism and decision-making heuristics as reasoning for why it may make sense to rely on a clear distinction of the public and private (Tilly 2006). In this chapter, we provide a rich variety of case illustrations from different contexts of hybrid activities.

There are number of analytic perspectives available for the study of hybrid governance. One can distinguish levels of hybridity according to the number of participants in social intercourse, which results in singular, dyadic, and triadic levels of analysis. Another way of separating hybrid activities is to see them as abstractions beginning from the low level of analysis (micro) and progressing into more general and larger levels (meso and macro). Yet another option is to see hybrids as entities. Most typically, hybrids are seen as organisational entities with a distinctive border

44 How to tame monsters

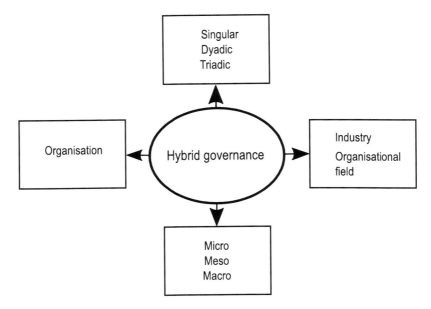

FIGURE 3.1 Analytic perspectives on hybrid governance

separating them from their environments, but it is equally possible to see collective entities of hybrids as comprising industries or organisational fields (see Figure 3.1). The following discussion elaborates on these perspectives in more detail.

Is there more than meets the eye? Hybridity as levels of societal activities

Hybrids and hybridity are often associated with the notion of hybrid organisations. In this association, we tend to assume that if an organisation incorporates features from both public and private forms of institutional action, it is regarded as a hybrid organisation. Such features, as previously discussed, may include ownership, objective setting, finance, and control (Perry and Rainey 1988; Bozeman and Moulton 2011). This type of reasoning has resulted in several studies and research programmes exploring how to delineate the public from the private and how to define hybridity in the context of modern organisations.

However, the argument that hybridity only resembles one form of organisational action in society is probably more an elucidation of us living amidst a world of organisations than a true representation of hybridity in social life (Simon 1991). To some extent, we have learnt to use organisations as an important frame for our thinking to inform ourselves of how social action takes place. We enjoy some of our dinners at business firms called 'restaurants,' educational activities are conducted by educational 'organisations' or 'schools,' and people are cured in health care 'organisations' or 'hospitals.' Organisational logics can easily be applied. Although almost anything can currently be reduced to the label 'organisation,' it is important to discuss what elements of societal activities are missing if such an argument is employed. This discussion is also conducive to our understanding of hybrid action and hybridity.

It may be easier for us to understand the important role of hybrid organisations in discussing hybrid forms of governance if we realise the fundamental underpinnings of organisational thinking. For instance, the objective of classic contingency theory is to simplify the complex institutional world by depicting the system under analysis using a clear-cut delineation of organisations and their environments. In other words, to investigate organisations, there is a need to distinguish that system from something that is outside its boundaries; that is, the environment (Scott 1991). Moreover, if organisations are able to adapt their structures to fit their environments, they are deemed successful. This is the conventional wisdom of organisational and managerial thinking.

However, this thinking assumes that an organisation can be easily distinguished from its environment. It is not easy to do this in the context of organisational settings, let alone in the context of hybrid organisations. Let us consider universities. What is the unit that is adapting to environmental conditions? Historically, universities bundled together two societal activities: the production of revealed knowledge and the socialisation of younger generations through teaching. In fact, the very first phase of unbundling these two activities in the nineteenth century was the unbundling of the primary obligation of higher learning to disseminate knowledge. For this purpose, research seminars were created, and new professions engaged with research that emerged and evolved. The university institution has organised itself to adapt to the changing nature of knowledge, thereby assimilating new responsibilities. To contend that a university (the organisation) is adapting to environmental conditions is to assume that the missions of socialisation and the dissemination of knowledge are bundled together (Neave 2002).

Furthermore, one of the most interesting things is, in fact, environment, the framework that sets the scene for organisations, policies, actions, and actors. It is obvious that, in practice, an environment partly consists of different organisations, but it also consists of other forms of relationships, influences, actions, and actors that have importance but not necessarily an explicit organisational focus. For instance, Scott (1991) refers to an industry system as a single, concrete, and stable network of the identifiable and interacting components (see Bain 1968) of the societal sector, which perform similar functions together with other members of their set that influence their operations in some manner. Whitley (2000, 7) talks about intellectual fields as a concept that describes 'a broader and more general social unit of knowledge production.' When we attempt to understand hybrid activities, organisational thinking may constrain us (Whitley 2000).

Levels of hybridity

In social life, hybridity may be observed in distinct settings of institutional, political, and economic action. Therefore, we can think of three different levels of hybridity:

hybrid systems, hybrid industries, and hybrid organisations. As the previous research discussion has primarily concentrated on hybrid organisations, our aim is to discuss further other levels of societal action influenced by hybridity; that is, levels of public-private interaction. Case illustrations of health policy (Case 3.1) and cleantech industry (Case 3.2) enable us to see hybridity as system- and industry-level development.

CASE 3.1 HYBRID GOVERNANCE FOR SOLVING TRICKY PROBLEMS OF HEALTH POLICY

Maintaining and developing health among people is a complicated task in society. At the level of health policy, societies struggle to balance different criteria of rationality: cost containment, access to health services, and service quality (Kissick 1994), each of which provides important, albeit to some extent mutually exclusive, criteria for the governance of health care service provision. For instance, while it may be legitimate to ease the access to health care services, it may be difficult to do this in the context of finite financial resources and providing marginal quality improvements for existing health service users. Therefore, health care systems struggle to cope with the wicked tension between the unlimited needs of health service and the limited financial and intellectual resources for providing services (Kork and Vakkuri 2016).

In governing such an effort, countries of the world have adopted different strategies and institutional practices with which they have attempted to solve simultaneous problems of access, service quality, and financial balance. Health care service provision reveals important examples of hybrid systems. Financing comes from both public and private resource bases; organising and provision includes business firms, public organisations, and nonprofit organisations; and forms of control entail both government oversight and private and professionally organised practices.

Health care systems show different levels of hybridity (OECD 2015a). For instance, the US's health care system is by definition a hybrid, as fundamental choices of health care activities are organised, financed, insured, and managed by both public and private interests and organisations (Sekhri et al. 2011). For instance, one half of the funding comes from private sources, and the other half comes from the government. However, even in publicly funded health services, the form of delivery is primarily private. The health policy is under intense scrutiny and policy debate in the US because, in addition to well-documented problems of access to services, health care expenditures per GDP are significantly higher in the US than in other countries (in the US it is 16.4 percent, and the average of all OECD countries is 8.9 percent) (OECD 2015a). Is this somehow associated with the hybrid nature of the US health care system, in which public services and goods are provided but also in which different sets of business profit-seeking motives are included and enacted? For instance, cost containment may be of different importance to different actors in the health care system. While it is too straightforward to make an argument about clear and unambiguous causal relationships between system properties and health impacts, there are several discussions and ideas emphasising the need for the systematic governance of health care systems as hybrid systems. These ideas have been labelled as, for instance, 'integrated governance' (Sekhri et al. 2011) or 'multisector partnerships' (Harris 2016).

As discussed in this book, it is complicated to talk about health as a purely private or purely public good. Health impacts may be wide-ranging and comprehensive, and they may spill over, but health can also be commodified and commercialised. Accordingly, the fundamental question in the governance of health systems is about selecting the best features of both public and private forms of health-maintaining activities and processes. But how to create solutions that would be able to utilise the best features of both systems? 'Integrated' modes of governance might be able to solve some of the problems that other forms of governance fail to address. What transaction cost analysis teaches us is to evaluate whether there is some concrete option to deal with governance problems other than the option that has already been adopted (Williamson 1985). Moreover, if a governance structure exists in the first place, it is viable, as it has already survived the institutional struggle of survival.

One could argue that hybrid systems have survived some important tests of institutional survival because they have been adopted in health care. In other words, there may be some important hidden rationalities in hybrid forms of governance when applied to health policy sectors. However, we could also contend that there are no viable alternatives for governance modes, which is why we cannot be certain whether distinct forms of hybrid governance are merely the lesser of two (or three) evils. To put hybrid systems or integrated partnerships to a real test, we would need to ask the following questions:

- How do hybrid forms of governance compare with other relevant alternatives in dealing with the problem of cost containment? For instance, to what extent are increasing health care expenditures in the US due to problems of hybrid forms of governance? Does the system have too much hybridity, or too little hybridity? Does the system lack the systematic governance of hybridity?
- What is the most efficient mode of governance in improving access to health care services?
- What is the link between different modes of governance and health care service quality?

There are multiple uncertainties and contingencies in different governance forms. In order to solve fundamental health problems, hybrid forms of governance require new types of system-level coordination, rethinking roles for government and private business firms, and disclosures of transparent and comparable information on service provision, as well as an understanding of the explicit and implicit forms of hybrid contracting (Williamson 1999b). It may be these contingencies which determine the actual possibilities of using hybrid forms of governance in health policy. However, an even more fundamental question is our approach to hybridity and our perceptions of how to define the success and failure of governance solutions. Do we think of these as a result of conscious and deliberate design, or as intended or unintended outcomes of institutional change with several conflicting interests and boundedly rational processes of intentions, compromises, and choices (Scott 2000)?

First, *hybrid systems* are a policy-level network of institutions and actors pursuing societal (public) macro-level goals but with different sets of institutional backgrounds, institutional logics, and decision-making rationales. For instance, a health system may be used as a case context for this level. Second, we are interested in *hybrid industries*, a cluster of public and private actors pursuing public goals but within a more specific institutional field of action (Padgett and Powell 2012). As a case context for this, we can think of the 'cleantech' industry, in which several actors – including public policy makers, business firms, and multiple associations – aim to contribute to the common good of ensuring clean air by producing environmentally friendly technologies and solutions for the global marketplace. Third, we can discuss *hybrid organisations* pursuing public goals by employing parallel institutional logics. The selection of different industries in our study represents the differentiated orderings of worth by default. As a field of activity, the area of health has been related to the civic order of worth in Europe, which is evaluated by the principle of collective welfare and its ability to distribute these services in an equal manner, whereas the US has valued the world of markets in emphasising competition and buying and selling while providing health services.

The cleantech industry signifies the green order of worth by supplying environmentally friendly products, emphasising sustainability, and working for ecosystems. These orders of worth are not natural in any sense, as they need institutional legitimation and justification. They have to be constantly negotiated, but they are also in a process of change, and they might include contradictory tendencies. Within R&D, there is an inbuilt impetus for an industrial order of worth, for technical efficiency, and for a long-term plan of the future combined with the world of markets, which does not always respect the features of the inspired world of creativity, innovativeness, and exploration. As a specific area of R&D, the cleantech industry is in its institutional infancy, as it combines features of the green, market, and industrial worlds. These ambiguities exemplify the difficulty of defining qualified objects within the cleantech industry. Is a low-emission diesel engine part of the green world on the basis of its modification, a part of the market world due to its ability to save on costs, or even a part of the industrial world due to its technical efficiency, to name a few possibilities?

CASE 3.2 HYBRIDIZATION OF INDUSTRIES

Going green through cleantech

The institutional emergence of industries is an interesting phenomenon and an extremely useful case for exploring hybrid forms of governance (Padgett and Powell 2012). Although many actors seek institutional clarity and wish to avoid uncertainty, this may not always apply to industrial fields. The current structure of industries is a social convention, which may be incongruous with what is happening in the real world of economic activities.

One such example is the cleantech industry, a nascent industrial field combining and transcending several categories of existing areas of industrial business firms and activities as well as distinct fields of public policies. According to O'Rourke (2009), in order to understand the emergence of the cleantech industry, two parallel trajectories of institutional changes should be considered. First, economic growth, particularly in North America and the US, has largely been stimulated by entrepreneurial actors operating with new technologies and innovations. Quite often, this goes hand in hand with venture capitalists (VC) willing to invest in such new innovative technologies. O'Rourke recognises such a development in the background of the cleantech concept's emergence, dating this back to the early 2000s. The second parallel development was the degradation of our physical environment. Long-standing discussions on climate change started to be grounded on explicit indicators of that degradation. People began to attach new meanings to environmental problems, such as environmental disasters, extinctions of species, acid rain, and changes in the ozone layers of the stratosphere. People also started to seek more sophisticated and eloquent evidence of climate change. They wanted to know more about what was going in their environments, and also how they would be able to contribute to solutions.

Interestingly enough, there had to be an intellectual shift to understand environmental problems in a new manner. The traditional idea of treating business and the environment as mutually exclusive elements of the market economy had to be changed. Environmental 'problems' had to be transformed into 'opportunities' for investments and VCs. This necessitated uses of new institutional logics, or frames, as O'Rourke (2009) names them, which indicate that new technologies are the most efficient means for solving environmental problems. In other words, as societal ends include environmental, ecologically sustainable, or social benefits to society, the most optimal means could be found in an effective system of business and entrepreneurial activities. Doing well by doing good began to be accepted as a proper form of business behaviour.

However, in terms of institutional clarity, cleantech has not been an easy concept. As Cooke (2008) points out, there have been several competing conceptualisations, not only about cleantech as such but also about the links between cleantech and other boundary concepts, for example, 'greentech.' Moreover, it could be argued that cleantech may remain a VC buzzword, such as what happened with 'biotech' and 'infotech' several years earlier. All these concepts link certain policy goals with the application of technologies: 'bio' with 'tech,' 'information' with 'tech,' and 'cleaner environment' with 'tech.' Cooke (2008, 378) illustrates these linkages, representing the several categories of the cleantech industry. Cleantech categories and their classifications may include the following industrial systems:

1. Advanced materials and nanotechnology: nonplatinum catalysts for catalytic converters, and nanomaterials for more efficient and fungible solar photovoltaic panels
2. Agriculture and nutrition: innovative plant technologies and modified crops that are designed to reduce reliance on pesticides or fungicides
3. Air quality: stationary and mobile emission scrubbers, testing and compliance services
4. Consumer products: biodegradable plastic ware and nontoxic household cleaners
5. Enabling technologies and services: advanced material research services and high throughput screening research equipment
6. Energy generation and storage: solar photovoltaic technology, wind power, hydrogen generation, and batteries and power management technology
7. Environmental information technology: regulatory and policy compliance software and geographic information services (GIS)
8. Manufacturing industrial technologies: hardware and software to increase manufacturing productivity and efficiency
9. Material recovery and recycling: chemical recovery and reprocessing in industrial manufacturing, remanufacturing
10. Transportation and logistics: fuel cells for cars; diesel retrofit equipment; hybrid electric systems for cars, buses, and trucks
11. Waste and water purification and management: biological and chemical processes for water and waste purification, fluid flow metering technology

The case of the cleantech industry reflects the basic idea of an industry transcending the boundaries between traditional business industrial activities and societal aims such as reducing carbon dioxide emissions and facilitating a clean-energy supply chain. However, it is also apparent that the introduction and emergence of the cleantech industry disturbs the institutional status quo of existing industries. For instance, consider manufacturing industrial technologies aimed at developing hardware and software to increase manufacturing productivity and efficiency (Cooke 2008). In terms of cleantech development, this makes perfect sense. For instance, in order to contribute to the reduction of carbon dioxide emissions, a system of production economics needs to drastically improve the eco-efficiency of production processes. However, not all manufacturing industrial technologies are related to environmental problems or cleanliness. Optimality is the fundamental aim and starting point of any production process (Koopmans 1957). Therefore, industries are not easily distinguished from each other, or, to put it another way, technologies of optimality may serve almost any context of institutional and industrial action (Porter 1995).

This illustration may be used as a way to discuss the mechanisms of the emergence of hybrid industries. The cleantech industry could be seen as an institutional change mechanism that Padgett and Powell (2012) label incorporation and detachment. The cleantech industry has come to solve 'new' social aims using both old and novel technologies. Old technologies implying that, for example, economising production manufacturing processes are indeed an 'old' concept are now utilised in a new context for solving social and ecological problems. In addition, we are also dealing with several new technologies in terms of inventions for reducing carbon dioxide emissions. In doing this, many of the elements of the cleantech industry have been detached from their old contexts in industrial activities. By connecting old and new networks of industrial activities, revised social aims, and new forms of technology, economising production processes have – step by step – become incorporated into the context of cleantech.

Meso as a constitutive level of analysis

There is a fertile debate in many fields of research about levels of institutional action in society. One common approach is to discuss micro, meso, and macro levels. In (neoclassical) economics, there is a long tradition of analysing two distinct levels of economic activities; that is, micro and macro. Micro concerns the choice of individual economic agents, and macro refers to the aggregated consequences of such individual choices. According to Dopfer et al. (2004, 264), 'The sum of micro is macro, and the decomposition of macro is micro.' Naturally, these levels have intrinsic value of their own in the economics discipline, as microeconomics aims to understand the behaviour of rational economic agents – such as consumers, firms, and public agencies – while macroeconomics aims to understand the overall economic system and the determinants of macroeconomic planning in society. An important area of methodological discussion concerns the extent to which the interlinkages between these two levels and systems of economic action can be assumed, observed, or intervened through policy design (Dopfer et al. 2004).

The level of societal analysis is indeed important, not only in economics but also in the social sciences in general. It is customary to separate micro analysis and macro analysis from one another, which is sometimes augmented by the introduction of the meso level in between these two categories. There is, however, no common reference among different disciplines for labelling and identifying categories. For instance, organisations might be considered to be at the macro level for social psychologists and at the micro level for economists. In this way, the level of analysis is often contextual and subject to specific heuristic devices that separate small-scale research objects from large-scale ones. Having said that, there is also a genuine interest in entangling the connections between micro and macro levels of analysis in social action. Evolutionary economics offers one such perspective for understanding economic exchanges.

Analysing evolutionary economics as a system of rules, Dopfer et al. (2004, 268) treat the meso level not as a transitionary or intermediary level between the macro and micro levels but as 'a thing . . . that is made of complex other things (micro) and is an element in higher order things (macro).' The meso level constitutes the basis for evolutionary process and change. Such a meso trajectory is represented in the three-stage process of emergence, diffusion, and retention, in which rule systems shape and reshape the underpinnings of economic change. For Dopfer et al., the meso level is necessary to understand the forces and mechanisms of economic change. The micro vs. macro distinction is not always sufficient for that purpose.

Dopfer et al.'s (2004) evolutionary levels of analysis view on evolutionary economics builds upon the tripartite distinction between the micro, meso, and macro levels of analysis. The distinction is not only a categorising tool for distinguishing economic phenomena in the production and consumption of goods and services but also a perspective for the analysis of the changing nature of economic circumstances. The starting point of evolutionary economics is that the standard economics viewpoint based on mathematical logic does not enable the analysis of structures, populations, or processes. Instead, the standard economics view replaces the micro economic agent with the notion of the representative agent, which covers all actors in the population who are able to choose rationally among all possible choices. On the macro level, the standard economics view sees economics as statistical aggregates of compiled economic actions. Both of these aspects makes it difficult to see economics as a dynamic open-system process embraced by evolutionary economics.

Research discussion in evolutionary economics has often referred to the natural sciences, biology in particular, in its goal to incorporate the temporal aspect of economic action. The problem with natural and biological analogies is that economic phenomena are not natural in an evolutionary sense but instead belong to the cultural realm of action that involves human information processing. One solution to include the information-processing ability of humans is to incorporate knowledge in dynamic economic processes. This leads to a number of implications. First, the economic actor or agent has the internal cognitive structurer's mind and the external structure-orienting individual choices towards society. The main manifestation of knowledge is found in the rule systems governing economic exchanges. Rules include subject rules (e.g. mental models and behavioural heuristics) and object rules (e.g. social rules governing the organisation of a firm or rules of the market and technological rules governing technologies) (Dopfer 2013). A system of rules manifests itself, for instance, as division of labour, organisation structure, and capability systems. According to this view, the underlying deep structure is the rule system governing economic exchanges, and actual economic exchange is a surface manifestation of the underlying rule structure. On the micro level, economic agents such as firms are individual carriers of generic rules. On this level, it is possible that economic agents have adopted idiosyncratic rules that do not extend to wider use. The generality of the rules is seen as a divisive line in the level of analysis issues. It is in the meso level that one can see rules that are generalised in a certain population as being of interest to economic analysis. The distinction between the meso and macro levels of analysis is based on similar logic. In the macro perspective, the totality of meso-level units constitutes the macro unit, such as an industry or whole economy. The distinction here is between a generic rule/population of rule actualisation (meso) and the connections and compatibility of generic rules between populations (macro).

According to this view, there is no direct link between the micro and macro levels of analysis. Rather, micro and macro are two perspectives that reveal structural aspects of the changes in meso populations. It is the meso level that constitutes the basic element of economic structure. The macro perspective offers a top-down view on the economic processes of the meso level, and the micro perspective signifies a bottom-up system perspective. The meso level of analysis includes industrial districts, regional knowledge clusters, learning regions, interfirm industrial organisations, national innovation systems, networks with weak and strong ties, and technical support communities. The dynamism of the meso level originates from the interplay between human experimentation and curiosity and the degeneration of rule structures, which guarantees that rule structures are prone to change. The meso view orients attention to single generic rules that have actualised in particular populations. In the evolutionary view, the application of rules in populations is a process. New regulation or technology opens up possibilities that are exploited through the adoption of rules in a range of contexts within a population. The tendency for a variant of a rule to become dominant over other rules is a meso-level phenomenon, which can be seen as the formation of monopolies on the micro level. Yet again, knowledge plays an important role in monopolistic tendencies. The emergence of a new monopoly is a sign of a new meso-level rule, but competition tends to collapse into monopoly when knowledge is fully exploited, and competition tends to grow out of monopolies when knowledge is new (Dopfer 2013).

CASE 3.3 NATIONAL INNOVATION SYSTEMS AS A HYBRID FORM OF GOVERNANCE

The discussions and developments of national innovation systems clearly point out some of the main features and challenges of a meso-level analysis of hybridity. National innovation systems represent an important area of public-private interactions within societies. Discussion of national innovation systems began in the late 1980s with the aim to provide an overall framework for a more systematic development of new technologies. In the background, there was a hope that the development of innovations would give mature industrialised countries a competitive edge over newly industrialised countries in Asia and elsewhere. There was also disillusionment about the linear innovation process, which begins with basic science and ends with a commercialised product through applied research, following the chain reaction from basic physics to large-scale development in big labs and leading to commercial applications and innovations. The development of the atom bomb and its aspired application to the production of nuclear energy was a (sad) showcase of such thinking (Freeman 1995). In its reliance on big science and the importance of national research laboratories, the linear model promotes the importance of the supply side in developing new technologies.

There were important links between different levels. National innovation systems appear in micro-level interactions. A triple helix grows out of the government-industry dyad into the government-university-industry triad. In this setting the third mission of universities (involvement in the socio-economic development of society) enables entrepreneurial universities to establish innovation-generating interactions with business enterprises aiming to commercialise R&D innovations aided by government funding. As a result, universities can adopt a position of advancing regional economic development (Ranga and Etzkowitz 2013).

The systemic view embraced by the national innovation system perspective promotes a more encompassing view of the innovation embedded in government policies, university research, industry structures, and their environment. This broader view of innovation activity coincided with the aim of the OECD to establish more coherent science and technology policies within industrialised nations. According to this view, advancement in technology requires the analysis of processes that link research and development expenditures with concrete outcomes, which cannot be properly examined with such aggregate measures as R&D spending or the number of patents. More often than not, these processes relate to the transfer of knowledge and know-how; that is, intangible assets in the form of human capital. The practical thinking of the OECD was also influenced by ideas promoting the continuing significance of nation states in the world economy. Following this view, countries tend to enjoy success in the same industries for long periods of time. It might be that the combination of the institutional context and the availability of particular technologies and capabilities provides a platform for the development of intangible human capital, which enables further development in a particular industry. Consequently, international trade emphasises rather than diminishes the initial differences of intangible assets between nations (Porter 1990).

Definitions of national innovation systems underline the interaction between national institutions in developing new technologies (Freeman 1987; Lundvall 1992; Nelson 1993; Patel and Pavitt 1994; Metcalfe 1995). This development orients the focus on systemic failures to mismatches between basic research in the public sector and applied research in industry, as well as between the malfunctioning of technology-transfer institutions and the lack of absorptive capacity (the ability to recognise, assimilate, and apply new information to commercial ends) of firms (OECD 1997). The basic flows of knowledge in national innovation systems deal with interactions among enterprises, universities, and public research laboratories as well as the diffusion of knowledge and technology to firms and the movement of personnel between institutions (OECD 1997). One of the challenges in mapping national innovation systems is the lack of proper statistics to account for the various aspects of interactions within countries not present in systems of national accounting. The measurement of industry alliances, industry university interactions, technology diffusion, and personnel mobility has to be organised through surveys, patent record examination and citation, and publication analysis (Godin 2009).

The lack of established measurement instruments contributes to the fact that many studies of national innovation systems are based on case studies of different countries. Empirical findings of a fifteen-country comparative study of national innovation systems in small and large high-income countries and some developing countries suggest that the countries did not have coherent industrial policies. Instead they employed selective protective measures to nurture infant and high-tech industries combined with some R&D subsidies. Where strong government industrial policies were executed, they led to failure as often as they led to success (Nelson 1992).

Focus on innovation systems is in itself problematic. It is difficult to extract innovation systems from other institutional factors of society, such as labour markets or trade and industrial policies. By narrowing the focus to the immediate surroundings of innovations, differences between industries emerge as the most important aspect of national innovation systems. In other words, innovation systems tend to be sector specific, without much connection to one another. For instance, R&D in the pharmaceutical industry has little in common with R&D in aircraft manufacturing in a particular country. The notion of national innovation systems implies more uniformity and connectedness than is the case in reality. In a broader sense, a nation's basic institutions related to the forming of new ideas show remarkable persistence. Most notably, the education system, which provides the workforce of knowledge-intensive industries, seems to never change its basic structure. Close links to public laboratories and universities make a difference in many industries, as do public infrastructure, laws, and financial institutions. Military R&D continues to play a role in many countries, such as the US, the UK, France, and Israel, but its spillover effect on commercial products is diminishing. The mode of directing government resources to the development of technology differs in national contexts. In the US, government spending circulates through universities, while European countries tend to directly support civil-industrial R&D (Nelson 1992).

An examination of the relative efficiency of innovation systems in OECD countries between 1999 and 2003 (Guan and Chen 2012) identifies different types of knowledge-creation challenges. Innovation leaders efficient in both knowledge production and commercialisation (e.g. Greece, Ireland) could benefit from additional knowledge production. Innovation followers (e.g. the Netherlands, the UK) with relatively low knowledge production and commercialisation require more efficiency in both aspects of knowledge creation. In the system framework, the discrepancies between inputs and outputs are interesting, as they point to problems in interlinking subsystems together. Some OECD countries (e.g. Canada, Finland, Korea, New Zealand) produce an ample amount of knowledge, but they encounter problems transforming it into marketable products. Elsewhere (e.g. Italy, Norway, Mexico, and Portugal), commercialisation efforts are efficient, but lack of innovation capacity hinders possibilities for further development.

An examination of the dynamics of national innovation systems in eighty-seven countries (Castellacci and Natera 2013) shows that the evolution of innovation systems is driven by the interaction between innovation capability (innovation input, scientific output, and technological output) and absorptive capacity (infrastructure, international trade, and human capital). The study covered industrialised OECD countries; middle-income countries (e.g. countries in East Asia, Latin America, and Eurasia); and developing countries (e.g. countries in Africa and South Asia) between 1980 and 2007. In a dynamic perspective, the accumulation of national wealth serves as both a result of knowledge creation and as source of that knowledge creation's augmentation. National wealth gives industrial countries a head start, as their high-income levels enable further promotion of both innovation and absorptive capacity. There are also differences among country groups. In industrial countries, inputs to R&D are a central aspect of innovation capability. In middle-income countries, infrastructure and international trade are the key aspects of absorptive capacity. In developing countries, weakly connected innovation systems show little connection between innovation capability and absorptive capacity, which provides meagre possibilities for growth or catching up with other countries.

This examination of national innovation systems (Case 3.3) illustrates the benefits and problems of developing new meso-level constructs to understand hybrid systems. A construct such as national innovation systems highlights knowledge-creation activities as an area of interest in their own right. Innovation systems invite us to examine information-processing activities within universities, public research facilities, and corporate R&D in private enterprises. However, this perspective of national innovation systems has turned into normative demands for more coherent innovation and technology policies. The examination of a new meso-level construct did not come about without problems. First, the lack of proper data regarding the most important features (e.g. interaction of industries and organisations in the process of innovation), systems, and problems of compiling data for new purposes not acknowledged by existing statistics eludes the exact measurement of meso-level phenomena. The problem is not made easier by the importance of public-private interaction within the perspective of national innovation systems. Case studies give rich description, but they are not able to give hard evidence. Reliance on approximate quantifiable measures (e.g. R&D spending or the export of high technology) does not grasp very well the internal functioning of meso-level activities (Godin 2009).

The extraction of a meso-level construct from the fabric of society is not only a methodological issue. In the case of national innovation systems, it is easy to see that a society's infrastructure makes a difference, but the adoption of a broader view makes it difficult to see innovation systems as independent parts of society. However, a more narrow perspective on innovation showcases the differences of industries within innovation systems. Neither of these options fits comfortably with the meso level as an important construct in itself (Nelson 1992). The comparative results of national innovation systems bring forth the differences between industrialised and developing countries. It seems that the integration capacity between research and development activity and commercialisation is visible in industrial countries but less so in developing ones. It is possible that innovation systems as a construct apply only to a limited population of wealthy nations and that developing countries might be able to follow other undetected causal routes to innovation. To put it differently, the actualisation of rules in innovation systems in different types of countries seem to be different, but it might also be that rules governing the actual activities vary across populations.

Public policy considerations

In public policy literature, it has been common to discuss the micro, meso, and macro levels. In this literature, the micro level is often associated with 'organisations,' the meso level with 'policy fields or areas,' and the macro level with the overall 'politico-administrative system' (Van Dooren et al. 2015). In this context, the levels may have slightly different roles than in economics reasoning. In order to achieve society-level goals, there needs to be a reasonable consensus on the macro level. However, achieving society-level goals necessitates the decomposition of abstract political goals into more governable, implementable, and manageable objectives. Often, this takes place at the meso level, in different policy fields where general ideological stances turn into more specific policy agendas. This is why the overall political objective of, for instance, a more secure society is transformed into a more transparent and operationalised objective of, for example, reducing crime and violence in cities. Politics and policies need to be implemented, and they need to be accompanied with the necessary economic and human resources because this allocation decision is an important political choice in society (Wildavsky 1986). Finally, as the micro level deals with organisations, in public policy areas this concerns public agencies, third-sector organisations, and business firms working to contribute to overall policy objectives.

All in all, if this book is about governing hybrid *organisations*, should we then focus only on the micro level of societal action? Moreover, if we accept the assumption that there are three levels of societal action, how would or should we modify these levels in the context of our discussion on hybrid governance and organisations? Can we presume that the same characteristics of institutional action that seem to work in economics, public policy, and organisational studies (i.e. there is a reasonably functioning division of labour for micro, meso, and macro concepts) will apply to our reasoning on hybridity?

Two important considerations need to be made. First, although it is not easy – even for us – one needs to be candid enough to loosen the absolute primacy of organisational reasoning. Instead, we need to understand the collaborative action that takes place sometimes between organisations but also between individuals, groups, and other types of institutional actors. These other actors may fulfil the criteria of hierarchical organising, but they are not necessarily organisations in the exact sense of the word (Powell 1990; Williamson 1999b). Therefore, we may be dealing with organising but not necessarily with organisations, with action instead of actors, with policies instead of policy organisations. Our notion of hybridity entails all aspects in order to grasp the multifaceted characteristics of hybridity.

Second, we may comprehend hybrid forms of action by discussing what is missing if we commit ourselves to organisational thinking only. Let us consider hybridity as a mix of public and private ownership, public and private sources of funding, public and private forms of control, and different and contrasting institutional logics and goal setting. Ownership is a pretty straightforward question in the context of hybridity. We may create typologies of public, private, and hybrid organisations in which hybrid organisations are usually referred to as ownership structures with both taxpayers' funding and private forms of capital (Thynne 2011). Funding is readily another issue, as we are moving to an area where the interest lies not in organisations as such but in projects and programmes. We may be dealing with PPP arrangements, private finance initiatives (PFI), etc. (Greve and Hodge 2007). Nevertheless, hybridity indeed manifests itself in this context as relevant, meaningful, and worth scrutinising. Many government activities are organised through different kinds of funding schemes. Goal setting and institutional logics are also important. Without this approach, it would be tricky to discuss shadow workers and outsourced activities of governments through which private business firms, using profit-seeking logics, provide services, sometimes doing well by doing good. Finally, forms of control do not only include 'controlling organisations.' Rather, they concern the control of activities and practices in society that include features of different levels of societal functions and activities.

Hybrids as singular, dyadic, and multilateral structures

In an analysis of numbers in social life, it is helpful to see social life as comprising three features. First, there are entities (actors, nodes), such as persons or organisations. Second, the actors possess attributes, such as size or legal structure. Third, there are edges or arcs that connect actors and nodes together in a social network. Connections can be diverse in their nature, including friendship, economic transactions, or subordination in a hierarchy (Wasserman and Faust 1994). In this sense, network concepts enable the analysis of any type of social life. In the following, we aim at using these concepts to find a possible space for defining hybrids in a meaningful way.

The number of participants is one of the building blocks of social and economic life (Simmel and Wolff 1964). The isolated individual (a singular being), the dyad (a group of two), and the triad (a group of three) are distinctive configurations which cover basic positions in social life (see Figure 3.2). First, a singular being is not isolated from a social environment, as the singular being cannot exist without the idea of separation from the group. In this way, an analysis of hybridity often denotes two separate aspects: (1) The very idea of hybridity refers to the idea of other forms that serve as a point of departure for hybrids to exist in the first place, and (2) a singular hybrid possesses attributes that give it its own idiosyncratic characteristics. In a theoretical sense, too much emphasis on the former delegates the role of the hybrid to a residual category of other beings, and emphasis on the latter gives it entitlement for its own existence. The evolution of organisational forms, the variety of legally defined organisation structures, and organisation typologies are helpful in detecting hybridity in organisational life. It becomes relevant to ask questions such as the

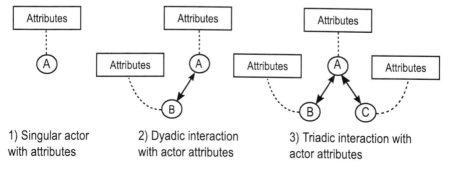

FIGURE 3.2 Hybridity as singular, dyadic, and triadic structure

following: What are the origins and basic forms of organisation structures, and how do we distinguish organisations in different populations?

Second, moving to groups of two, the important feature of the dyad is that it does not possess supra-individual characteristics. If you remove either party of the dyad, the social structure ceases to exist. In an organisational setting, the organisation itself poses rights and duties to both parties, which brings about a shadow of a third party. The dyadic interaction often creates intimacy and also the need to protect the intimacy against third parties. Any large social structure can be decomposed into a number of dyadic pairs, such as managers and subordinates or buyers and sellers. Now, hybridity may refer to a particular kind of interaction pattern among the partners in a dyad, a combination of their attributes, or a mixture of both of these features. In empirical analyses of organisation interactions, dyadic analyses of hybrids have included, for instance, the examination of cooperative ties between firms (Dyer and Singh 1998), exchange relations (Larson 1992), strategic alliances (Kale et al. 2000), and Japanese keiretsu networks composed of diverse business firms gathered around major banks (Lincoln and Gerlach 2004).

A fundamental transformation in sociability emerges when moving from the examination of dyads into the examination of triads. A triad is composed of three elements that connect to one another, forming a group. Many basic properties of social and political life first appear in triads. There can be a brokerage role or majority and minority positions, and any one of the members can leave the group without dissolving the group completely, which diminishes the power of one against the others. As conflicts arise, triads are better equipped to solve them, as the third party can mediate conflicts between the other two. The important characteristic of the triad is that the addition of more members into it does not necessarily pose a qualitative change in its social structure (Krackhardt 1999). An increase in the number of actors increases the possibilities of defining hybrids in a more elaborate way. In addition to hybridity's connections and attributes, hybridity may appear as a function of the minority and majority in a group as well as the different social roles of one party in connection to other parties.

While not restricted solely to triadic interaction patterns, the governance perspective offers a viewpoint on multi-actor structures in society. Here we assume that governance takes place between many rather than a few actors. Networks play an important role in the study of governance, signifying not only the number of actors but also the different types of actors, such as public and private organisations or types of voluntary civic engagement. The levels of governance add an additional layer to the analysis as activities emerge out of the interaction between global, regional, and local interactions. There is also an emphasis on the processes of governing rather than on structures of government. In other words, such processes highlight 'soft' coordination mechanisms, such as negotiation, alliance formation, and cooperation, which are in contrast to the 'hard' methods of command and control (Kersbergen and Waarden 2004).

CASE 3.4 HYBRID STRUCTURES IN GLOBAL AIR TRAVEL

The international airline industry showcases public-private interaction on the grandest scale. Developments after World War II represented sharp increases in air travel on a global scale, even though the regulatory regime was founded on intergovernmental agreements and detailed restrictions on establishing new routes. Here, business models in the US and other countries differed from one another. In the US, transborder (legacy) carriers and domestic carriers were carefully regulated but were mutually competitive private enterprises, whereas in many other countries airlines were national monopolies under government ownership (flag carriers). After the World War II era, international air travel was developed according to bilateral agreements of governments for the operation of routes between two countries after the World War II era. The initial political constellation was such that the US aimed for liberalised world markets in air travel for obvious reasons. The US's commercial airline industry covered over 70 percent of global air travel, and, unlike many other countries, its air fleet was left unaffected by the war. Other countries feared the global dominance of the US airline industry if an outright market-based solution was chosen. As a compromise, a Chicago convention on international air transportation in 1944 established rules by which international air traffic would proceed. Most importantly, the convention gave sovereignty to governments to rule their airspace, which meant that foreign aircraft needed domestic government approval to enter its airspace, and commercial airlines could not negotiate agreements involving two or more airspaces. Consequently, the commercial rights of airlines in international routes were governed by bilateral agreements between each country pair. The developments of the regulatory environment, however, signified two different regimes during the postwar period. The first was highly regulated, the second less so (Hanlon 2007).

The old bilateral agreements included agreements on traffic rights, capacity, designation, and other issues. Traffic rights defined the routes airlines could fly, including destinations that could be served within, between, and beyond bilateral partners. The details of these rights were defined through principles known as 'freedoms of the sky.' Capacity defines the number of flights that can be operated or passengers that can be carried between bilateral partners. Designation refers to the number of airlines bilateral partners can nominate to operate services. Some agreements required airlines to submit ticket prices to aeronautical authorities for approval, and the agreements may have contained ownership criteria that airlines had to meet to be designated under the bilateral agreement. In the old regime, capacity restrictions were open to renegotiation, designation was limited to one or a few airlines, and the pricing of fares was based on the principle that, if the host country was unsatisfied with the fare of the foreign carrier, it could unilaterally adjust it. In the old regime, the details of coordination extended to setting rules for other aspects of aviation services, such as food service and in-flight entertainment. The bilateral agreements and national monopolies, connected by strictly regulated international markets in which airlines supplied identical services at identically high prices, produced a mixture of public and private institutions in a de facto cartel of international aviation services (Richards 2001).

In the new regime, the contractual arrangement of the Chicago convention still exists, but the restrictiveness of such contracts has eased greatly. The US policy of open skies agreements after 1977 gave the initial impetus for more liberalised markets of international air travel. In these agreements, no host country can unilaterally limit the volume of traffic and frequency of service provided by the partner's carrier. Agreements allow the partner to name multiple air carriers for designated routes, and, in pricing, partners can unilaterally change the fare without the other partner's approval. According to these agreements, any carrier from a partner country can fly into any domestic airport with as much capacity and frequency as it wishes. These agreements also allow unlimited arrival at or departure from third countries (the fifth freedom). The open skies initiative began at the time of US carrier dominance, and the US government was persuaded that greater access to outbound routes would compensate for the opening up of inbound travel. The deregulation has increased airline competition and decreased ticket prices. The establishment of major hubs gathering domestic and short-distance travel for international destinations enables legacy and flag carriers to respond to the competition of new low-cost carriers entering the aviation markets. Also, the mounting cost of operating an airline has resulted in the privatisation of airlines (Hanlon 2007, 16).

Probably the biggest change eroding the basis of the post–World War II regulation regime was change in the European Union, which affected the bilateral nature of the air traffic agreements. Measures for the liberalisation of air transport in the European Union came into force in 1993, largely replacing the bilateral air transport agreements signed in the past between EU member countries and making it possible for EU nationals to establish air transport activity anywhere in the European Union. The measures also provided free access to all intracommunity routes and flexible fares for the services operating on those routes (OECD 2014).

Despite deregulation in the European Union and in some other countries, the principles of the original Chicago convention remain in most parts of the world. Agreements are still bilateral, countries basically do not allow foreign air carriers to operate services between cities in a host country, and foreign ownership restrictions on airlines still apply in many countries. However, the overall direction is to rely more on market-based solutions, not only those dealing with airlines but also with other services, such as air traffic control, airport management, and the management of landing carriers (slots) in more and more congested airports. In general, there seems to be more willingness to allow foreign ownership and flexible route entry and pricing, but many governments are reluctant to abandon their sovereignty in defining traffic rights (Hanlon 2007, 8).

To circumvent restrictions on bilateral agreements when operating in foreign countries, and due to restrictions on the ownership of airlines, many airlines began to build alliances with other airline carriers. The obvious gains of partnering can be found in scheduling, enhanced use of capacity, and the provision of connecting flights to other destinations. By forging an alliance with another carrier, an airline can expand its network and provide customers with many more itinerary combinations than it could on its own. Most of the airlines take part in some sort of alliance with other partners. Most notably, there are three global airline alliances in the world: Star Alliance, SkyTeam, and Oneworld. Each alliance was founded with a major US carrier, one of the 'big three' European carriers, and a major Asian carrier. Consequently, Star Alliance includes United Airlines, Lufthansa, Scandinavian Airline Systems (SAS), and Thai International. SkyTeam includes Delta Airlines, Air France, KLM Royal Dutch Airlines, and Korean Air. Oneworld includes British Airways, American Airlines, and Cathay Pacific, among other partners. More than a decade after their formation, half of the seating capacity in the world and around 80 percent of intercontinental traffic between Asia, Europe, and America were served by airlines enrolled in these alliances (Tugores-García 2013). Alliances now involve a form of code sharing in which the participating carriers all indicate that a specific flight being operated is their own (Chan 2000).

Government ownership has withered away from some of the global alliances' major airlines (e.g. Lufthansa, British Airways). Still, the interesting public-private feature of the global airline alliances is that they tie together private enterprises and flag carriers, some of which still hold major government stakes (e.g. SAS, Thai International), minor government stakes (e.g. KLM, Air France), or indirect government stakes (e.g. Cathay Pacific of Air China).

This airline case illustration (Case 3.4) relates to the different kinds of hybrid groupings in the following ways:

Singular

The most obvious demarcation line between airlines as singular entities is the ownership structure, which might involve purely private shareholders (private), both public and private shareholders (mixed or hybrid forms), and predominantly government-owned entities (public). Formerly, airlines have been viewed as public utilities that provide everyday necessities, such as water, electricity, natural gas, and telephone service, among others. Most public utilities enjoy a monopoly position due to the excessive cost to build and maintain the infrastructure for their operations. It makes little difference whether utilities are in public or private hands, as the monopoly position requires government regulation to guarantee that utilities provide adequate service at reasonable prices. However, the institutional context for utilities has changed over the past two or three decades. Deregulation and technological change has eroded the rationale for some public utilities, such as national telecom operators. Within the airline industry, deregulation has been slow, which is also related to the nonfinancial aspects of international air travel. For one thing, upholding national sovereignty makes it difficult to allow foreign carriers to operate within national borders, added to which is the possible importance of national air fleets in times of crisis.

The privatisation and hybridisation of airlines have seemingly reduced governments' financial control of airlines. The combined influence of deregulation, increased competition, and the introduction of low-cost operators also signifies that operating an airline is a burden for public finances, as witnessed in the bankruptcies of some flag carriers, such as Sabena in Belgium in 2001, Swissair in Switzerland in 2001, and Air Canada in 2003, and also as witnessed in the continuing difficulties of others that have required government aid, such as Alitalia in 2005, Cyprus Airways in 2007, Olympic Airways in 2008, and Austrian Airlines in 2009 (European Commission 2014). These examples indicate that government-owned flag carriers pose a genuine financial risk and that reducing government ownership stakes enables the minimisation of such risks.

In terms of ownership, out of the top 100 airlines, the top sixty have private ownership, fifteen have mixed ownership, and the remaining twenty-five have state ownership (Hanlon 2007). Apart from the US, where airlines have always been in private hands, public ownership has been part of the airlines operating on designated routes. In contrast, charter airlines have always been mainly private everywhere around the world. The trend has been that formerly government-owned national flag carriers have been privatised. There is, however, significant regional variation in the ownership structures of the airlines. The US, Europe, and Latin America are dominated by private airlines, whereas emerging airline markets in the Middle East are dominated by government-owned operators, and airlines in Africa and Asia Pacific are divided roughly into equal shares of public and private operators (IATA 2011).

Basically, modern airlines have the option to choose from three different business models: (1) the full-service carrier model (FSC), (2) the low-cost carrier model (LCC), and (3) the charter carrier model (CC) (Cento 2009). Most of the remaining and former national flag carriers (and legacy carriers in the US) are attuned to the FSC model in their operation, which includes cargo, passengers, and maintenance as the core business. The FSC model also includes global reach through a hub-and-spoke network, which gathers passengers from regional airports to international hub airports for connecting flights, alliance partnership, and customer loyalty programmes. The LCC model typically concentrates on passenger traffic, point-to-point networks – which directly connect departure and arrival destinations – and the extensive use of secondary airports combined with no-frills service and the maximal utilisation of often single-aircraft fleets. The charter model is also passenger based, but carriers typically do not sell their own tickets. Instead, tickets are sold as part of some overall holiday package. Most often, charter carriers operate from small- and medium-sized airports, which do not have any scheduled flights (Cento 2009).

The change of the business model into full-service carriers and low-cost carriers has altered the significance of the ownership form. Most importantly, it has pushed traditional airlines, including those under public and mixed ownership, into the full-service carrier group. This group aims to combat tightening competition with participation in alliances and offers a variety of destinations through hub-and-spoke networks, as compared to point-to-point travel combined with secondary airport destination offered by low-cost carriers. In this sense, the different business model has become more important than the form of ownership structure, government and mixed ownership structures being integral parts of the full-service carrier group.

The financing of airlines has been changing since the debt crisis of 2008. Traditionally, European banks have been the key source of finances for airlines. The new regulation governing liquidity ratios and the financial stability of banks, combined with more difficult access to US dollar funding, is expected to increase the cost of finance from European banks, which is likely to increase financing from Asian sources and other Eastern sources. Aircraft manufacturing is capital intensive, and the market is dominated by very few manufacturers (Bombardier in Canada, Boeing in the US, Airbus in Europe, and Embraer in Brazil). For widebody aircrafts, there are only two producers (Airbus and Boeing). Another change has been that, formerly, many aircraft-manufacturing countries (the US, the UK, Germany, France, Canada, and Brazil) provided guarantees for commercial banks through their export credit agencies in the case of losses in lending to risky airline companies. In the aftermath of the financial crisis of 2008, even well-off airlines have resorted to government-backed guarantees when arranging their finances, often with less cost than with purely private arrangements. Another development has been that operating and lease arrangement has become a more common practice in airline operations. Some 40 percent of all aircrafts were leased rather than owned in 2012. For airlines, this alleviates burdens on raising capital, but it also opens up new possibilities in investing in aircraft-leasing businesses for institutional investors (Hampson and Shamsad 2013).

Dyad

The dyadic nature of air travel originates from the bilateral air service agreements between national governments that made decisions about how transborder traffic between two countries operated (Prokop 2014). Despite liberalisation, the basic structure of bilateral agreements on the use of domestic airspace is still operational, which gives national governments ample possibilities to control incoming air traffic. At first, it seems that there is very little hybridity involved in such procedures, as the agreements are made between public authorities. The hybrid twist originates from the fact that such agreements aim at establishing operating rights for commercial airlines. To put it differently, bilateral contracts include airlines as a shadow of a third party. In a formal sense, every agreement introduces a link between national government airlines (public) and approved foreign airlines (private). Hybridity thus originates from the different attributes of the parties.

In terms of financial and social control, the concentration of aircraft manufacturing is likely to influence the nature of the industry. For a long time, US aircraft-manufacturing companies, such as Boeing, Lockheed Martin, and McDonnell Douglas, could benefit from government contracts when developing new designs, mainly for defense purposes (Battershell 1999). In Europe, the French, German, and Spanish governments have direct stakes in the Airbus Group. As there are only two players manufacturing planes for long-distance routes, Boeing and Airbus, politics continue to play a role in aircraft purchases. For instance, the lifting of sanctions against Iran led to an agreement to order over 100 planes from Airbus in 2016.

Triadic governance

The global constellation of the airline industry has resulted in a tripartite alliance structure of three major alliances, which together account for the majority of global travel. All three alliances include an internal triadic constellation of US, European, and Asian carriers. The literature on the airline industry seems to be in favour of more liberalised and competitive markets, in which there is little need for government intervention or ownership. However, the issue of competition has not been neutral in the past, nor does it appear to be neutral in the present or future. Government ownership is more significant in middle- and low-income countries, which are not as prepared for full-fledged global competition as North America and Europe. The historical fear of US airlines dominating world air travel has changed into the fear of well-established competitive airlines taking over the traffic of airspaces in the developing world.

The airline industry is global in its nature, but it continues to bear domestic interests as well. The highly regulated bilateral agreements enabled the subsidisation of some of the less lucrative domestic routes through the more profitable international routes. Intensified competition has meant that maintaining unprofitable routes is no longer possible for the flag carrier and legacy companies. In some cases, low-cost carriers and charter carriers have been able to cater to the travelling demands of some of these destinations, but it seems that remote, sparsely populated areas might not benefit from the internalisation of global air transport (Zuidberg and Veldhuis 2012).

The most obvious hybridisation development has taken place at the global level. The formation of three global air alliances is a typical hybrid constellation according to transaction cost logic. They are not organisations arranged under unified command or a hierarchical, vertical division of labour, nor do they represent unsecured transactions of atomistic markets. Instead, the alliances are tied together through cooperative agreements in code sharing, scheduling, and shared loyalty programmes. These practices have been flexible enough to allow changes and restructuring in the partnership structures. In a more speculative tone, it can be argued that the restrictive bilateral agreement regime, combined with national ownership restrictions, was instrumental in the current network formation. A less regulated environment would have enabled the establishment of larger and more unified global conglomerates in the air travel industry.

Within the airline industry, hybridity appears in many forms. On the organisational level, private stock-hold companies, government-owned flagship carriers, and hybrid ownership formed by both public and private shareholders continue to operate in airspaces. The main change in the institutional logics has been the abandoning of the airlines as public utilities and the introduction of competition to replace government regulation. Despite deregulation efforts, governments hold considerable influence in the final say of allowing or denying the operation of foreign airlines in national airspace. The financing of airlines has been in the hands of commercial banks, but lending has recently been aided by government guarantees to compensate for possible losses. The aircraft-manufacturing business is concentrated to only a few manufacturing firms, which are connected to national governments through direct government stakes, contracting deals, and/or military aircraft development.

Making sense of public-private distinctions: the world of classifications

Decision-makers construct public-private distinctions by making judgments at several levels. According to Ranson et al. (1980), this process takes place through interpretive schemes that create provinces of meaning for actors by providing the behavioural schemata to understand the societal world. Interpretive schemes are a set of assumptions that provide mental explanations as to why things happen as they do and what should be done to influence the course of events in a social context or organisation (Bartunek 1984; Thomas and Janowitz 1966; Giddens 1979). For regulating, organising, and managing public service delivery, decision-makers intend to do the following:

- Comprehend the overall context of society and service provision (What is going on?)

- Create plausible explanations for what contributes to policy solution (What should be done?)
- Predict outcomes of future activities (How should the outcomes of the efforts be evaluated?) (March 1988b)

Schemes on how things should be organised, or how organisations should be managed, are not constantly questioned. Often, schemes include several taken-for-granted assumptions on how society works and how to change and intervene in activities. The institutional process through which interpretive schemes become 'real' sometimes precludes deliberate reasoning and communication within an organisation and sometimes more implicit exchange of ideas (Thomas and Janowitz 1966). One important instrument for the sense making of human beings is their ability to classify and categorise things and subjects.

The principles of the classification process have their strongest tradition in the natural sciences. In the tradition of the natural sciences, taxonomy is an empirically derived hierarchical system. Conversely, the word 'typology' is used to classify data into types based on theoretically derived, and more or less intuitively categorised, qualities of observed phenomena (Rich 1992). Eighteenth-century scientist Carl Linnaeus used the form and structure of organisms to categorise them. He first divided all organisms into two kingdoms, plantae (plants) and animalia (animals), and then he proceeded with hierarchical steps to generate more specific classifications of particular species. For the most part, the modern system of classifying organisms follows Linnaeus's basic idea in the following fashion:

- Each kingdom is divided into phyla
- Each phylum is divided into smaller groups called classes
- Each class is divided into orders
- Each order is divided into families
- Each family is divided into genera
- Each genus is divided into species

With the aid of Linnaean taxonomy, it is rather straightforward how to pigeonhole beings in flora or fauna with remarkable precision. If I were interested in bobcats living in Canada, I would be able to get the information that their kingdom is animals, their phylum is Chordata, their class is Mammalia, their order is Carnivore, their family is Felidae, their genus is Lynx, and their species is Lynx Canadensis. These features give plenty of information on these animals. They have a flexible spinal column, they are beasts of prey, they are part of the family of small cats, and they are different from their relatives living in Spain or in Nordic countries, among other things.

The main difference between biological and organisational classifications is that organisations do not possess inbuilt mechanisms, such as DNA, that dictate their birth, life, and death. Furthermore, unlike biological organisms, organisations can inherit acquired characteristics from their ancestors through a number of mechanisms, such as mergers, imitation, or learning from written sources. Consequently, organisations are not only units in the physical world but also creations of the human mind, or, to put it differently, artefacts of human imagination. They are not stable or passive objects of classification. Instead, they react to social categorisations. They may wish to belong to certain categories, or they may resist certain types of categorisations. The difficulties of providing valid classifications of organisational life do not liberate us from the need to make such classifications. Classifications are needed to make institutional action and systems 'real.'

CASE 3.5 ADMINISTRATIVE PRAGMATISM IN ACTION – THE DEVELOPMENT OF THE SYSTEM OF NATIONAL ACCOUNTS

The structure and development of the System of National Accounts is a representative example of an important macroeconomic classification that has a profound impact on the way in which we view organisational populations. The impetus for national accounting grew from the need for public intervention to combat the Depression in the 1930s, from developments in economic theory in the 1930s that emphasised the role of government in economy, and also from the need to calculate the available resources for the war effort and recovery after the war. Originally, the national accounts were designed to inform macroeconomic policy by supporting macroeconomic analysis and providing a conceptual basis for the formation of long-term strategic development and reform (Ward 2006; Vanoli 2005).

The System of National Accounts (SNA), first published in 1952, is the internationally agreed upon standard set of recommendations on how to compile measures of economic activity according to accounting conventions based on economic principles. The recommendations are expressed in terms of definitions and accounting rules that comprise the internationally agreed upon standard for measuring such items as gross domestic product (GDP) (United Nations 2009, 1). Such classification serves as a conceptual framework that provides consistency of definitions across various fields of activity, and, as an accounting device, ensures the consistency of data originating from different sources (Kendrick 1996, 3). The SNA provides an overview of economic processes, recording how production is distributed among consumers, businesses, governments, and foreign nations. It shows how income originates in production flows to these groups and how the groups allocate these flows for consumption, saving, and investment.

The SNA is designed to provide information about the behaviour of institutional units and the activities in which they engage, namely production, consumption, and the accumulation of assets. This is achieved by recording the exchange of goods, services, and assets between institutional units in the form of transactions (United Nations 2009, 2). By identifying the distinct roles of different institutions, national accounts give guidance on the mandates and incentive structures of corporations, households, governments, and nonprofit institutions (Ward 2006, 329).

For the purposes of the SNA, institutional units that are resident in the economy are grouped together into five mutually exclusive sectors composed of the following types of units:

1 Nonfinancial corporations
2 Financial corporations
3 Government units, including social security funds
4 Nonprofit institutions serving households (NPISHs)
5 Households

The five sectors together make up the total economy (see Figure 3.3). A reference to Linnaeus's typology represented in Table 3.1 gives insight on the importance of divisions in moving from general to more specific categories. The first and fundamental distinction of the SNA is the geographical location of institutional units: those that reside within national territory and those that reside outside national borders (or the 'rest of the world' in the vocabulary of the SNA) (United Nations 2009). The second distinction is between households and institutional households; 'households' refers to the family unit, and 'institutional households' refers to groups of people staying in hospitals, prisons, or retirement homes for a considerable amount of time. The third distinction between market and nonmarket producers depends on whether the majority of the unit's production is offered at economically significant prices or not, but this distinction has been problematic in dealing with government activity in particular. For instance, questions to be solved have included the following: Are taxes treated as services or transfers? How can users of the output be defined, as the government produces both collective and individualised services? (Muller 2003). The main distinction within nonmarket producers relates to whether the unit is government controlled or not. The financial corporations sector includes all resident corporations whose principal activity is providing financial services, such as financial intermediation, insurance, and pension fund services. Nonfinancial corporations are corporations whose principal activity is the production of market goods or nonfinancial services. From the bird's-eye view of the government, it makes sense to differentiate market activity according to control criterion. Those under government control are the easiest to influence, in contrast to those under foreign control, those under private control, and those holding a position somewhere in between.

TABLE 3.1 A hierarchical classification of institutional units in the System of National Accounts

Level of analysis	Main distinction	The result of distinction
Level one All institutional units	No distinction between institutional units is possible (kingdom)	Totality of units
Level two Geographical location	Distinction between resident and foreign (rest of the world) institutional units (phylum)	Domestic, foreign
Level three Type of institutional unit	Distinction between types of households (class)	Institutional households, households
Level four Pricing	Distinction according to market principle (order)	Nonmarket producer, market producer
Level five Area of activity	Distinction between the institutional nature of organisations (family)	Nonprofit institutions serving households, nonfinancial institutions, financial institutions, government
Level six Control	Distinction according to controlling entities of the unit (subarea of activity only) (genus)	Public, private, and foreign control of market producers

This basic division of institutional units clearly reflects the top-down character of the SNA. The area of activity gives only rudimentary insight into what organisations actually do. Therefore, the species of an organisation is difficult to decipher when following the hierarchy of the classification. A further complication of the classification is that it allows variation in the divisions between subsectors to accommodate for national differences. It would be very difficult to classify a particular organisation to a specific category without examination of the ownership, control, or market orientation of the organisation. To put it differently, a layman's view of observing empirical reality without deep theoretical knowledge does not work in this context. In line with the top-down orientation, the SNA does not properly reach the observable features of organisational life.

Some other problems of the classification relate to fundamental issues of valuation, such as how change in national income relates to change in economic welfare, how environmental sustainability can be taken into account, what role the value of human capital should play in the assessment of economic value in calculations (Muller 2003), and how to assess

72 How to tame monsters

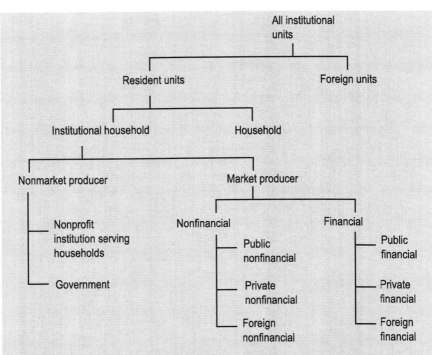

FIGURE 3.3 Hierarchical classification of institutional units in the System of National Accounts

Adapted from United Nations (2009, 64).

the economic impact of totally new fields of activity, such as information and communication technology (ICT).

For the purposes of our examination, the practices of dealing with borderline cases are an interesting part of national accounts. They also show how one must tackle different perspectives when taking into account the emerging classification problem of the grey area between public and private sectors, on the one hand, and the grey area between nonprofit institutions and institutional sectors and units on the other hand. The former area has been handled by introducing classification principles to guide the choice between public and private spheres of activity without changing the existing categorisations. The latter distinction between nonprofit institutions and other economic activities has been solved by introducing extra categorisations (satellite accounts), which are external extensions of the basic structure of the SNA but not an integral part of it. Typically, satellite accounts allow for the provision of additional information on particular social concerns and the use of alternative concepts and alternative classifications, among other things (UNESCO 2009).

> In the case of public-private interaction, the 2008 SNA gives instructions for the distinction between general government and public corporations. It offers guidance on when certain entities created by government units should be included in the public sector or not. The entities concerned include public-private partnerships, quasi corporations, restructuring agencies, special purpose entities, joint ventures, and supranational authorities.

Dealing with public-private interaction

Public-private partnerships are long-term contracts between two units whereby one unit acquires or builds an asset or set of assets, operates it for a period, and then hands the asset over to a second unit. Such arrangements are usually between a private enterprise and the government, but other combinations are possible, with a public corporation as one party and a private NPISH as the second party. These schemes are described variously as public-private partnerships (PPPs), as private finance initiatives (PFIs), and, lastly, as build, own, operate, transfer schemes (BOOTS). The basic principles of all are the same and are treated the same way in the SNA. A general description that includes the most common arrangement is as follows: A private enterprise agrees to acquire a complex of fixed assets and then use those assets together with other production inputs to produce services. Those services may be delivered to the government either for use as an input for its own production (for example, motor vehicle maintenance services) or for distribution to the public without payment (for example, education services), in which case the government makes periodic payments during the contract period. The private enterprise expects to recover its costs and earn an adequate rate of return on its investment from those payments (United Nations 2009).

The earlier version of the SNA did not include the handling of PPPs. In practice, two issues needed resolving. The first issue was deciding whether the private enterprise or the government was the economic owner of the fixed assets. The second issue was deciding the appropriate recording of transactions between a private enterprise and a public unit during the period covered by a PPP arrangement. One solution to this has been the assessment of risk. Depending on the bearer of the risk, PPP assets and liabilities should be considered either public or private. This is not fully satisfactory, as, according to the risk criteria, PPP assets and liabilities might be classified as private in national accounts, although they influence fiscal sustainability and public funding obligations in the future (Vries and Yehoue 2013).

Quasi corporations are treated in the SNA as if they were corporations – that is, as institutional units separate from the units to which they legally belong. Thus, quasi corporations owned by government units are grouped with corporations in the non-financial or financial corporate sectors. An example of a restructuring agency is an agency mainly concerned with impaired assets, primarily in the context of banking or other financial crises. Restructuring agencies must be analysed according to the degree of risk they assume considering the degree of government financing. Some governments may set up special purpose entities (SPEs) for financial convenience, the SPEs being involved in fiscal or quasi-fiscal activities (such as the securitisation of assets or borrowing). Resident SPEs that function in only a passive manner relative to general government and that carry out fiscal activities are not regarded as separate institutional units in the SNA and are treated as part of general government, regardless of their legal status. If they act independently, they are treated as separate institutional units and are classified in a sector and industry according to their principal activity (United Nations 2009, 440–441).

A joint venture involves the establishment of a corporation, partnership, or other institutional unit in which each party legally has joint control over the activities of the unit. The units operate in the same way as other units except for their joint control over the unit. As an institutional unit, a joint venture may enter into contracts in its own name and raise finances for its own purposes. If a joint venture operates as a nonmarket producer, the government is effectively in control, and the joint venture is classified as part of the general government. Some countries may be part of an institutional agreement that involves monetary transfers from the member countries to the associated supranational authority and vice versa. The supranational authority also engages in nonmarket production. In the national accounts of member countries, supranational authorities are nonresident institutional units that are part of the rest of the world category (United Nations 2009, 441).

Dealing with nonprofits

Under the guidelines of the SNA, data on the nonprofit sector are merged with data on other sectors, which obscures the view of nonprofit institutions as a part of the economy. Approved by the United Nations Statistical Commission in 2002, the UN *Handbook on Nonprofit Institutions in the System of National Accounts* aims to resolve this problem by offering countries a standard set of guidelines for highlighting data of the nonprofit sector so that the data can be seen and analysed through a system of satellite accounting, which allows the expansion of the scope of the SNA while not being an integral part of it (United Nations 2003).

Broadly, two types of satellite accounts are popular. One focuses on the details of an industry without the expansion of the SNA framework, for example, satellite accounts for agriculture, tourism, NPISHs, health care, and education. The other type of satellite account expands the framework beyond the boundaries (related to production or assets or both) of the SNA, for example, satellite accounts for the environment, households, and human resources (UNESCO 2009).

The SNA identifies two bases for classifying nonprofit institutions (NPI), one according to their economic activity (international standard industrial classification, ISIC), and the other according to their function or purpose (classification of the purposes of nonprofit institutions serving households, COPNI).

Three of the components of the definition provide necessary clarification for the features of NPIs:

1. The institutionally separate from government criterion places additional emphasis on the nongovernmental nature of NPIs, a crucial feature in most understandings of this set of institutions.
2. The self-governing criterion usefully distinguishes NPIs from organisations that are essentially controlled by other entities, whether governments or corporations.
3. The noncompulsory element of the voluntary criterion distinguishes NPIs from entities that people belong to by birth or legal necessity, which distinguishes NPIs from families, tribes, and other similar entities and represents another central feature of the common understanding of these organisations.

(United Nations 2003, 17)

Thus, for the purposes of the satellite account on nonprofit institutions, the nonprofit sector comprises organisations that (a) are not-for-profit and, by law or custom, do not distribute any surplus they may generate to those who own or control them; (b) are institutionally separate from government; (c) are self-governing; and (d) are noncompulsory. NPIs, as defined above, may take a variety of legal or organisational forms – for example, associations, foundations, or corporations – and they serve a variety of purposes. They may be created to provide services for the benefit of the persons or corporations who control or finance them. They may be created for charitable, philanthropic, or welfare reasons to provide goods or services to other persons in need. They may be intended to provide health or education services for a fee, but not for profit. They also may be intended to promote the interest of pressure groups in business or politics.

Dealing with entities in the grey area

Even an illustrative analysis of the SNA shows clearly that the existing categories of institutional units do not form uniform categories in a precise fashion. This is not to argue that the system represents poor quality or judgment. On the contrary, national accounting shows remarkable flexibility in accommodating changes in the economy without losing the system's basic structure. This, however, comes with a price. First, economic developments have meant constant repairs and amendments to existing categorisations, which means that the categories lose their intuitive appeal and require expert judgment to validate the essence of institutional units. Second, the increasing number of exceptions and the delegations of these exemptions to existing categories make the categories themselves less uniform and less pure.

The most interesting feature of dealing with anomalies that do not fully conform to previously formulated categories is the 'conceptual waste' that represents the residue of the existing categories. In hindsight, the entangling of nonprofit institutions with the service of households does not appear to have been a very good choice for the great variety of existing nonprofit institutions. Another development that many governments have faced over the last few decades has been the hollowing out of the state, or, put differently, the delegating of the government to private sector operators. The solutions for dealing with these two types of developments of conceptual waste have been quite diverse. As regards the public-private debate, the procedure has been to give guidance on how to specify a particular activity as belonging to either the public or private sphere of operation using a variety of rules of thumb. In contrast, the variety of nonprofit institutions has been taken into account by building new external classifications to appreciate their abundance.

The beauty of simplification in distinguishing public from private

How should we approach the distinction between public and private activities in society? Does that distinction reflect the 'true' state of affairs in organising, or is it more a reflection of the ways in which we as human beings perceive that distinction? To what extent is it real, and to what extent is it socially constructed, a product of human sense-making procedures, or an outcome of administrative pragmatism (Berger and Luckman 1967; Sokal 1996)? We come across ontological and epistemological problems as to what our assumptions are regarding institutional life and existence, and we also wonder how we are able to actually understand societal life and social forms of organising (Padgett and Powell 2012). One obvious conclusion may be that we cannot possess any understanding of public and private distinctions without the social and linguistic constructions we have created to conduct such a process of comprehension.

However, it would be unfair to maintain that the dichotomy of the public and private does not incorporate rationalities, albeit hidden rationalities, for decision-makers. Rather, there may be several hidden rationalities, interpretive schemes, and locked-in histories that make sense, as our previous discussion on the SNA demonstrated. It is important to discuss the beauty of black-and-white constructions of organisational and institutional life. We can do this by asking what attracts actors and decision-makers to abstain from adding levels of complexity and ambiguity in policy making. We need to address the beauty of simplification, which is not a normative, prescriptive approach but a descriptive perspective of decision-making.

We can use Daniel Kahneman's work (Kahneman 2003; Kahneman 2012; Tversky and Kahneman 1974) on human cognition and human perception as one pioneering perspective in order to understand the mechanisms of distinctions, simplifications, and heuristics in human decision-making. The deliberate choice to focus on distinctions between the public and private can be seen as a decision that is shaped by different societal, political, and individual rationalities and guided by several decision-making rules and interpretive schemes of human decision-making (Vakkuri 2010). Those rationalities are limited, bounded, and, as such, associated with a large research tradition on bounded rationality in human choice. Bounded rationality is a theory of decision-making that attempts to take into account the two aspects of scissors: the cognitive limitations of decision-makers and the structures of their working environments (Simon 1955). Cognitive limitations include, for example, memory, limitations in the comprehension of complex causal relationships, and shortage of time. The structure of environments – the context to which public managers have to adapt – is a source of ecological rationality indicating external limitations (Gigerenzer 2000). Understanding decision-making as it happens in practice necessitates an analysis of both aspects.

Daniel Kahneman is well-known for his thoughts and theories on the two systems of human cognition. System one includes automatic and quick controls and procedures, whereas system two is defined by effortful processes and the complicated rule systems of decision-making. While system one directs human attention to fast, intuitive choices, system two looks for more careful consideration, calculation, and weighing of costs and benefits. Therefore, with system one thinking, decision-makers tend to focus on existing evidence and ignore absent evidence (Kahneman calls this WYSIATI; that is, What You See Is All There Is) (Kahneman 2012). Accordingly, decision-makers try to avoid ambiguity in their choices by suppressing doubt in all forms.

Tversky and Kahneman have based their theories of heuristics and decision-making on the idea of two systems of cognition (Tversky and Kahneman 1974). Classic forms of heuristics include representativeness heuristics, according to which people tend to count on the resemblance of phenomena in making judgments on the representativeness of things. In doing so, people may be insensitive to the prior probability of outcomes and to the sample size of what their judgments are based on. Hence, in their judgments, people search for confirmation of their prior beliefs rather than analytically questioning the existing assumptions and principles of choice. Moreover, we can think of availability heuristics as referring to decision-making situations in which people evaluate the frequency of a phenomenon by the ease with which relevant instances can be brought to mind. More than we may expect, decision-making cognition prefers intuition instead of sophisticated analysis and calculations. Lastly, we may think of anchoring effects that emphasise the significance of initial starting points and reference values in decision-making. For instance, in order to evaluate the performance of a hybrid organisation, we should focus on marginal changes; that is, it is important to understand how performance has changed with respect to some previous relevant reference point.

As Tversky and Kahneman argue, decision-makers' assessments are biased and often neglect baseline effects. In other words, initial starting points are sometimes too significant for ultimate choices. Therefore, there may be important gains, or 'scale economies,' when relying on the clear-cut distinction between public and private. Pierson (2000, 263) writes about contingencies defining the momentum for instigating institutional or political change. Even small events may reshape the trajectories of reforms. Reforms emphasise the timing and sequencing of policy events to enable increasing returns to reform processes. The lesson for a policy reformer would preferably be to influence the course of reform actions earlier, not later. Accordingly, the costs of shifting reform paths from distinctions between public and private to more ambiguous and hybrid forms of governance tend to become higher in the long run. Institutional locked-in structures and ergodic institutional processes are known to persist in time, particularly in complicated areas of societal change and public policy. We may discover different forms of inherent administrative pragmatism within distinctions of public and private (Pierson 2000).

Decision-making heuristics are one type of rule system. There can be search rules of two types: searching for alternatives for action (defining the choice set) and searching for cues for judging the alternatives (Hey 1982). Search can be random, ordered, or based on imitation and emulation. Furthermore, there are stopping rules originating, for instance, from the theory of aspirations (Simon 1955). The acceptable level of aspirations provides satisficing search procedures. A search is discontinued when an acceptable level is achieved.

When should a specific decision-making rule or heuristic be employed? Would this help us understand why and how the strong commitment to public and private distinctions develops? An answer may be found in the individual history of a decision-maker. For example, if a manager of a hybrid organisation learns to use a rule when there is little time to make a decision, the use of such a rule will more likely be used later in choice situations with time pressures. It is obvious that the preceding situation makes it possible to influence judgments and choices by designing situations in which tasks incorporate or simulate initial learning conditions (Einhorn 1982). Therefore, for example, the amount and schedules of reinforcements and the number of trials should be considered when understanding modelling behaviour. Another explanation is outcome feedback. Since outcome feedback is the main source of information for evaluating the quality of judgment rules, knowledge of how task variables both affect outcomes and influence the way outcomes are coded and stored in memory becomes critical in explaining heuristics. This makes it important to understand the perceived causalities of public managers in their decision-making (Weiner 1986). In other words, decision-makers using the clear-cut distinction between public and private need to be convinced of the assumed cause-effect relationships between decisions made and outcomes produced. Decision-makers ask themselves how they can determine the relationship between the distinction and the outcome achieved. Where can they see the benefit in the distinction? How do they value those benefits?

4
SETTING THE PATH FOR MONSTERS

How do hybrids explore their strategic options and objectives?

This chapter elaborates on the three modes of strategy formation – strategic design, internal strategic scanning, and strategic governance – in the business enterprises and public and hybrid organisations formulated in the introduction of this book. Our focus is on assessing and applying strategic thought mostly developed in the private sector context for the use of public and hybrid organisations. The analytic framework for this discussion comprises the role of strategy, assumptions of environment, primary types of capital, management control regimes, and challenges for the strategy modes. Business enterprises, public agencies, state-owned enterprises (SOEs), and social enterprises serve as respective empirical platforms for the application of strategic thought.

The main issue is not whether the discussion of strategy is relevant in public and hybrid settings, as they have already adopted the same management techniques as their private counterparts to implement their policies. Short-term financial concerns are not the essence of strategy. Strategy is about purpose, direction, and goals, which are equally important in all types of organisation settings. The questions are what purpose, what direction, and whose goals. The answer, as always, depends on one's view of strategy. One of the common themes around strategy is that it orients focus when shaping future circumstances that do not yet exist. The goals of sending humans to Mars or finding a cure for cancer exemplify the nature of strategic goals orienting resources to endeavours that are not feasible in the present.

The role of management – top management in particular – is central to strategic thinking. It is the duty of the top manager to formulate and communicate the strategic orientation to subordinates. There is only a limited role for middle management, and there is either a very small or nonexistent role for operative employees. Still, the fundamental significance of strategy might be that it gives us confidence in the future during conditions of uncertainty. The following extract illustrates this point:

> The young lieutenant of a small Hungarian detachment in the Alps sent a reconnaissance unit into the icy wilderness. It began to snow immediately, snowed for two days, and the unit did not return. The lieutenant suffered, fearing that he had sent his own people to death, but on the third day the unit came back. Where had they been? How had they made their way? Yes, they said, we considered ourselves lost and waited for the end. Then one of us found a map in his pocket. That calmed us down. We pitched camp, lasted the snowstorm, and then with the map we discovered our bearings. And here we are. The lieutenant borrowed this remarkable map and had a good look at it. He discovered to his astonishment that it was not a map of the Alps, but a map of the Pyrenees.
>
> *(Weick 1995, 54)*

The lesson provided by the extract above is that in many cases the power of strategy is not found in its accuracy or level of detail but in its ability to give guidance and comfort in ambiguous situations. Moreover, genuine belief in the strategy enables concentration of effort, even if the belief proves eventually to be faulty.

In the following, we present a description of strategic orientations within public, private, and hybrid contexts. The basic idea is that strategy in itself contains two main aspects: thinking and doing. The main avenues for the thinking part of strategy are design for future circumstances, focus on the availability of relevant resources, and emphasis on the partnering structures in both intra- and interorganisational settings. However, design, resources, and partnering structures all point to different types of actions. The design orientation aims at establishing constant and stable routines (action sequences) that can be programmed in advance. Resource orientation points to another direction. This activity consists of finding novel resource combinations that benefit the organisation but cannot easily be copied by others. Lastly, emphasis on partnering aspects focuses on finding the most fruitful partners and lucrative positions in the network as a whole. Some of the most prevalent features of strategy, such as foresight acquired through different types of planning, are ubiquitous aspects of organised action, but resource-based thinking and cooperative relational aspects are more context specific, signifying different positions of public, private, and hybrid arrangements in modern societies.

There is growing literature on strategic management in the public sector (Bryson 1995; Nutt and Backoff 1992; Koteen 1997; Joyce 1999; Rabin et al. 2000; Scholes and Johnson 2001), but some of this scholarly work has been more oriented towards introducing tools of strategy implementation than elaborating on the nature of strategy itself. Public sector strategy literature often includes discussion of nonprofits as well. Hybrid arrangements have gathered focused attention in organisation literature (Koppell 2006; Billis 2010), but this discussion has not been particularly attuned to the strategic aspects of hybridity. The private sector discussion of strategy is not always helpful either because of its overwhelming emphasis on achieving market share and growth through competition – key elements that are not always strong in hybrid contexts and that are lacking in the public sector environment.

Public agencies and hybrids

Public agencies

In contrast to private enterprises that are owned by shares and aim to increase shareholder value, public agencies and hybrids represent entities that possess unique features that deviate from the market principle. In the following, we discuss the strategies of these different organisational forms. Public agencies serve as a showcase for government organisation strategies and SOEs, and social enterprises serve as examples of strategies in hybrid arrangements. Public agencies are part of government and are intended for the administration of law, which sets them apart from privately owned firms and other nonprofit organisations (Gortner et al. 1997). Administrative duty makes public administration a legally proscribed entity. In this sense, public agencies are not sovereign powers; rather, they execute government functions under delegated authority by way of legal obligation. The legality of administration defines what agencies are supposed to do, and legal statutes define the limits of administrative action such that agencies cannot initiate their own policies or programmes without legal mandate (Harlow 2006). In strategy formation, the distinction between public and private organisations is clear: Public organisations cannot invent their own business in the way stock-hold companies can. The variety of legal systems and national traditions makes it difficult to define a public agency with accuracy. The formation of agencies has been a vehicle for market-based reforms in some countries, especially in the UK. In other countries, particularly in Sweden, both central and local agencies have traditionally been responsible mainly for the execution of public policy, and strong and independent regulatory function has been a prevalent feature of agencies in the US. The unifying features of agencies include the following:

- Some degree of autonomy from political direction
- Pre-established strategic direction through political decision
- Budgeting autonomy
- Financing from a combination of the agencies' own revenues, earmarked contributions, and subsidies from the state budget
- Publicly owned assets
- Public accountability defined by law and tradition

(OECD 2001, 14)

Hybrid organisations: state-owned enterprises and social enterprises

The hybrid area of organisations covers a number of quite different institutions that cannot easily be grasped with the use of a single organisational form. For illustrative purposes, SOEs and social enterprises exemplify differentiated strategic options for hybrid organisations. State-owned organisations operate in the market environment, but they include public policy goals in their strategic orientation. Some state-owned organisations are an integral part of the government, but the separation of ownership and control in SOEs has meant that governments can retain control of SOEs with minor ownership stakes (Bruton et al. 2015). Social enterprises represent hybrid organisations that fulfil a social mission as their strategic goal and use profit generation to support the achievement of their social missions. The notion of social enterprise is, in itself, an ideal typical construct that covers various types of non-profits and enables a comparison of hybrid action in different institutional contexts (Defourny and Nyssens 2010).

State-owned enterprises

Globally, SOEs account for 20 percent of investment, 5 percent of employment, and up to 40 percent of output in some countries (World Bank 2014). Most SOEs were created through the nationalisation of the Western world in the post–World War II era. At that time, the establishment of state-owned entities did not occur in the US, which followed an approach of regulation rather than ownership of private industries. Typical areas of activity for SOEs were and still are banks; insurance; social security; education (public universities); health (public hospitals); basic goods industries (coal, oil, atomic energy, steel); and public utilities, communications, and transportation. There were different motives for nationalisation: political, ideological, social, and economic motives. First, there was an aim to decrease the role of private capital in favour of increasing the power of the labour force and the belief in the ability of the government to solve economic problems. Second, social motives for nationalisation centred on achieving full employment, and economic motives included the correction of market failures and the encouragement of economic activity in underdeveloped countries and regions. The demise of SOEs beginning in the 1970s included orthogonally opposite motives. The inefficiency of SOEs, the aim to reduce public debt through privatisation, the aim to increase the role of the markets in society, and the erosion of natural monopolies through technological progress (e.g. telecommunication, electricity) have downplayed the position of SOEs. As a consequence, the role of SOEs has diminished in industrialised countries. Interestingly enough, the same type of decline has not happened in the developing world (Toninelli 2008).

In a more fundamental tone, Bremmer (2010) suggests that there are two types of capitalist systems. These are state capitalist and free market capitalist systems, which are both based on long-term strategic policy choices. State capitalist systems see markets as a tool for serving mainly national interests or interests of the political elite. A state-owned enterprise is but one vehicle to exercise state influence. It is therefore possible that state involvement in the economy in countries such as China or Russia is not a transitory phase towards pure market society; rather, it is an integral feature of the countries' long-standing institutional structures. The aim of state capitalists is to use international and domestic markets for the advancement of their political and economic influence. In contrast, free market capitalists see that the private sector is the key engine of economic expansion and sustainable economic growth. The Anglo-Saxon model in English-speaking countries is built on mistrust of the government and strong reliance on markets guaranteeing individual freedom. The Central European variant is based on stronger government influence and employee protection in particular, but, together with the Anglo-Saxon model, these two types of capitalist systems are variants of the same market-based approach (Bremmer 2010).

The OECD (2015a) guidelines for state-owned organisations point out common features of SOEs:

- State ownership and control
- Engagement in economic activity
- Inclusion of public policy objectives

SOES are companies under government ownership limited by shares. Moreover, statutory corporations, with their legal personality established through specific legislation, should be considered SOEs if their purpose and activities are of a largely economic nature. The state can be the ultimate beneficiary owner of the majority of voting shares or otherwise exercise an equivalent degree of control. Examples of an equivalent degree of control include continued state control over an enterprise or its board of directors. Some borderline cases need to be addressed on a case-by-case basis. For example, whether a 'golden share,' which gives superior voting rights, amounts to control depends on the extent of the powers it gives to the state. An economic activity is one that involves offering goods or services on a given market, which could be carried out by a private operator in order to make profits. Public policy objectives benefit the general public within an SOE's own jurisdiction. They are implemented as specific performance requirements imposed on SOEs and/or private enterprises and are not related to the maximisation of profits and shareholder value. Public policy objectives could include the delivery of public services, such as postal services (OECD 2015b).

Within the context of SOEs, there are a number of governance issues that complicate the supervision and/or internal functioning of SOEs:

- Multiple principles
- Competing goals and objectives
- Protection from competition
- A politicised board of directors
- Low levels of transparency and accountability
- Weak protection of minority shareholders

(World Bank 2014, 13)

Social enterprises

The concept of social enterprise bridges the discussion of different types of third-sector organisations; that is, cooperatives such as worker-driven cooperatives and nonprofit organisations. The concept emphasises the production aspect of third-sector organisations instead of their advocacy role. The idea of a voluntary organisation as an enterprise puts forward the need for the professional management of voluntary activities. This does not mean that nonprofits would turn out to be another industry; instead, the idea signifies a response to changing social and economic circumstances which requires professionalism in the management of any organisation in the Western world (Defourny and Nyssens 2008).

Social enterprises are not-for-profit private organisations that provide goods and services that are directly related to their explicit aims to benefit the community (Defourny and Nyssens 2010). More specifically, social enterprises meet the following ideal typical economic and social criteria.

The four economic criteria:

- A high degree of autonomy
- A continuous activity producing goods and/or services
- A significant level of economic risk
- A minimum amount of paid work

The five social criteria:

- An explicit aim to benefit the community
- Decision-making power not based on capital ownership
- An initiative launched by a group of citizens
- A participatory nature, which involves persons affected by the activity
- Limited profit distribution

(Defourny and Nyssens 2010, 43)

The fundamental distinction between social enterprises and other organisational forms is that social enterprises are based on the activity of civil society, not on business interests or government intervention. The aspect of voluntary labour is another unique feature of social enterprises. The aim to benefit the community and democratic decision rules give social enterprises a public flavour, whereas the profit distribution of social enterprises, limited as it may be, and their economic risk emphasise social enterprises' business nature. The following discussion shows that the view of social enterprises as belonging to the third sector (Billis 2010) represents a rather restrictive and probably Eurocentric view on the activities of social enterprises. Having said that, social enterprises are a well-suited illustration of hybrid organisations. While the origin of social enterprises lies in civil society, they occupy the same ground as other entities in the grey area between public and private spheres when acquiring resources and the legitimacy necessary to fulfil their goals.

Analytic dimensions

The role of strategy

Since deterministic strategy formulations refer to events that have no random aspects but proceed in a fixed, predictable fashion, it is possible to direct future events by planning. The emergent formation of strategy emphasises that, in uncertain conditions, it is likely that the results of a project will be affected by unknown factors and that planning has only a limited effect on outcomes. Between these two perspectives, there is a considerable grey area in which categorical thinking does not apply. Even in a predictable world, the complexity of the specific environment and the cognitive limitations of human thought (Tversky and Kahneman 1974) elude rational calculation.

Assumptions about environment

Since an organisation uses strategy to deal with changing circumstances (Chaffee 1985), strategies are based on some explicit or implicit assumptions about the environment. Open-system, closed-system, and nonsystemic views are alternative strategy-relevant views on organisation-environment interfaces. The open-system view constitutes self-maintenance based on a process of resources deriving from the environment and interaction with the environment. Along these lines, Emery and Trist (1965) describe four types of environment that influence the nature of organisational strategy: (1) a placid randomised environment, (2) a placid clustered environment, (3) a disturbed-reactive environment, and (4) turbulent fields. Regarding the first type, a randomly organised environment requires no strategy. In the second type of environment, survival is linked with knowledge of environment. Easily attainable goals may prove to be dangerous, and tackling difficult issues may reveal rewarding opportunities. In the third type of environment, there are a number of similar organisations, each of which has to take account of the others and also has to consider that what it knows may also be known by others. In market competition, the revelation of business secrets to rivals is always a threat. The organisation has to both make sequential choices and choose actions that will draw the other organisations off. In turbulent fields (the fourth type), dynamic properties do not simply arise from the interaction between participating organisations; these properties also arise from the field itself: The 'ground' is in motion. To put it differently, there are not only changes in the position of the players in the game; the rules guiding the game itself transform at the same time. The consequences of organisational actions become increasingly unpredictable, and organisations have to rely on their own innovativeness (Emery and Trist 1965). A practical example illustrates the situation. If you were playing a game of chess you would have to anticipate not only the moves of the opponent, but also changes in the rules in moving the objects on the board. In contrast to the open-system view, neofunctionalists take a closed-system approach by pointing out that the environment is in fact an organisational feature and that the inability to adapt to demands of the environment is an anomaly of organisational identity (Luhmann 1995, 176–209). Furthermore, both real-life changes (Grandori and Soda 1995) and theoretical developments (Thompson 2003) challenge the importance of the organisation-environment distinction. What these advancements imply is that organisational boundaries are becoming more fluid and that interorganisational networks rather than organisations are becoming more important producers of value.

Types of capital

A discussion of types of capital shows differences between types of activities. Most strategy literature deals with manufacturing, and only scant attention is given to service provision. This emphasis on manufacturing orients the perspective to the utilisation of tangible assets, such as facilities, equipment, and finances, whereas an emphasis on service orientation shifts the attention to human and social assets. In addition to financial capital, the current literature also identifies human and social capital, both of which are assets that yield income and other useful outputs over long periods of time. 'Human capital' refers to expenditures on education, training, and medical care, producing individual benefits such as knowledge, skills, and health. The human aspect of capital is less mobile than the aspects of physical or financial capital because it is more difficult to transfer knowledge and skills than it is to move machines or money (Becker 1993). Social capital literature emphasises the relational aspects of capital, such as goodwill (Adler and Kwon 2002), networks, shared cognitions, and shared trust (Nahapiet and Ghoshal 1998). One particular feature of social capital is that no single actor can fully own it, like other types of capital. The relational basis of social capital implies that assets reside at least partially in relationships between actors.

Managerial control

'Control' refers to the evaluation of correspondence between actual and intended outcomes of work assignments (Kaufmann et al. 1986). The idea of control implies that there is either an explicit or implicit assumption of acceptable behaviour (Horwitz 1990). Thus, managerial intervention cannot take place efficiently without legitimation. In voluntary work, the mission of the organisation is the most important device for achieving coordinated action, in which there are only meagre possibilities for management command. In public organisations, the authority of management stems from the internalisation of rules, assumptions that are taken for granted, and accepted, legally rational bases for constraining action (Clegg et al. 2006). Overall, the efficient use of authority includes the indifference of subordinates such that they obey orders without consciously questioning authority (Mahoney 2005).

Traditionally, management control refers to the application of financial measurement for the use of managerial decision-making, but, in strategic terms, financial control is a rather remote way of directing activities that lacks any substantive emphasis on the actual activities of the organisation (Goold et al. 2001). Recently, the area and methods of managerial control have been expanding beyond the financial aspect of organised action in order to process control of daily activities, administrative control of organisational structures, and control of culture in the form of beliefs, norms, and symbols (Hared et al. 2013). Moreover, methods of financial control have been changing within public agencies and hybrids to emulate practices within the private sector. In addition, control over the organisational design defines another area of managerial influence by which activities can be directed. The most notable change in the large conglomerates of the World War II era has been the adoption of a multidivisional form (M-form) consisting of a number of semi-independent units under the overall guidance of the headquarters aided by staff units (Freeland 1996). Another area of management control is communication with the environment of the organisation, which cannot be supervised through internal control devices. Basically, top management is responsible for the 'foreign policy' of any organisation by defining the approach to external stakeholders and constituencies (Donaldson and Preston 1995). The following discussion elaborates on the features of the three strategy modes sketched in Figure 4.1 and represented in Table 4.1.

FIGURE 4.1 Three modes of strategy formation

TABLE 4.1 Three modes of strategy formation

	Strategic design	*Strategic scanning*	*Strategic governance*
The role of strategy	The strategy defines ways to expand and organise current actions (programming)	The strategy enables the mapping of novel ways to match resources to fulfil goals (combining)	The strategy defines the basis for sharing work with external partners (relating)
Assumption about the environment	Disturbed-reactive	Turbulent fields	Turbulent fields
Primary type of capital	Financial	Human	Social
Managerial control	Budget	Division of labour	Contract
Main challenges	Unanticipated situations	Rigid resources, misinterpretation of resources	Contracting costs, overwhelming external stakeholders

Adapted from Johanson (2009, 14).

Strategic design mode

Twentieth-century strategic thought after World War II has been rational, emphasising the possibility of calculating all options, the attunement to profit-maximising behaviour, and, as strategy is prescriptive, the opportunity to supply guidelines on how to apply strategy instead of simply describing it.

The fundamental assumption of strategic design is that organisations can face future circumstances with current understanding. While it is obvious that strategy by its very nature incorporates planning, the strategic design mode relies heavily on predetermination. The future can be programmed in advance (Whittington 1993; Mintzberg et al. 1998). The anticipation of future events, along with the subsequent programming of actions, is in its essence a very practical task that does not separate actions between types of organisations. Formally, the strategic design mode does not much consider differences between types of activities, whether public or private. The five-year plans of the Soviet Union did not formally differ much from the long-term projections of major American corporations in the post–World War II era.

A discussion of public value (Moore 1995; Moore 2013) might be helpful here. The strategic task of the public manager is the use of value in creating imagination when combining the tasks of an agency (e.g. services/regulation, operational/professional) and authorising environment and operational capabilities. While business enterprises provide services to paying customers, government agencies often provide services to citizens free of charge or with nominal cost to the customer. To be able to provide services, public agencies require the authorisation of the environment and organisational capabilities, which establishes the legitimacy and support of public action. Following due process (e.g. auditing or disclosing government information) is one part of gaining legitimacy for public action. Sometimes tackling new problems requires authorisation of change and innovation. For instance, increasing awareness of a sustainable development gives public authorities a better mandate to tackle threats to the physical environment. In terms of operational capabilities, public agencies usually consist of multiple production lines, which require coordinated effort. Most often, one agency is but one part of a production chain, which brings forward the importance of coordination between public bodies. The satisfaction of citizens is an integral part of public value creation, but public value as a product of government agencies eludes exact measurement, as it can be detected more in the collectively defined outcomes of government action than in the direct output of public agencies.

Design in private enterprises

The possibility of programming the future necessitates that the environment remain relatively stable, but the environment also should be complex enough to make any planning exercise worthwhile. In theory, no change in implementation is necessary if the planning has been done carefully enough. Strategy literature has questioned the straightforward implementation of a defined strategic direction (Mintzberg 1994). There is an eminent threat that plans become ends in themselves and that embracing a predefined, deliberate strategy path hinders the possibility to see the potential in an emergent strategy, which surfaces without any conscious attempt.

Sanchez and Heene (1997) see business strategy as originating from three main sources in the 1940s and 1950s: industrial organisation economics, general management at Harvard, and Edith Penrose's analysis of the growth of firms (see Penrose 1960 and Lockett and Thompson 2004 for evaluation). Industrial organisation economics gave the impetus to analyse industry groups and strategic groups within industries. The analysis of the growth of firms was one of the building blocks for the resource-based view of firms, while general management laid the foundation for strategic human resource management and strategic leadership studies.

Later business developments related to the design mode (Porter 1980) were built explicitly on economic theory, in particular industrial organisation economics. The structure-conduct performance hypothesis in industrial organisation assumed that industry structure determines corporate conduct, which in turn dictates economic performance. The reason for such an analysis was initially to spot industries with a lack of competition, which would require government intervention to make them more competitive (Barney and Hesterly 1999). The classical formulation did not give much weight to the conduct of corporations, emphasising the importance of industry in defining performance. In its newly formulated version, corporate conduct also plays a role in rivalry within an industry, especially among strategic groups following similar strategies. The idea is that organisations should try to find defensible positions in industries that provide above-normal profits because of a lack of competition. Thus, government tools for detecting market failures have become a business instrument for surviving competition.

Design in public agencies

The analysis of public sector policies has included a relevant discussion of planning. The rational comprehensive model implies an exhaustive consideration of all possible options, and the incrementalist approach suggests looking only at very few options. Lindblom (1979) argues that policies evolve from their initial positions in small incremental steps. In this incremental view, any rational comprehensive plan is likely to fail because all of the consequences of any policy cannot be taken into account in advance. Etzioni (1986) suggests that one way of overcoming the distinction between comprehensive and incremental planning could be the mixed-scanning approach such that policy formulation involves an appreciation of the overall problem and a consideration of alternatives without rejecting incremental strategies for existing policies and programmes. Public administration literature provides a historically rich source for examinations of the challenges of implementation, such as the strict assumptions under which implementation can succeed in a predicted manner (Hogwood and Gunn 1984), the power of street-level bureaucrats in moulding initial preferences (Lipsky 1971), and the bottom-up implementation model (Hjern and Porter 1981), which reflects the ambiguity of policy objectives and thus the ambiguity of external strategic direction.

Economics literature on the public sector context records anomalies of economic thought, such as collusion between competing firms in an industry. Collusion among competitors is problematic in the industry structure view, as collaboration between rivalries usually represents unethical patterns of behaviour (e.g. the formation of cartels), which distort competition. In the public sphere, cooperation among agencies is a welcomed practice and is not ethically questionable. However, the tendency to form agencies according to monopolies so that duties related to particular areas of operation are handled within a single agency does not particularly encourage cooperation.

The politics of bureaucracy discussion points out that administrators and agency heads take part in the policy process, and they have their own goals in defining public goods and services. In essence, the enlargement of an agency and/or the increased autonomy of an agency are two alternative goals that agency heads may strive for in their struggle with other actors. To put it briefly, the enlargement argument states that the amount of employees, the size of the budget, and the breadth of operative duties enable agency heads to gain personal prestige (Niskanen 1971). Alternatively, the autonomy argument in the bureau-shaping model argues that agency heads behave in such a way as to maximise their personal utility in their work. The size of the budgets is not the main issue for bureau chiefs; instead, bureau chiefs' main concerns are interesting work and low-risk work environments. Therefore, positions in small executive agencies close to political power are tempting for agency heads, because such positions offer interesting work without the risks and discomfort of large operative agencies. Following the same line of reasoning, senior public officials favour the outsourcing and privatisation of government functions in order to avoid excessive internal risks (Dunleavy 1991).

Design in hybrid organisations

For one thing, hybridity brings forth the problem of industry. To begin with, hybrids' current classifications are exemptions to existing categories or are residual categories that do not fit with existing divisions between public and private organisations. As a consequence, it is extremely difficult to identify the industry context in hybrid settings, as hybrids do not comprise organisations following the same purposes, seeking similar strategies, or serving a shared clientele. If the type of goal is the divisive line separating public and private strategic design, the key aspect of hybridity is the mixture of public and private goals. The emergent position of SOEs serves to illustrate this point on hybridity. First, the reasons for the existence of SOEs are different in various contexts. In industrialised countries, the establishment of SOEs is typically related to the expansion of government into private activity in competitive markets. On the other hand, in the developing world, SOEs might represent the only option to raise capital for the formation of large-scale business operations in nonexistent or poorly developed market conditions (Koppell 2006).

According to a recent review of the literature (Bruton et al. 2015), there are some common themes in SOE research: (1) a dichotomous view of the ownership issue, (2) disagreement about the influence of state ownership on firm performance, and (3) a focus on SOEs in the Chinese economy. It is easy to see that the dualistic view of SOEs fails to see the hybridity of ownership and control arrangements. The dilution of full state ownership signifies the presence of private investors, which gives rise to following parallel institutional logics at the same time. Such an arrangement enables the harvesting of legitimacy, enhancing elements from both the public and private spheres. Meanwhile, the issuing of different types of shares can guarantee governments' considerable control over the functioning of firms, even with only minority stakes in the enterprise. In other words, ownership and control form a continuum that contains a considerable hybrid area between the public and private. Disagreement over the performance of SOEs might partially originate from the failure to identify levels of government control in various ownership arrangements. The challenges of SOEs in the developing world is illustrated in Case 4.1. In practice, the dual goals of public policy and profit generation are difficult to mix in the microprocesses of everyday work, as witnessed in Swedish SOEs (Alexius and Cisneros Örnberg 2015). If employees concentrate on an SOE's performance efficiency, they run the risk of a 'mission drift' to the financialisation of targets, and, if they aim to preserve the value plurality of the SOE, they face the criticism that they are inefficient and political.

The case (Case 4.1) of a Vietnamese state-owned power corporation illustrates the difficulties in adapting to changing circumstances with tools of planning.

CASE 4.1 HYBRID GOVERNANCE IN STATE-OWNED COMPANIES

The case of PV Power in Vietnam

The Petro Vietnam Power Corporation (abbreviated as PV Power) is one of the first leading organisations of the state-owned Vietnam Oil and Gas Group (abbreviated as the PVN), which contributes about 30 percent of GDP to the country annually. The main duty of PV Power is to invest in power supply, operate several types of power plants, and supply electricity to ensure national power security – a political mission assigned by the government of Vietnam to PV Power's business. Accounting for 10 percent of total market shares in electricity production, PV Power became the second-ranked position among electricity suppliers in Vietnam and the biggest producer in terms of gas-fired power generation. In addition to the gas-fired, hydro, and wind power plants, PV Power is operating two coal-fired power plants consuming domestic coal. Furthermore, the PVN is investing in three coal-fired power plants, which will consume around ten million metric tons of import coal from foreign markets per year.

Having been a coal export country for many years, Vietnam is now increasingly importing coal. According to the Ministry of Industry and Trade's assessment of the balance of supply and demand, domestic coal mining met Vietnam's demand until the end of 2015. Since 2016, Vietnam has had to import coal to serve local consumers, especially for electricity production. The requirement of importing coal creates challenges and difficulties, not only for PV Power but also for almost the whole system of Vietnam's power generation due to the interaction between buying coal and selling electricity.

Only three organisations were allowed by the government to import coal for the electricity-generation sector in Vietnam: (1) PV Power, (2) the Vietnam National Coal and Mineral Industries Holding Corporation (abbreviated as VINACOMIN), and (3) the Dong Bac Corporation. Based on government regulation, the price of coal imported for electricity must be accepted by the electricity buyer (Vietnam Electricity, abbreviated as EVN). The domestic coal price mechanism and regulations were issued by the government and the Ministry of Industry and Trade, but the importing coal price mechanism for electricity generation has not been stipulated yet. This has led to the embarrassment of coal importers who try to purchase coal from foreign markets and have to determine coal's price in electricity prices.

Actually, the Law of Bidding allows state-owned organisations to purchase input fuel for production bases according to their own regulations, provided that those regulations meet the targets of fairness, transparency, and economic efficiency. Thus, PV Power should choose, for instance, importing coal suppliers through bidding in order to prove the competition on price and thereafter get EVN's acceptance of the fuel components of electricity prices. However, bidding for importing coal purchases has the following difficulties:

1 The coal specification must be within the range of the designed specification of the power plant, and coal suppliers have to ensure long-term supply, as coal specification varies from mine to mine.
2 The target of bidding is to choose suppliers who not only meet the requirements mentioned in item one above but also offer competitive prices.

Also, some owners who have big coal mines that satisfy technical requirements and long-term supply may not be willing to participate in bidding, and brokers who are eager to offer competitive prices may not be able to guarantee long-term supply, as they are not coal mine owners. Thus, if PV Power only pursues bidding to buy imported coal, it may miss opportunities to sign contracts with big coal mine owners. Bidding may solve short-term purchases but might not be a sharp solution for the long-term security of supplying coal stably.

The abovementioned situation leads to difficulties in seeking coal resources and negotiating contracts. As importing coal is a new activity in Vietnam, guiding documents or regulations applicable for this activity have not been issued yet. For this reason, the state governance unit for coal imports is the Ministry of Industry and Trade, which established a state committee to guide and manage coal imports to the country. The head of the committee is the minister of industry and trade, and other members of the committee are deputy ministers, presidents, and CEOs from related ministries and state-owned organisations, such as the PVN, PV Power, VINACOMIN, and the Dong Bac Corporation. The main mission of the committee is to advise the minister of industry and trade and the prime minister on how to form and issue policy and manage coal imports to Vietnam.

The consultancy of the state committee with the minister of industry and trade and the prime minister should be based on the electricity market, the long-term and short-term strategies of coal mining in Vietnam, and the consideration of rules governing activities of electricity production and trading. For state governance, the Ministry of Industry and Trade is able to get policy advice from major economic groups related to the production and trade of electricity, such as the PVN, PV Power, EVN, and VINACOMIN, which can create synchronous policies for the whole system.

In social enterprises, community-serving missions entangle nonprofits with business enterprises and public agencies. Here, the US and European approaches show different positions on the importance of social missions. In the US, discussion of social enterprises covers the corporate philanthropy and social responsibility of business organisations as well as the partnering of social enterprises with business organisations in cause-related marketing, but, in practice, the rules for the tax exemption of nonprofits do not allow profit distribution. In Europe, discussion of corporate social responsibility is similar to the US's debate, but there is also a more restrictive idea that social enterprises belong to a specific group of third-sector organisations, together with cooperative organisations striving mainly for social benefits. In practice, European social enterprises are able to distribute some limited profits. In the US, foundations have encouraged social enterprise activity by providing help in starting and operating social enterprises, but local, federal, and state governments have provided only limited and indirect support for social enterprises. In contrast, many European countries have established new legal organisational forms for social enterprises (Kerlin 2006).

Strategic scanning mode

The use of biological analogies is commonplace in organisation research, as already witnessed in the previous chapters of this book. Still, there are dangers in seeing organisations as living organisms. In particular, organisations have no genetic constitution dictating their death (Penrose 1952). The comparison between the growth patterns of organisations and the growth patterns of animals originates from the fact that there is a lag between managerial capability and the possibilities created by growing resources. In animal life, growth patterns are often directly linked to the availability of nutrition. More generally, experience and knowledge in management define both the production of services from resources and the demand that management considers suitable for its activities (Penrose 1960). In a somewhat similar vein, evolutionary economics (Nelson and Winter 2002) builds on notions of change and bounded rationality. Environment constantly poses new and unfamiliar problems for organisations, and the internal decision-making processes of firms often deviate from economic rationality. Moreover, the organisation's history in terms of organisational routines plays an important part in defining future action. Organisational routine is a collective equivalent to individual skill. Routines enable the storage and retrieval of knowledge, and routines help solve internal grievances within organisations. Going back to the biological analogy, the idea is that routines are 'genes' that can be passed on to other organisations.

Scanning in private enterprises

An important compilation of ideas combining features of growth and evolutionary economics is the resource-based view of the firm. The success of an organisation cannot be found directly in the organisation's adaptation to its environment; success is instead found in the unique resource combination of the organisation. The important feature of strategic scanning is that it directs attention to strengths and weaknesses rather than to the opportunities and threats of the environment espoused by the strategic design mode. All organisations have unique resources, which produce a sustained competitive advantage if they are rare, inimitable, or difficult to copy and can be used by an organisation (Barney 1991; Barney et al. 2001). More often than not, resources are intangible combinations of knowledge and skills rather than physical objects. The ability to combine resources is usually socially complex and tied to an organisation's history. Resources are the inputs of the production process. The use of resources determines organisational capabilities that, in essence, are organisational routines. There are, however, no predetermined functional relationships between the resources of a firm and its capabilities. A recommendation for strategy formation is to develop strategies around the most important resources and capabilities (Grant 1991).

Due to the primacy of resources, their identification may involve a fundamental reorganisation of the existing structures. The obvious problem in combining identified resources lies in the organisational structure itself, which does not allow the deployment of existing resources to new uses. However, the ability to combine resources in a novel way might also necessitate a novel way of identifying the resources themselves. Some of the more practical developments related to the resource-based view are highly relevant in public and hybrid contexts. The core competence perspective encourages the use and deployment of capabilities across internal organisational boundaries. To put it another way, multilayered hierarchies and the detailed division of labour into individual offices might be a structural hindrance when trying to determine the strategic direction of an organisation (Prahalad and Hamel 1990).

The human side of capital comes to the fore in the internal scanning mode. Intellectual capital is tied up in the knowledge of employees, and the knowledgeable worker is a premium commodity in the production process. Petty and Guthrie (2000) see human capital as comprising employee competence: employees' knowledge, formal qualifications, and energetic attitudinal and behavioural orientations. In this way, the abilities of employees might be related to informal practices and work-related learning; that is, tacit knowledge (Nonaka and Takeuchi 1995), which eludes verbal utterance and management intervention.

In promoting the uniqueness of every single organisation, the strategic scanning approach turns away from any management technique that is readily available to other organisations because they allow imitation. In a hybrid context, it makes sense to identify inimitable capabilities when faced with competition, but, even more importantly, the resource-based view warns against the mindless copying of practices that work in another setting and are embedded in the history and culture of an organisation.

The ideal mix of capabilities or competences is not easy to define in advance, and, if organisation-based unique resources are taken seriously, there are hardly any options to formulate ubiquitous principles to take the resources into account. The empirical evidence of success in matching resources rests more on the post hoc analysis of successful organisations than on predictions of particular resource combinations (Mahoney and Pandian 1992). A consequence of the study of hybrid arrangements is the use of the case study approach in pointing out challenges and the ways in which successful managers have either surmounted these challenges or failed to succeed in their work. In the spirit of internal scanning, such analysis should not create generalisations; rather, the analysis should be a learning exercise for other organisations facing the same types of circumstances. As heuristic devices, case descriptions offer a valuable tool for managerial self-reflection.

Scanning in public agencies

The most important resources in public agencies are tied to the knowledge and capabilities of administrators: administrators' expertise, abilities in generating information and advice, and possession of a dominant profession (Ellison 2006). The specialisation of duties is an avenue for the clear mission of an agency. The agency is able to strengthen its position if it is able to master complex technical duties that

96 Setting the path for monsters

cannot easily be adopted by the general public. The technical language of engineers, lawyers, and medical doctors illustrates this point. In addition, successful agencies are able to generate information and provide advice on the policy-making process. The result of this ability in the information generation is that agencies are able to control the information flow circulating in the policy process.

The possession of a dominant profession signifies a situation in which the agency is occupied by members of a single profession. Thus, a regulatory agency dealing with financial control that is occupied by economists is likely to be more successful than a similar agency that is occupied by a number of occupational groups. The position of an agency is further advanced if the professionals within the agency belong to a group that performs highly valued duties in society. Interestingly enough, focus on internal administration is not the main avenue for the success of an agency. The reason for this is that agencies tend to be evaluated on the basis of the success of the policies they are engaged in, not on the basis of their internal operations. This does not rule out that successful agencies are sensitive to the internal needs of their employees (Ellison 2006).

Scanning in hybrid organisations

In the hybrid context, the dual nature of organisations provides avenues for resources that are not available to others, for instance, the ability of state-owned organisations to enjoy the benefits of government financing and access to resources that are regulated by public bodies. The use of natural resources, such as oil or minerals, is often subject to government control due to these resources' nature as strategic national assets. In such a setting, those that are part of the government decision-making structure are in the best position to enjoy the benefits of superior access to these resources (Okhmatovskiy 2010). From the perspective of a hybrid organisation, the availability of government resources and resources acquired from market transactions highlights external resources as internal assets of the organisation which can be denied for other possible users (see Case 4.2).

CASE 4.2 COXA

Public-private interaction in hospital development in Finland

The Coxa Hospital is located in Tampere, the third largest city in Finland, and serves almost 450,000 inhabitants in the region. Coxa is a hospital specialising in the insertion of prostheses that fit inside the body, such as replacement bones and joints. The company was established in February of 2001. Several factors contributed to the development of the hospital. The management of the Pirkanmaa hospital district started to invest in management and business training with the aim of increasing its clinical and research capability in the 1980s. A major catalyst emerged when a national study revealed quality problems in performing surgeries in the 1990s. A further impetus for change originated from new government legislation that encouraged municipalities to purchase procedures from the private sector in order to shorten queuing times (Dowdeswell and Vauramo 2009).

The Coxa team focused on consultation with key stakeholders. The real breakthrough in changing the way of thinking and achieving commitment to the project came through a time-consuming series of informal conversations, briefings, and negotiations. These developments prepared the way for public agreements with key stakeholders. The organisation form of a stock-hold company limited by shares promised to free Coxa Hospital from the rigidities often ascribed to public institutions. The hospital would no longer need to queue for public sector capital and negotiate constraints associated with public financing. The main reason favouring limited company status was the fact that, as a company limited by shares, the hospital would be able to keep its own profits. At Coxa, the corporate strategy was shaped by public and private interests which are also represented in the company board. The hospital took advantage of the freedoms available to limited companies during the capital financing and procurement stages. When the hospital opened in 2002, it was possible to make some tentative judgments about its initial performance. Overall, Coxa exhibits many characteristics of success. Financially, the hospital seems to be viable. Coxa Hospital has made a successful transition from the public sector to the public-private sector, and it has capitalised on investment in management training, research innovation, and business skills. The hospital's organisational model was based on a partnership among a group of institutions (local government, hospitals, universities, and commercial interests), all with strong intertwined strategic interests (Dowdeswell and Vauramo 2009).

In discussion on state-owned organisations, the ability of SOEs to continuously resort to government funding has been seen as source of inefficiency, because the munificence of financial resources decreases the need for adaptation to market competition and changing economic circumstances. However, it is also possible that the soft budget constraint enables a more long-term perspective on strategy and the future, which in turn improves economic performance. Institutions signify another aspect of SOEs. In studying the relationship between economic freedoms (e.g. financial, monetary, investment, trade, and labour freedoms), it was found that there is no correlation between enterprise-friendly economic freedoms and government ownership, but, interestingly enough, government control was connected to limited institutional development supporting private enterprise (Bruton et al. 2015). It is not easy to decipher the significance of macro-institutional developments. Is an SOE a solution for an underdeveloped institutional environment that is unable to gather capital or organise functional firm structures, or is an SOE in fact the cause of institutional underdevelopment, which favours public intervention and crowds out purely private initiative?

In regards to social enterprises, developments in securing resources have been different in the US and Europe. In the US, the expansion of public services in the 1960s progressed through the financing of the nonprofit sector instead of the building of new public bureaucracies in areas of social policy, education, and health. Correspondingly, the economic downturn and corresponding cutbacks of public spending in the 1970s directly hit the funding of nonprofits, which then sought for new ways of gathering resources through markets to secure the fulfilment of social missions. In Europe, structural unemployment was a problem in many countries in the 1980s, and many initiatives within social enterprises were connected to a more active labour market policy. Strategies for garnering new resources have been different in the US and Europe. Social enterprises in the US established market activities to advance their social missions, but these market activities were often unrelated to the social missions. Scouts selling cookies to finance their camping trips is one example of such an activity. In Europe, resource gathering followed more the social mission of social enterprises. For instance, preoccupation with unemployment led social enterprises to establish opportunities for work within social enterprises, often with government aid (Defourny and Nyssens 2014). The different developments in the US and Europe signify the embeddedness of hybrid activity in a variety of institutional contexts. Increased reliance on market-based activity has been a lifeline for social enterprise survival in the US, whereas in Europe the backing of national governments and the European Union has given the impetus for social enterprises. Having said that, US government contracts are one source of revenue for social enterprises not commonly used in the European context. In the US, the government has earmarked budget appropriations for purchases from nonprofit producers (Kerlin 2006).

Strategic governance mode

The third mode of strategy formation, strategic governance, is emerging from the increased interdependence of the world at the global as well as national and local levels (Kersbergen and Waarden 2004). Networks play an important role in the study of governance, signifying not only the multitude of actors but also the different types of actors, such as public and private organisations as well as voluntary organisations. The idea of triadic governance in putting forward a triadic constellation (three actors in a group) points to unique constellations of social structures. Triadic constellations might involve market by competition, cooperation, and power relationships.

First, the connecting node can seek his or her own benefit by exploiting the role in connecting others (Burt 1992). An obvious case is a real estate agent raising the price between competing and unconnected buyers. The disconnection of different parties in a competitive 'structural hole' situation gives the connecting point an advantage. Second, the actor in the middle connecting other actors can be a neutral mediator of resources, information, and knowledge between the other actors (Fernandez and Gould 1994). An arbitrator who aims at solving grievances between other actors illustrates the neutrality of this role. Third, the connecting actor can exploit his or her position of power by forming an alliance with one of the other parties or having total domination over others with the help of superior power resources. The divide-and-rule strategy is efficient in weakening foreign and domestic opponents. Rulers can exploit grievances between others in advancing their position (Simmel and Wolff 1964).

Governance in private enterprises

An analysis of business organisations shows interorganisational networks as an extension of the resource-based view, transaction cost analysis, and the relational view. In the resource-based view, the aim of forming alliances is to create economic value by pooling resources, as alliances provide access to the resources of another organisation. The rationale for forming alliances is to garner resources that cannot be purchased from markets or to acquire ownership (Das and Teng 2000). Transaction cost economics (Williamson 2000) provides another platform for strategic governance. Organisations need to pay attention not only to production cost but also to such things as transaction costs, searching for sellers and buyers, negotiating terms, and writing contracts. Forming alliances can also be understood in terms of transaction cost logic. If the transaction costs are high compared to production costs, it is efficient to coordinate activities within the firm, but alliance formation is lucrative when transaction costs are intermediate and not high enough to justify vertical coordination (Das and Teng 2000). In contrast with transaction cost economics, social capital literature suggests the idea of organisational advantage (Nahapiet and Ghoshal 1998). An organisation is not only a solvent for market failure but also a productive vehicle for the creation of innovation and knowledge.

The relational view represents a third relevant economic formulation for interorganisational relationships, which draws together some of the ideas developed in the transaction cost framework and the resource-based view. The benefits of an interaction increase if the partners are secure in the continuation of their relationship, the magnitude of exchange is high, partners are able to learn from each other, their resources and capabilities complement each other, and interchange takes place informally without formal contracting (Dyer and Singh 1998).

The transaction cost framework, the relational view, and stakeholder analysis share a dyadic approach to intra-organisational relationships; that is, they examine relationships between pairs of actors at a time. By doing so, these perspectives offer little theoretical guidance as to what would be a suitable network structure as a whole. Social network analysis might be a relevant source of inspiration here. For instance, a central connecting position at the core of the network structure provides the organisation with a rich structural source of information and can advance performance in information-reliant industries (Powell et al. 1996; see Borgatti and Foster 2003 for a review). The principal idea here is that the benefits of networking depend not only on the dyadic relationships between actors but also on the positions in networks as a whole. Pivotal positions in networks offer control over others (Burt 1992). This is in sharp contrast with the positive notions of information society (Castells 1996), which assume that any one actor's power in the network is quasi-automatically overwhelmed by the power of the network as a whole.

Governance in public agencies

Constituency support is important for public agencies. The success of an agency seems not only to depend upon the control of the most important information flows, but also on the ability of agencies to gain continuous political support for their role and the acceptance of rival agencies and other actors over which the agency has a superior position. The provision of an agency's tangible results gives an additional boost for strengthening the agency's role, because the results enable agencies to mobilise interest and client group support and provide quantifiable measures for agency actions. Successful agencies are able to protect and defend their proposals when negotiating with external constituencies (Ellison 2006).

In public agencies, the outsourcing of duties puts public officials in between the public and private spheres. The problem is that we cannot easily allow public and private interests to form a hybrid. There is always a need to protect government actors from the harmful consequences of profit maximisation, as interaction with business interests potentially corrupts government actors. Financial gains can be enjoyed individually and do not necessarily have any collective balancing mechanism similar to the balancing of interests between opposing political parties. The problem of the dual roles of civil servants has been tackled, in one example, by 'firewall protection,' meaning officials responsible for dealing with business organisations cannot take part in decision-making while performing their administrative duties. In addition, the profit interest of privatised organisations and business partners in public-private partnerships (PPPs) cannot be supposed to advance society's public interests as their sole purpose, which brings about the need to establish government watchdogs to oversee the fairness of the competition and to protect customers from the harmful consequences of profit maximisation (Stern 2000).

In the public sector, the influence of stakeholders has an important role in defining the area of operation for public agencies. Stakeholder mapping offers some insight into the identification and relationship formation stages of possible partners. This mapping makes organisations sensitive to the power and interests of external constituencies. The features of relationships between agencies and interest groups depend on the distribution of benefits and costs. For instance, entrepreneurial politics is the result of cost being directed to one industry, profession, or locality and benefits being spread over many people (Wilson 1989, 76–78). For example, the forest industry, faced with more stringent measures for waste management by a regulating agency, would surely oppose tightened regulations, but, as the benefit of purer water is dispersed among everyone affected by the water system, it is difficult to establish an interest group favouring more detailed regulation. Consequently, the environmental regulating agency faces a strong and uniform stakeholder influence from the enterprise and only weak influence from the citizens affected by the production.

While the governance perspective opens up avenues for strategic manoeuvring, some of the features related to outside contracting make public organisations even more competitive than their private sector counterparts. Practices such as competitive tendering and competition for public contracts imply that the public sector divests itself of the ability to form long-lasting relationships with its interacting partners. Instead, public organisations are forced to resort to a single-minded use of market contracting. This is in sharp contrast with some of the hoped-for benefits of interorganisational networks, particularly the diminished transaction costs achieved through repeating interactions and partner-specific investments. Furthermore, informal governance mechanisms, which emphasise trust instead of formal contracting, informal control, and obedience to rules, do not coincide well with the legality of public sector organisations. Public agencies are thus ill equipped to enjoy the benefits of informal, interorganisational social intercourse with business enterprises.

Governance in hybrid organisations

The most relevant feature of strategic government in the hybrid context is the structure of interaction patterns. Hybrid relational configuration consists of both public and private actors. The development of public-private interaction has increased interorganisational interaction. For one thing, networks arise from the need to coordinate actions between government agencies and outsourced activities. Another related development has been the incentive to form PPPs, which introduces the need to construct methods for interaction across different organisational forms. Moreover, the tendency to decrease the size of government agencies implies that, in shrinking agencies, resources are more likely to reside in the environment of an organisation.

The main role of strategy in the governance mode is formulating principles for identifying possible interaction partners and establishing appropriate interaction patterns. By forming interaction patterns with surrounding organisations, hybrids may stabilise the local environment among its network partners. A negotiated order with the partners of the organisation does not have to be local in any territorial sense. Since relevant interacting partners may well reside in other countries or other areas of operation, the governance mode assumes that the environment is highly unpredictable, but it offers the solution of stabilising the local network through cooperative relationships. In a sense, the strategic governance framework combines the environmental assumptions of the strategic design and internal scanning modes. The assumption of turbulence within the environment connects the strategic governance framework with the internal scanning mode. In addition, the formation of networks to stabilise the environment relates strategic governance with the planning orientation of the strategic design mode.

The developments of Chinese SOEs illuminate the features and challenges of combining corporate governance with state influence. The taxonomy of (1) state-centric, (2) shareholder-centric, (3) open/entrepreneurial, and (4) mixed SOE governance systems gives insight into the developments of SOEs in China (Hua et al. 2006). According to survey results, the traditional state-centric regime dominates one-fourth of Chinese SOEs. The main governance bodies are in the hands of the so-called old three committees consisting of the Communist Party Committee, the labour union, and employees' representatives meetings. The contrasting shareholder-centred regime rules in some 10 percent of Chinese SOEs and consists of shareholders' general meetings, the board of directors, and a supervisory board with employee presence. This structure is required for the listed enterprises. Interestingly enough, the structure follows the Central European two-tier government structure rather than the Anglo-Saxon single-board structure. In addition to the state-centric and shareholder-centric enterprises, some 10 percent of Chinese SOEs operate under the open or entrepreneurial regime, with a strong leadership role filling the weak role of state and shareholder institutions.

Over half of Chinese SOEs follow a mixed governance system, which combines the traditional state-centric and more recent shareholder-centric approaches. The old three committees and the shareholder regime committees are present, resulting in a highly decentralised management structure and the integration of native Chinese and Western corporate culture. The mixed regime also seems able to accommodate multiple goals at the same time: (1) strong incentives for managers; (2) big advantages for employees through shareholding; (3) excellent integration of duties, power, and interests; and (4) good democratic management. In a mixed setting, the state-centred regime can prevent managers from corruption through the political education of party members, while the shareholder-centred regime enables the motivation of employees through financial rewards rather than symbolic compensation (Hua et al. 2006).

In Russia, some important sectors of the economy are dominated by SOEs: mass media; the military-industrial complex; infrastructure (railway transport, pipelines, nuclear energy); the extraction of natural resources (oil and gas, diamonds); and financial services (banking, insurance, pension funds). Together, the public sector accounts for 40 percent of stock market capitalisation in Russian stock markets (Sprenger 2010). The affluence of SOEs is only the tip of the iceberg of government-economy interactions, which encompass patron-client structures within the economy as a whole. In the Russian context, the political elite dominate the most important parts of export in natural resources, energy, and banking through direct ownership stakes in the largest companies, such as Gasprom, Rosneft, and Sperbank (Sprenger 2010). What is more, the economy is concentrated around major business groups headed by a major business leader oligarch ruling typically through holding company industry-level divisions and individual plants (Guriev 2010).

The position of subsidiary managers within a business group is dependent upon their connection to the leading oligarch, and the success of a business group as a whole is defined by the patronage of political leaders, those in the vicinity of the president in particular. The same type of patron-client structure prevails in regional and local levels as well, resulting in parasitic business-government relationships in all levels of society (King 2007).

The governing structures of US and European social enterprises signify different views on stakeholder involvement. In Europe, the beneficiaries of nonprofit activity are often expected to participate in the production of services and products, following the practice of cooperative movement. Furthermore, a democratic ethos encourages the involvement of stakeholder groups in the management of social enterprises. For instance, an extension of social enterprises in the form of multi-stakeholder cooperatives is given a legal form in Italy, Portugal, and France. Such arrangements acknowledge three types of stakeholder groups: (1) lending or funding members, (2) beneficiary members, and (3) volunteer members that can be represented in governing boards. The discussion of US social enterprises has been more geared towards the professional management of the business side of nonprofits, which supports their social mission and puts less emphasis on stakeholder involvement in governance (Defourny and Nyssens 2008; Kerlin 2006).

Strategy formation in business, public, and hybrid contexts

What would be the ideal position for private enterprises, hybrid organisations, and public agencies in connection with the three strategy modes of strategic design, strategic scanning, and strategic governance? According to the modified industry structure view, a permanently strong position in the most lucrative industries would be ideal for a business firm. In a hybrid setting, the ideal position would be straddling the public and private spheres. Serving public policy goals enables legitimation from the government and the recipients of the services. In addition, engagement in business activity gives hybrids autonomy from government decision-making. Within bureaucratic politics, possible long-term goals for agency heads include the enlargement of bureaus or enjoyable positions in small public agencies in the vicinity of political power (see Table 4.2).

A unique combination of resources and capabilities offers business enterprises their competitive edge. More often than not, these resources reside in the internal structure of a firm. To provide continuity, these combinations should, at best, be inimitable for competitors. It is quite easy to see that in an ideal situation hybrids would be able to combine both public and private resources through privileged access to both of these sources, which often reside outside the borders of the hybrid organisation. The challenge for hybrids is to maintain privileged access to these resources. For instance, SOEs able to get financing from both government budget appropriations and private banks are well equipped to satisfy their investment needs. In the US and Europe, there are different developments in the resource gathering of social enterprises during times of economic austerity. US

TABLE 4.2 Private enterprises, public agencies, and hybrid organisations in the strategic context

	Private enterprises	*Public agencies*	*Hybrid organisations*
Strategic design	Strong position in lucrative industry	Ideal position in proximity to power or the enlargement of bureaus	Beneficial position between private and public spheres
Strategic scanning	Inimitable and unique combinations of internal resources	Command of valued expertise and information in the policy process	Privileged access to both public and private resources
Strategic governance	Exploitation of lack of contact between other firms	Brokering in the policy-making process, divide-and-rule through power and alliances	Exploitation of lack of contact between other organisations, brokering between government bodies and business enterprises

social enterprises are more attuned to exploit market activity in order to fund their social mission, whereas their European counterparts resort more to public institutions to satisfy their financial needs.

The governance of relationships is markedly different in private enterprises, hybrid organisations, and public agencies. Despite the emerging trend of cooperative arrangement between firms, the most obvious relational strategy for business enterprises to get an advantage in competitive settings is exploiting the lack of contact between other firms (a structural hole). Hybrid organisations may resort to the same type of strategy if they operate in competitive markets. In contrast, non-profit voluntary organisations built upon egalitarian memberships are instrumental in producing social capital, which lubricates the smooth functioning of political institutions (Putnam et al. 1993; Putnam 2000). Also, social enterprises may enjoy information benefits, such as the formation of innovations, by brokering between both business enterprises and government bodies. Relational attachment to both public and private spheres enables the balancing of sector-specific downturns and upturns in terms of resource gathering, and institutional contexts might give the impetus to resort to either public or private resources. By definition, bureaucratic politics are connected to power stakes acquired by public agencies. This discussion, however, suggests that, within government circles, an earned prestigious position requires genuine expertise, the ability to provide valuable information for the policy-making process, and constant legitimation of this superior position when brokering information flows between agencies and political decision-makers. In public agencies, the aspect of power politics is most eminent in the external relationships of public agencies' jurisdictional area when avoiding the influence of regulated industries (Bó 2006) and securing the fair allocation of government grants from local and regional levels of government (Oates 2005).

Combining business goals, public policies, and social goals enables hybrid organisations to settle in between the public and private spheres. The possibility of using external public and private resources as if they were internal resources offers hybrid organisations options to gather a variety of resources from multiple sources. The mere existence of hybrid organisations connecting private industry and government circles produces social capital in society. Furthermore, the diversity of contacts in different areas of society is conducive for the emergence of new ideas, whether they include technical innovations benefiting industry or social innovations serving public policy implementation and the functioning of communities. Empirically, the developments in China and Russia illustrate the different ways of mixing private enterprise and government influence, and the different approaches to social enterprises in the US and Europe signify the influence of the institutional context in orienting the strategies of nonprofit organisations.

The strategic design mode represents an established strategic orientation that is well tested and thoroughly criticised in business environments, but the importance of planning as such has hardly faded away. Many future service needs related to areas such as pensions, education, and health can be assessed in advance through an analysis of the characteristics of populations. Whether the planning takes place in a comprehensive or incremental way or through a combination of these is more a matter of form than content, as the main idea behind all of these approaches is the possibility of programming future operations in light of current understanding. Internal strategic scanning does not offer the possibility of predicting future events. An unpredictable environment focuses attention on the internal features of an organisation, such as the division of labour among horizontal units and vertical levels of management, and considers external resources as internal to the organisation, as is the case with hybrid organisations. This discussion suggests that the strategic governance mode represents a middle ground. The environment contains unforeseeable elements, but an organisation can achieve some stability through building networks with other organisations. The strategic governance framework is not yet a well-established theoretical view on strategy formation, even in the private sector context, but it represents an emergent strategy field. What the strategy talk entails in all modes is the need for some understanding of the organisational environment. The environment is not the same for all organisations, and conceptions of environmental interfaces are becoming more fluid.

5
TRACING THE FOOTPRINTS OF MONSTERS

The performative orientation of organisations

This chapter elaborates on performance regimes and the notions of performance in the public, private, and hybrid settings of organisations. This discussion deals with fundamental ambiguities in both making things measurable and in enabling institutional action through measurements. Irrespective of the nature of the adopted performance regime, the demonstration and evaluation of results puts forward questions of accountability and legitimation. Furthermore, the polysemic nature of performance implicates that the definition of success and failure in any institutional context is highly dependent upon the measurement perspective. The perspective of those doing the measurement can diverge from the perspective of those being assessed within the confines of measurement systems and measurement results. This chapter begins with a discussion of the nature of performance in an organised activity, which is then applied in the examination of performance regimes in public, private, and hybrid organisations alike. Discussion of measurement principles precedes the case illustrations of hybrid universities and public-private pension systems. In this chapter, the three *E*'s – economy, efficiency, and effectiveness – and their conceptual extensions serve as a common ground for understanding, comparing, and measuring performance in these different domains.

Performance, performativity, and quantification of performance

Talking about performance includes information and management. We are dealing with information designed to contribute to more intelligent and rational choices in society, public administration, and business. We are interested in the conceivably rational allocation of resources and the extent to which different institutional actors and policies have achieved their goals and objectives. In different contexts of institutional action, this focus may yield distinct representations. While for-profit business contexts may rely upon bottom-line performance indicators, such as profit or loss statements or return on investment (ROI) for shareholders, public sector policies and agencies need – in addition – to count on alternate modes of information production and concepts to describe the value and worth of taxpayers' 'investments.' The nature of performance information design is thus contingent upon the context we are thinking of. This may be associated not only with accounting or calculative practices but also with distinct hybrid forms of professional expertise (Hopwood 1996a; Noordegraaf and Abma 2003; Miller et al. 2008).

Performance is also associated with management. Based on several studies, it has become almost common knowledge that performance is not only about information design; it is also about the uses of performance information for different policy purposes. This is clearly reflected in definitions regarding performance measurement and performance management. Often these two concepts appear to overlap with each other. They both address the measurement of performance and the management of performance measurements (Van Helden et al. 2008). However, it is also fair to argue that performance management doctrines more systematically emphasise the utilisation of performance information for different institutional purposes, whereas performance measurement regimes have a systematic emphasis on the design stage of performance measurement systems (Van Helden et al. 2012).

Despite the inherent ambiguity of institutional performance, societies have learnt to trust that performance quantifications are sensible, useful, and real. For many, Lord Kelvin's dictum, 'When you cannot express it in numbers, your knowledge is of a meagre and unsatisfactory kind' (McCloskey 1983, 323) has come to serve as one of the most persuasive arguments for developing the valuation and evaluation of business sector organisations, public administration, and hybrid arrangements between the public and private sectors (Vakkuri 2010). Quantification of performance, in this context, can be seen as another effort to reduce human uncertainty in institutional decision-making. Performance measurement systems have become an instrument for creating order, maintaining the legitimacy of public service, and making sense of complicated societal problems. Quantifications are not necessarily considered a panacea, yet they appear to permeate the activities of society and economy in many ways. Quantifications provide a conceivably impersonal basis for making difficult resource allocation decisions. They also may serve as centres of calculation (Miller and Rose 2008). Furthermore, quantifications enhance reliance on performance numbers as technologies of distance and as forms of political justification (Porter 1995; Boltanski and Thévenot 2006).

Whether and to what extent decision-making uncertainty in public management can actually be diminished through quantifications remains a puzzle. Performance metrics may easily become a magical concept (Stark 2009; Pollitt and Hupe 2011) or a residual explanation for complicated cause-effect relationships in political decision-making (March 1978; Noordegraaf 2008). Although they are both theoretically and intuitively incomplete, performance metrics systems are used for two important purposes: first, to distinguish good performance from bad performance in societal activities, and second, to determine who is to receive credit for good performance or who is to blame for poor performance (Allen 2012). Questions of accountability (i.e. 'Who is accountable to whom?' and 'What is one accountable for?') have remained in the development agenda of institutional systems for a long time (Mayston 1993). Moreover, accountability has a significant impact on the ways in which performance measurement systems are developed, designed, and utilised, and also on the kind of problems decision-makers are confronted with when they apply performance measurement systems to hybrid settings.

Despite the claim (Porter 2008) that economic measurement is – more than we think – shaped by fairly pragmatic procedures of bureaucratic oversight and regulation, doctrines of quantification are fundamentally based on scientific realism, which makes strong assumptions about how social reality can be described and understood (Davis and Hersh 1981). 'Reality' is something objective and identifiable, something that in an ideal world can be conceptualised and measured. Quantifying performance is not a problem per se. The problem is identifying the correct surrogates. 'Pi' is in the sky; the world is quantitative (Barrow 1991). Moreover, the world can be measured, intervened in, and changed through technocratic design (Davies et al. 1999; Vakkuri 2003). This has served the ideal of scientific objectivity and the plethora of forms of technocratic ethos.

In contrast, sociologically oriented research on organisations and managerial practices emphasises the structuration approach to performance measurement and management. Performance measurement can be discussed as calculative practices that are related to what people actually do with performance information in their recurrent and contextual practices (Orlikowski 2000; Orlikowski 2002; Giddens 1979; Orlikowski 1992; Lave 1988; Wenger 1998). Figure 5.1 introduces performance measurement as part of a larger social structure consisting of three elements: performance measurement, human agents interacting with performance measurement, and institutional properties (Vakkuri and Meklin 2006).

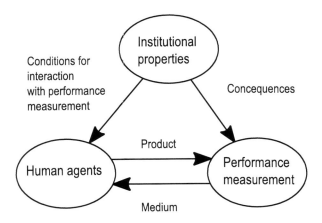

FIGURE 5.1 Performance measurement as part of social structures

These elements, on the one hand, influence the users and uses of performance metrics, but, on the other hand, these elements are influenced by performance metrics and their uses. Figure 5.1 provides four approaches to understand the interaction between performance measurement, human agents, and institutional properties.

First, performance metrics are social *products* that have been created and invented by somebody. Measurements can be regarded as social artefacts and outcomes of creative human action, design, and development. Second, performance measurement may be analysed as a *medium of human action*. Metrics are employed by users: stakeholders, organisations, service users, and citizens. The information created mediates the activities of actors and stakeholders (Lave 1988). Two aspects need to be considered. On the one hand, performance measurement cannot determine social practice. This is because users are always left with an option to act otherwise, to practice unique forms of rule following. However, performance measurement may condition social practice. In doing so, performance measurement may both facilitate and constrain. For instance, when the members of an organisation act upon performance information, they do so within the institutional setting of that organisation. This has an impact on the methods of designing, adopting, implementing, and using performance measurement and management systems. Third, these are the *conditions for interaction with performance measurement* (Chaiklin and Lave 1993; Vakkuri 2013). Finally, performance measurement has *consequences*. These consequences include an effect on institutional properties. By using performance measurements, the members of an organisation may wish to sustain the status quo by reinforcing certain institutional properties or change the status quo by transforming other institutional properties.

It is widely known that performance measurement research could be advanced by scrutinising more thoroughly how processes and policies of quantification aim to alleviate uncertainty in making decisions for and about public sector performance, including the extent to which they actually manage to do so (Kurunmäki and Miller 2006; Van Helden et al. 2012). There is a need to understand the role of performance quantifications and their impacts on creating new problems and facilitating long-term institutional change (Vakkuri 2013). Here, quantification policies could be studied more as a process of long-term institutional development in which such policies are understood as products of human design (Van Dooren 2005), outcomes of political and institutional action (Modell 2001), instruments for mediating the activities of public policies (Noordegraaf 2008), and the intended and unintended consequences of public interventions (Bevan et al. 2006). Such a comprehensive approach would be particularly useful in the context of hybrid activities and institutions (Grossi et al., forthcoming).

Polysemic performance

The concept of performance is subject to distinct, contrasting, and polysemic interpretations (Vakkuri 2010; Vakkuri 2013; March 1987). Performance is an ambiguous concept (Stark 2009). Ambiguity is associated with both the design of performance information and the uses of performance metrics to make more intelligent choices. To put it bluntly, there are uncertainties in conceptualising and quantifying performance in institutional settings, and there are multiple possibilities for institutional uses of performance information. Hence, there are limitations as to how performativity may be produced and constructed in institutional settings (Miller and Rose 2008).

The polysemic notion of performance is easy to observe merely by looking at a large variety of definitions that have been used to talk about performance. Lebas and Euske (2007, 67–68) introduce a list of definitions of performance using several dictionaries. Performance can be the following things:

1   Something measurable
2   Something accomplished intentionally
3   The result of an action associated with measured value that has been created
4   The capability or potential for increasing value
5   A result of a comparison process of searching for benchmarks or other types of reference points
6   A surprising result-expectations ratio
7   'Acting out': deceptive illusion of control
8   A 'show,' including actors, process, and input from the audience
9   A judgment (by comparison).

It is no wonder that performance may yield several distinct conceptual connotations in day-to-day discussions. In fact, these various definitions confirm the conclusive argument of a long-standing research discussion that there can hardly be any consensus on how performance should be conceptualised and measured and how the outputs of the measurement process should then be used to rationalise decision-making (Cameron 1984; Cameron 1986; Meyer 2007). Let us explore the implications of such obscurity when the notion of performance is applied to different institutional contexts.

Performance measurement in private enterprises: in search of relevance

There exists an in-depth research discussion concerning the question of second-best performance measures in business firms. Meyer (2002) refers to the time lag of most performance measurements, and, subsequently, to the relevance of performance indicators in business decision-making (Johnson and Kaplan 1987; Cooper and Kaplan 1991; Neely 2007). As there may be considerable differences as regards the uses of performance measurement in small entrepreneurial-based business firms vis-à-vis large multinational corporations, some common problems exist. Otley (2007) refers to three major functions of financial performance measurement in the context of a business firm. First, performance measurement is intended to provide instruments and tools for an efficient allocation of financial resources in an organisation. By doing this, performance measurement, at its best, may assist in achieving the wider goals of the organisation. Second, financial performance measurement is designed and used to represent the most important function of a business firm; that is, to create profit for shareholders. Finally, Otley refers to the motivational role of financial performance measurement. The organisation should be able to make sense of the cause-effect relationships between the firm's financial performance and employees' input, which enable performance (Otley 2007).

It is also important to discuss the role of financial performance vis-à-vis other dimensions of performance in the context of business firms. In contemplating the multifaceted nature of performance, Meyer (2007) discusses problems with the second-best performance metrics of business firms:

- There is not a proper balance between financials and nonfinancials in the performance measurement of firms. The idea that nonfinancial indicators (e.g. employee motivation, customer satisfaction, learning, and growth) will systematically drive financial performance has been a strong assumption (Kaplan and Norton 1996), but it is not consistent. There are nascent links between customer satisfaction and financial performance. Decision-makers are not able to create convincing models that combine financials and nonfinancials (Norreklit et al. 2006).
- The number of performance measures is not always manageable: 'Firms are swamped with measure sand, and the problem of too many measures is, if anything, getting worse' (Meyer 2007, 115). The large number of indicators may provide a sophisticated picture of performance, but using that picture to make sense of performance is almost impossible. There seem to be significant opportunity costs in searching for validity in performance measurement.
- It is complicated to use comparable indicators across a large business firm. Therefore, the processes of rolling up and cascading down within an organisation become difficult (Meyer 2002).
- Performance measurement systems never stand still, which makes it difficult to enhance learning processes over time. In addition, performance measurement systems tend to become sporadic and disposable.
- It is not easy to compensate people by using performance metrics. Thus, the motivation and commitment of employees become a problem, as top executive pay-for-performance schemes are used instead.

In their comprehensive literature review and meta-analysis, Richard et al. (2009) express their almost identical surprise about the ambiguity of the concept of performance in business management. Surprisingly enough, performance appears to be a significantly open question with hardly coherent definitions and measurement solutions (Richard et al. 2009; Richards 2001). Richard et al. call for more comprehension of the relevance of performance measurement for distinct stakeholders, the heterogeneity of the environments where performance measurement takes place, and performance judgments and comparisons over time. The authors do this by discussing three sources of performance measurement data. The first source is 'accounting measures,' which include, for example, profit margins, return on assets (ROA), return on equity (ROE), and return on investment (ROI). The second source is 'financial market measures,' which include earnings per share (EPS), price-to-earnings ratios (P/E indicators), and beta coefficients. The third source is 'mixed accounting/financial market measures,' for example, a balanced scorecard, economic value added (EVA), and Tobin's q ratio. Based on their meta-analysis, Richard et al. (2009, 740) provide five suggestions for research on business performance measurement:

1 Conscious and systematic scrutiny of the relevance of performance measurement for different stakeholders
2 Analysis of links between performance measurements and the heterogeneity of institutional environments, strategies, and managerial systems and practices
3 Systematic emphasis on the time properties of firms' performances
4 Performance measures that are valid enough to depict different, both objective and subjective, dimensions of organisational performance
5 More detailed understanding of the relationship between different measures that contribute to overall performance

Interestingly enough, despite the commonly held assumption that in business firms (in comparison with the public sector) it may be easier to detract bottom-line indicators for performance, most of the methodologically rigorous research discussion maintains that there may not actually be a single 'bottom line.' In fact, bottom-line measures can be discerned in business performance, but they should not keep us away from the fact that they are not the whole story. Multiple multidimensional measures are required to comprehend business performance with all its characteristics. There may be several bottom-line indicators, and there may be indicators other than bottom-line indicators that are still of high relevance to business firms. There is a special need for understanding the role and interlinkages of bottom-line indicators for different contexts, different areas of operations, and different stakeholders.

To conclude, the notion of business performance perfectly meets the criteria for conceptual and methodological ambiguity (Noordegraaf and Abma 2003; Vakkuri and Meklin 2006; March 1987). However, depending on the institutional context, the level of ambiguity varies. Perhaps here we are just stating the obvious: Quantifications are always imperfect, and we should be concerned about to what extent and in what respects this imperfect characteristic manifests itself and how distinct institutional contexts vary with respect to such imperfect characteristics. Accordingly, it is fair to argue that, for business firms, and in comparison with public policy domains, the domain of market activities nevertheless constitutes a more consistent basis for performance quantifications.

Public sector performance: problems and origins of value

While to some extent similar performance measurement problems may apply to public policies and agencies as much as in business firms, there are additional dilemmas associated with the characteristics of politico-administrative systems of government. Performance measurement is partly about information design, which is why the mechanisms and characteristics of that information are an important issue in the public sector (Lapsley and Mitchell 1996). With the absence of market price information, there are high expectations for a public sector performance measurement. There is a need for information depicting the financial process of public sector agencies and particularly rational and efficient uses of taxpayers' money. As these perspectives do not always go hand in hand, there is a particular need for an integrative perspective to combine financial information with performance information (Mayston 1993).

Let us consider an example. Take a business firm willing to understand its impact on customers and the marketplace. In order to draw conclusions on impacts, the firm may conduct a traditional customer survey, but the firm can also analyse its revenue structures. The logic here is that, the more satisfied the customers are, the more likely it is that they will come back to the marketplace to buy the company's products. The customers' satisfaction would ultimately result in increased revenues. Using this chain of logic, a business firm can make judgments on the impact or effectiveness of its products and services. And what about a public agency? In many of the contexts of public sector activities, the link between customer satisfaction and revenues is missing for two reasons. First, quite often it is the case that there is no price or fee for the service, as there may be policy rationales contending that a public service should be free of charge to the user (not to the taxpayer, though). This is due to different forms of market failures or deliberate aims to create positive externalities or mitigate negative ones. Therefore, a public manager or policy maker cannot look at revenues to judge the agency's effectiveness or user preferences. Revenue collection is based on a separate process of public politics and policy. Second, it may even be the case that the customer, or citizen, does not want the service, as the service delivery principles are based on the provision of public or common goods (e.g. public defense, infrastructure), or the services are mandatory based on government authority (e.g. authorised cheques, tax collection). In this context, using the service does not necessarily indicate one's preferences. Instead, there may be a situation in which a public service is delivered despite the dissatisfaction of the citizen. The provision and delivery of all 'goods' are not necessarily grounded on the dogma of satisfaction (Kelly 2005; Fountain 2001).

This approach necessitates performance evaluation and measurement. Due to the lack of price information and revealed customer preferences, there is a need to ascertain whether public services are provided and delivered in an efficient and effective way. In fact, the need for this type of information is quite striking. During the last thirty years, performance information design has loosely followed the general doctrine of the three *E*'s in public service delivery (Pollitt 1986; Lapsley 1988). As previously mentioned, these conceptual typologies consist of the following:

- *Economy*: the amount of costs that service provision accounts for (the ideal being minimum costs for delivering public services)

- *Efficiency*: the relationship between the inputs and outputs of service delivery processes (the ideal being an optimal ratio with respect to given standards or other units, peers, or benchmarks)
- *Effectiveness*: the extent to which public agencies and policies have achieved their goals and objectives, as well as the extent to which these policies have accrued to expected and unexpected, intended and unintended, consequences of policy action

While economy and efficiency are usually understood as the criteria of the internal optimalities of a public organisation, effectiveness is often referred to as indicating the external optimality of a public organisation or agency. Furthermore, these concepts are well known to be enmeshed with complications that may lead to dysfunction or several perverse effects of public policies (De Bruijn 2002). Just consider the link between economy and effectiveness: The objective of minimising the costs of public service provision (economy) may be achieved, but at the expense of the service's quality and impacts on users (effectiveness). Partly due to this reason, there has been an ongoing discussion on what the actual purposes of performance measurements are. Behn's (2003) formulation for the purposes of public sector performance measurement derive from a simple question: Why measure performance in the public sector? He defines eight purposes of performance measurement in government:

1. Evaluation, which ascertains how well public agencies are performing
2. Control, which makes sure that employees are doing the right things
3. Budget, which includes asking how and on what grounds the actual targets for resource allocation in government should be defined
4. Motivation, which includes figuring out how to demonstrate for public sector personnel, stakeholders, and partners what performance improvements are needed
5. Promotion, which persuades political decision-makers, the media, etc. about agency performance
6. Celebration, which includes identifying sources of success and celebration
7. Learning, which includes pinpointing strengths and weaknesses and sources of learning
8. Improvement, which involves what should be done to actually improve public sector performance

(Behn 2003, 588)

More so than in the context of business firms, performance measurement in public sector settings seems to involve an assumption of the preexistence of organisational purpose. Organisations are collections of activities that are guided by ex ante exogenous preferences for action. Goals are defined exogenously and externally. Furthermore, in order for action to occur, goals have to be already in place; therefore, goals come first, and action comes afterwards. This is consonant with the long tradition of teleological and consequentialist thinking in the area of rational choice, which takes ends as a given. The purpose of scientific analysis is to optimise the means for achieving those ends (Porter 2008). In addition, the assumption of value neutrality has been criticised in an ordered fashion from the perspective of ethical desiderata in social science (Weber and Winckelmann 1985). The proposition that goals are exogenous and external may be somewhat confusing from the standpoint of organisational action. What is the source of exogenous preferences (March 1988b)? If, in an analysis of the optimality of means to ends, the ends are taken as a given, what is the origin of the ends? We may also ask to what extent human behaviour is also about creating new goals, not only acting upon prestated goals.

Consequentialist logic is not without ethical problems (Vickers 1997). That line of reasoning can be seen as providing an opportunity to refrain somewhat deceptively from normative or ethical comments. The attempt to insist on ethical neutrality, the *Wertfreiheit* principle, was historically regarded as pushing academic research into a more scientific and a less value-loaded mode of arguing about social action. Instead of going into deontological problems about the ends of social action and decision-making, the aim is to evaluate the consequences of actions in terms of their optimality (Koopmans 1977; Caldwell 1984). The attempt is in fact oriented towards separating goals from action, because distinguishing them from each other allows an analysis to focus on elements that are assumed to be neutral targets of scientific inquiry. Indeed, an important rationale behind public sector performance metrics systems is that they are intended to be neutral and objective. They are designed to increase the certainty of human choices by being noninstitutional (Porter 1995). This thinking has its roots in classic general scientific reasoning, in which quantification has traditionally played an important role for verification, analysis, and solid judgment (Porter 2006). Consequently, quantification of social activities has long been influenced by technocratic ethos and the related decision-making imperative, which is very much present in public performance metrics systems (Porter 2008).

It is also interesting to think about why and how different forms of economic measurement historically came to be adopted in areas of social life, in which it is extremely complex to assign value to things. Just consider the value of extending life or physical or social well-being (health) and the value of education and intellectual capital. Paradoxically, in the early stages of quantification, measurement techniques and devices of cost-benefit analysis were much more common in political life and public sector activities than in profit calculations among actors and private companies in the marketplace. According to Porter (2008), economic measurement and quantification became an instrument that was more important in the area of public policy than in understanding and analysing the behaviour of market firms and other market actors. For Porter, this is more a historical story of administrative pragmatism and technocratic ideals than a description of scientific achievements and rigour in mathematics, physics, and engineering. In contexts with complicated problems of evaluation, quantifications provide instruments perceived to be legitimate in order to mitigate subjectivity, political influence, and blame avoidance. Quantification was probably not about the 'truth' as such; rather, it was a way to negotiate about the truth, but within a strict rule set (Porter 2008).

For performance measurers in public administration, the goal dilemma is fundamental for two reasons. First, the attractive assumption seems to be that of understanding organisations as targets of performance measurement and as a set of data-based and flexible entities attaining different ambitions. Thus, this analysis would be able to introduce 'revealed' best practices. This is constrained by the measurement process. Even though the problem of goals may be somewhat limited, it still exists. It merely expresses itself in a different form. Second, there is a measurement perspective on the problem of goals. In performance measurement, there are no external goals in terms of empirical verification unless there are external and given criteria for the measurement of outputs and outcomes. To complete the search procedure, the methodologist is forced to make an empirical operationalisation of goals. In fact, the methodologist creates 'super-goals' for organisations (March 1988b), a fixed set of values and preferences across different organisations over time. The super-goals make it possible to evaluate the actions of organisations and interpret them as 'optimal' behaviour or 'deviations' from optimal behaviour. For example, in performance evaluations of university organisations, the super-goal is an average approximation of the preferences and goals of university organisations with distinctive sets of academic disciplines, including goals for creating and warranting scientific knowledge as well as goals concerning different epistemic cultures with scientific ambitions and endeavours (Knorr-Cetina 1999). A super-goal is not a goal of organisations. It is a proxy created for measurement purposes.

In addition to the fact that explicitly stated goals of organisations may be different from goals that are pursued, and also the fact that goals pursued may differ from goals that are used to rationalise actions ex post (Brunsson 1989), all these goals are distinct from the super-goals used for measurement purposes. During the search process, organisational goals are modified to meet the methodological rationales of performance measurement. In this regard, it is difficult to see performance measurement only as a 'device' or 'technicality.' Performance measurement instead is an institutional process that creates new goals in the public sector (March 1988b).

Performance measurement problems in hybrid organisations

There is a lack of a theoretic-conceptual understanding of the evaluation of value and worth in hybrid arrangements (Boltanski and Thévenot 2006). Following Stark (2009), research lacks understanding on the impact of dissonance; that is, diverse and ambiguous criteria for performance evaluation. More particularly, the gap lies in understanding the design and uses of systems of performance evaluation and measurement in hybrid forms of governance (Hodges 2012).

As stated previously, Thévenot et al. (2000) put forward seven regimes of worth, or 'common worlds': market, industrial, civic, domestic, inspired, fame, and green, which differ from one another in terms of evaluation modes, forms of relevant proof, qualified objects and human beings, and time and space formation. Previous research has concentrated on institutional forms and organisations in hybrid settings, but not so much on the ways in which governments, decision-makers, service users, and citizens assign value to these arrangements. This accounts for two major problems. First, theories of hybrid governance are inapt to explore one of the most important decision-making rationales of current legitimacy-seeking institutional life (Stark 2009). Second, in the changing landscape of government activities, it is of utmost relevance to understand methods of evaluation and measurement, as they drive the institutional legitimacy of societal activities. Trust in performance numbers has become the zeitgeist for valuing social activities (Porter 1995).

Assessing the value and worth of hybrid arrangements and organisations through performance metrics involves two theoretical approaches: those of design and those of use (Van Helden et al. 2012). The problem of design refers to the conceptualisation and measurement of the performance of hybrid arrangements. How should one define accounts of worth in hybrid settings (Stark 2009; Boltanski and Thévenot 2006) and how should one differentiate high performance from poor performance in hybrid arrangements (Allen 2012)? Furthermore, we can ask how these valuations are actually made in society (Dewey 1939). Performance metrics aim to provide evidence for making choices and making sense in different contexts of institutional action: hybrid organisations, central and local governments, private business organisations, charities, and other stakeholders. There are different legislations and social and institutional norms of conduct for this purpose. However, the design problem is particularly complicated in hybrid settings. There are no ready-made statistical or bookkeeping codes for hybrids. Instead, there is a vast collection of data on the finances and other aspects of the performance of individual entities and organisations. There are several entities and systems of distributed intelligence (Stark 2009), which in practice collaborate and contribute to common service delivery outcomes but are counted as separate, discrete entities and organisations.

A comparison of performance dimensions in three contexts of institutional action

Institutions have a persistent interest to survive over time (North 1990). For this to happen, institutions need to make ends meet in one way or the other. They need to cope with a complicated balance between institutional aims and objectives as well as the scarce economic and intellectual resources available to advance those aims. The notion of performance, as we discuss it in our book, is one of the modern representations of that timeless dilemma (Kurunmäki and Miller 2006). We have found, as many others before us, that demonstrations of performance are subject to several ambiguities in the context of business firms and public entities, let alone hybrid activities.

However, for us, this is not to state that, due to such ambiguities of performance representations, we feel compelled to treat performance measurement as a problem that cannot be solved. In accepting that, we would simultaneously need to argue that survival over time would not matter to institutions, because they would be unaware of the historical record and value of their past achievements. This is probably not the case. Instead, institutions invent instruments, methods, and metrics of performance that are socially legitimate and acceptable, that make sense to them, and that help institutions (albeit with limitations) distinguish high performance from low performance (Stark 2009; Allen 2012). In this respect, for us the question is more about exploring whether there is something comparative we could say about the distinctive characteristics of performance demonstrations in these three contexts of institutional action, and whether the contexts may vary with respect to inherent ambiguities of performance demonstrations.

But what reference point should be used to compare different contexts? Let us make some observations by using a simple conceptual and measurement scheme as a framework for comparison: the three *E*'s model (economy, efficiency, effectiveness). This scheme could be understood as a kind of boundary object that is 'both plastic enough to adapt to local needs and the constraints of the several parties employing them, yet robust enough to maintain a common identity across sites' (Leigh Star and Griesemer 1989, 333). There may be problems in applying a common framework originally used in a specific institutional context (i.e. the public sector) to other contexts. However, the three *E*'s model may serve as a lowest common denominator for different institutional contexts in exploring the characteristics of each of the types of institutional performances. We aim to provide modifications for the model when needed.

Table 5.1 utilises the three *E*'s model to explore performative dimensions in the contexts of business firms, the public sector, and hybrid activities. Let us discuss the

TABLE 5.1 Private enterprises, public agencies, and hybrid organisations in the performance context

	Private enterprises	*Public agencies*	*Hybrid organisations*
Economy, the principle of parsimony	Minimising product costs in a competitive environment, minimising transaction costs	Minimising public expenditures and the financial burden to taxpayers	Minimising the cost of collaborative governance and joint production
Efficiency, the principle of optimality	Technical efficiencies, optimal input-output relationships, scale efficiencies emphasising the volume of production, economies of scope emphasising the benefits of joint production	Scale efficiencies emphasising the volume of production, allocative efficiencies ensuring the equal distribution of outputs and outcomes	Economies of scope beyond organisational boundaries, producing a complementary variety of services and goods
Effectiveness, the principle of value creation	Value for customers and shareholders (the profit motive and the concept of profitability)	Value for society, taxpayers, and the public	Value for society, taxpayers, and the public, value for customers and shareholders (the profit motive and the concept of profitability)
Motto	'Doing good by doing well'	'Doing good by doing good'	'Doing well by doing good'

approaches in more detail. First, economy is associated with the classic principle of parsimony, the Occam's razor of economic thinking, which states that the economic means for achieving desired ends should be minimised (Simon 1979b). In other words, less is better. If we compare this principle across the three institutional contexts, we may see different interpretations of the same general principle. In the context of business firms, the interpretation may indicate two things. First, as many business firms operate in competitive markets where it is important to be able to compete with prices, the principle of parsimony may contribute to successful price strategies. Moreover, for business firms, it is important to be able to minimise the transaction costs of governing economic exchange (Williamson 1999b). For public sector agencies and actors, economy usually implies the imperative for cutting public expenditures. Cutting down public expenditures has become particularly important during the age of austerity (Grossi et al. 2016). However, there is an intrinsic mechanism of public finance and budgeting, according to which – in the context of complicated political preferences – public budgeting serves as a heuristic of relative priorities and the weighing of allocation decisions (Wildavsky 1986). Budgets are instruments used to make ends meet, sometimes with institutional and political force. In this process, the notion of economy incentivises public sector actors to minimise the financial burden of taxpayers. For hybrid activities, the concept of economy primarily concerns parsimony in collaborative arrangements. As hybrid activities, by definition, emerge from interaction between the public and private sectors, it may be important to mitigate the costs of such collaborative governance. The successes and failures of hybrid arrangements, in terms of economic parsimony, are thus contingent upon the ways in which the costs of such collaborative designs can be controlled.

Efficiency concerns the optimality of means and ends in different institutional contexts. More specifically, efficiency has been understood as the optimality of input-output relationships (Koopmans 1977). In business firms, this may be associated with technical efficiencies, with an emphasis on the optimality of transforming inputs (e.g. labour, capital, and infrastructure) into outputs and goods that are sold on the markets or associated with scale efficiencies, which make optimalities dependent on the size and volume of business operations (Charnes et al. 1994). In the public sector, the notion of efficiency is primarily related to both scale efficiencies and allocative efficiencies, with an emphasis on the fair and equal distribution of outputs and outcomes. In hybrid activities, the focus of efficiency is on a complementary variety of goods and services. In other words, certain services may appear inefficient when evaluated separately from the other parts of the service provision system. Optimality originates from the complementarity of the separate parts. Panzar and Willig (1981, 268) discuss economies of scope in the context of a modern firm: 'There are economies of scope where it is less costly to combine two or more product lines in one firm than to produce them separately.'

Effectiveness, as we understand it in our book, is first and foremost about value creation (Moore 1995). For institutional survival, business firms need to create value for two important stakeholders: customers and shareholders (owners). Value creation for customers is an important condition for succeeding in the marketplace. Naturally, the condition varies to a significant extent, as business industries vary as regards the nature and intensity of competitive dynamics, and, in fact, as also regards the notion of the customer (Nelson 2005). In addition, business firms need to create value for their owners and shareholders. From this perspective, the concept of profitability, which relates to profit-seeking motives, is often used as an important concept to characterise this type of value creation. In this respect, effectiveness and profitability may be boundary objects in the vocabulary of economic rationalism.

The public sector intends to create value for society, taxpayers, and the public. This process is largely influenced and shaped by legitimacy. Democratic societies, with an emphasis on the openness and transparency of public policy and administration systems, have important difficulties in pursuing desired impacts without simultaneously paying considerable attention to the appropriateness of the process. The process needs to be a due process. Therefore, although the notion of effectiveness is often addressed as the most important area of value creation in public administration, there are limits to which value creation is possible due to legitimacy concerns. Interestingly enough, we argue that value creation in hybrid activities is a 'hybrid' of the two abovementioned forms of value creation. Effectiveness in hybrid activities is almost by definition polysemic, as it stems from both of these sources of value creation. Sometimes the effectiveness of hybrids concerns value creation for society, taxpayers, and the public, while in other cases hybrids intend to create value for customers and shareholders.

A comparison of performance dimensions in the public sector, business firms, and hybrid activities provides a few important aspects for understanding hybrid performance. First, the performance of hybrid activities is naturally contingent upon the type, level, and characteristics of the hybrid institutions that we are referring to. It may be complicated to produce a generic application of performance schemes to distinct types of hybrids, such as SOEs, PPPs, social enterprises, or let alone R&D systems. However, it is also obvious that the criteria for economic rationalism are general enough to serve as boundary objects to explore performance among hybrid activities. Any institutional system needs to cope with the balance of means and ends, the optimality of complementarities, and the creation of value outside the system's own boundaries. Therefore, economy, efficiency, and effectiveness include some characteristics that are useful in conceptualising hybrid performance. However, it should be noted that the problem of applying general conceptual models to the heterogeneous populations of hybrid activities and institutions is not actually drastically different from that of private firms or public sector entities. One of the key dilemmas in applying forms of economic rationalism to public sector activities has been the problematic 'whole-of-government' approach, in which managerial systems may provide benefits and gains in some areas of public administration while creating problems in other sectors (Christensen and Lægreid 2007). Perhaps we do not have enough conceptualisations to play with when discussing the performances of hybrid activities.

For our purposes, the concept of economy in hybrid activities emphasises the principle of economic parsimony in organising collaboration and the joint production of services and goods. Efficiency refers to the ideal of optimal complementarities and economies of scope that go beyond organisational boundaries. Effectiveness, as a source of value creation in hybrids, has a mixed character. In the ideal world, hybrids should be able to provide two categories of value simultaneously: value for society, taxpayers, and the public, as well as value for customers and shareholders. By no means is this easy, for two reasons. First, the value categories are excessively fluid to make conceptual sense. Sometimes the categories may go hand in hand conceptually, and sometimes it is difficult to distinguish value categories from each other, which is why performance appears to remain polysemic and ambiguous. 'Doing well by doing good' is thus a difficult case to demonstrate in terms of performance quantifications.

Finally, it is important to point out that it is possible to conceptualise hybrid performance using some of the traditional notions of performance. The fact that the performance of hybrid activities has been understood as a complicated and fuzzy process may be due to the fact that the previous tradition has attempted to apply performance conceptions to hybrid contexts through reasoning with residuals. However, the idea that the performance of hybrids should be understood as something that is different from the performance of public or private institutions may not take us too far. At least, we should not engage ourselves with a research strategy in which hybrids and hybridity are not analysed as an institutional space of their own (Skelcher and Smith 2015).

Measurement principles applied to hybrid settings

In its simplest form, performance measurement concerns the process of determining an isomorphic relationship between 'principals' and 'surrogates' (Ijiri 1967; Ijiri 1975). In this context, the 'principal' is the object to be quantified, and the 'surrogate' is a device, a method, to transform the principal into valid measurements (Swoyer 1987). In order to quantify, one needs an idea – specifically, a conceptualisation of an idea – and a method to operationalise that idea in terms of performance measures. Quantification as reasoning involves discussion on the thing that is measured (e.g. performance or efficiency) and the ways in which that thing is quantified in terms of available data (measures of performance or measures of efficiency). Thus, economic measurement always includes an aspect of performativity: Our notions of performance are representations of, and influenced by, the calculative devices we use. Thus, measurement results are never neutral about the uses and users of calculative devices (Vakkuri 2010; Miller and Rose 2008; Porter 2008).

Let us consider a simple model for understanding performance measurement problems in hybrid settings (Ijiri 1967; Ijiri 1975) (see Figure 5.2). In a hybrid context, a performance measurement exercise incorporates four elements:

- A person or organisation conducting the quantification process (*measurer*)
- The object of measurement (*measuree*)

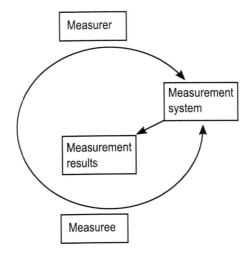

FIGURE 5.2 Elements of economic measurement

Adapted from Ijiri (1967, 22).

- The rules of evaluation and calculation, according to which performance is conceptualised and quantified (*measurement system*)
- The results of measurements to be used for the decision-making of public policies, organisations, and relevant stakeholders (*measurement results*)

Furthermore, such a model implicitly includes two approaches to performance metrics systems: those of design and use. While design is associated with the initiation, conceptual content, and construction of a performance metrics system, use refers to the objectives and styles of the adoption of performance metrics by individuals, organisations, programmes, and other relevant stakeholders. Design and use approaches have been extended to cover other stages of the life cycle of performance management models, such as implementation and assessment (Van Helden et al. 2012).

The measurer and the problem of accountability in hybrid settings

One of the most pervasive problems in the performance measurement of hybrid settings is the question of who conducts the measurement; that is, who is the measurer? Conventional reasoning would require that there be a clear system of accountabilities that distinguishes between accountor and accountee, or principals and agents. The interaction between these parties is defined as a relationship of information exchange. The accountor provides an account of her performance through formal channels of information and informal channels of verbal communication and discussions (Mayston 1993; Schillemans 2011). Schillemans (2011) also refers to the debating phase, during which the accountor has an opportunity to provide further evidence and interpretations regarding her performance, and the consequence phase, during which possible sanctions or rewards are assigned and determined. This is usually known as a basic formulation of an accountability system, particularly in a hierarchical setting in which the relationship between the accountor and the accountee is based on the traditional command-and-control philosophy of following rules in institutions (March et al. 2000; Van Dooren, forthcoming).

However, in hybrid contexts, the system of information exchange between accountors and accountees does not comply with the traditional vertical accountability mechanisms of hierarchical systems (Brandsma and Schillemans 2013). On the contrary, accountability relationships are often horizontal; that is, accountees are not necessarily hierarchically superior with respect to accountors (Schillemans 2011), which creates complexities in determining two important perspectives in any accountability relationship: Who is accountable to whom, and for what? (For practical illustration see Case 5.1.) In such a context, it is not easy to attribute credit and blame, let alone sanctions and rewards, because there are multiple audiences (Taro 2016). Who, then, should be given credit for successful outputs of coproduction or collaborative governance between public agencies, nonprofits, and private firms? This is also a question in the service provision context, in which citizens may have provided an important input for the actual service provided. The attribution problem is much more difficult in hybrid settings, in which accountees are numerous, expectations regarding the information content of accountees may be of different types and extents, the boundaries of accountors are fluid and elastic, and information exchange is about lateral instead of vertical information flows (Koza 1988; Hopwood 1996a).

CASE 5.1 ACCOUNTABILITY IN PUBLIC-PRIVATE PARTNERSHIPS IN THE EUROPEAN OLD-AGE PENSION PROVISION (SORSA 2016)

Over the last few decades, the boundary between public and private responsibility in old-age pension provisions has been redrawn throughout Europe. Pension privatisation has led to the large-scale emergence of mandated private pensions, as well as privately managed but publicly defined mandatory pension schemes. The adoption of such public-private partnerships in pension provisions was among the most typical pension reforms in the 1990s. These schemes refer to mandated pension schemes that include at least one genuine public policy element, as well as some elements of private governance.

There were nineteen PPP-type pension schemes in eighteen of thirty-one European countries in 2013. They represented three types of partnership arrangements: *public leverage, franchising,* and *licensing.* Public leverage refers to the provision of coercive backing (e.g. making private services legally obligatory for certain groups) or direct financial subsidies for certain products or producers in order to improve the conditions for establishing private sector activities. This rarely includes follow-up accountability mechanisms, since the public policy rationale is to facilitate private activities with private accountability mechanisms. Franchising refers to partnerships in which the government defines the product and then grants a mandate and a license to private sector actors to offer the product. This form of partnership may include various types of accountabilities depending on the nature of services and the mandates of service providers. In licensing, the products are not purchased by the government; instead, they are sold to private actors. Licensing includes a compliance-oriented mode of accountability in that service providers need to comply with the public specifications of a service in order to continue providing that service (Skelcher 2005).

There are three typical features that nearly all the schemes share. First, all the schemes are legally mandated, earnings-related pension schemes for private sector employees that are implemented by private entities. All schemes enjoy very little direct public financing. Schemes are typically financed with collective contributions paid by employers or shared by employers and employees, or with earmarked taxes or earmarked user contributions withheld by the employer.

The type of partnership varies quite significantly among the nineteen schemes studied. Four schemes – Italy, Netherlands, Norway, and United Kingdom (Scheme 2) – are based only on public leverage. The government usually makes the provision of occupational pensions mandatory for employers, who then select the providers and participate extensively in the financing of the schemes. Eleven schemes are based on licensing: Czech Republic, Estonia, Iceland, Latvia, Lichtenstein, Netherlands, Romania, Slovak Republic, Sweden, Switzerland, and United Kingdom (Scheme 1). In most cases, all providers are private for-profit firms. In the typical form, the government defines a pension scheme and then provides operating licenses for pension providers to provide a variety of investment plans. There are five franchising-based schemes (Bulgaria, Finland, France, Lithuania, Poland) which define both a uniform pension plan and special purpose pension providers. These schemes have somewhat mixed accountabilities to their supervisors, members, and/or owners.

In one-half of the schemes studied, parent companies own and govern pension provision. In the other half, ownership or at least management is in the hands of employers and, in varying scopes, employees. Employees have very limited 'exit' options from the schemes. While parent company owners dominate decision-making in licensing-type schemes, employees are represented in most franchising schemes and in some public-leverage-based schemes.

> Europe can be roughly divided into two worlds of public-private pension provision, each of which have distinct rationales and challenges of accountability. The first world of accountability is characterised by the fact that the providers of mandatory schemes are made directly accountable to their key stakeholders. The providers are typically special purpose organisations established through franchising or collective bargaining, and key stakeholders are members in the partnership and sometimes the owners of pension providers. Otherwise, owners and investors have little say over pension provision. In most cases, employers and employees have representation in the governing boards of pension funds and can thus directly call providers to account.
> The second world of accountability is characterised by business- and quasi-market-based pension provision. In this world, the government defines the available pension plans and makes the scheme mandatory, and employees as individuals choose what kind of investment plan and which provider they have. The rationale here is to make pension funds accountable to the government for implementing a pension policy. The members of the scheme have no effective voice or exit options available.
> The majority of European countries have adopted some types of public-private partnerships to organise a part of their earnings-related pension systems. Private management of publicly defined pensions can increase user choice and accountability to citizens in their pension regimes, but the analysis suggests that these opportunities have hardly been seized in the PPPs of European pension provision.

Accountability in hybrid contexts involves tensions or even 'pathologies' that originate from the combination of public and private logics in institutional action (Koppell 2005; Skelcher 2005; Sorsa and Johanson 2014). First, there is the limited degree of constitutional oversight over hybrids, which may instigate conflicting criteria as to whether and to what extent accountability controls are required. In some regards, hybrids have to suffer from audit explosion, an excessive amount of audit systems that evaluate hybrids and that are organised by different control rationalities (Power 2000). Also, there may be absolute caveats in terms of controllability and appropriate audit trails. Hybrids may not just fall short of 'public accountability'; they may more generally fall outside any aspired forms of accountability. Second, there may be disparity between procedural regularity and transparency vis-à-vis the involvement of private actors with their distinct institutional logics. Accountability cultures, within which different actors operate, may be fundamentally different from each other. Third, the relative importance of public and private goals may collide in the interaction. A hybrid may have to, or wish to, compromise public goals and the role of government as an impartial regulatory actor. Therefore, accountability structures may lead to subordinating public responsibilities in favour of private goals.

In some sense, problems of accountability in hybrid organisations may be associated with something Koppell (2005) has named 'multiple accountabilities disorder' in public agencies. Conceptual ambiguities of accountability may lead governments to undermine performativity in two ways. First, a hybrid organisation attempts to be accountable, but in the wrong sense of the word. The organisation may be held accountable in areas that are not in its control. From this perspective, adding new layers of accountability may indeed cause audit explosion, control of things that are not relevant, or improvement in public performance. Second, the problem of multiple accountability audiences may motivate hybrids to be accountable in every possible sense. As Koppell (2005, 95) frames it, 'Organizations trying to meet conflicting expectations are likely to be dysfunctional, pleasing no one while trying to please everyone.' There may be a clash of performance criteria in particular with respect to 'responsiveness,' which may mean different things to different audiences depending on the conceptual perspective. A hybrid is expected to simultaneously respond to customer demand and to policy needs, which creates considerable problems in terms of performance data systems, evaluation and measurement procedures, and, of course, related accountability conclusions (Koppell 2005; Kork and Vakkuri 2016).

The discussion of accountability in hybrid contexts epitomises the fundamental problem of performance measurement, the idea that interests of measurers vary to a significant extent. The purposes of measurement, and, accordingly, the interests of measurers, are different in various contexts of institutional action. They vary, first of all, for the simple reason that in hybrid settings there are several measurers, measurees, and audiences of measurements. Therefore, it is almost unavoidable that unanimous consensus regarding the most important characteristics of the performance of hybrids cannot be constructed. Measurements, being representations of 'real performance,' are contingent on those institutions and actors who are in a position to construct representations of performativity.

The minds of measurers are boundedly rational in terms of cognitive, political, and institutional constraints. Although the intentions may be rational (intended rationality) (March and Heath 1994), decisions regarding measurements are significantly constrained by limited cognitive capabilities and incomplete information (Roslender et al. 2015). The talk on measurements may make sense, but the action may be something drastically different (Brunsson 1989). Therefore, we observe different kinds of ambiguity among measurers due to several reasons:

- Ambiguities in *focusing attention* to relevant areas of performance measurement in hybrid contexts. This is associated with the complexity of attention allocation (Radner and Rothschild 1975) and the complexity of determining what is relevant. The process of determining relevant areas of performance measurement among hybrids involves several conflicting interests, which is why there is hardly any common interpretation of relevance (Hodges 2012; March 1987; Johnson and Kaplan 1987).
- Ambiguities in *understanding the cause-effect relationships* of complex policy interventions and collaborative governance. This is especially important for most

hybrid settings where the valuation of activities cannot always be conducted through market prices, or where final outcomes are determined not by individual public agencies or business firms alone, but by their collaborative interaction. Causal mechanisms between inputs, outputs, and outcomes are complex cases for modelling in hybrid forms of governance.
- Constraints in the *recording and data systems* of hybrid activities. This is important for the verification of performance. As Griliches (1994) has maintained, there are prominent misrepresentations of data in many areas of economy and society, in particular in service sectors. A widely used argument by Griliches is that, as an example, a good portion of the measured productivity growth may be, in fact, an indication of changes in the quality of outputs and measurement errors rather than 'real' productivity growth (Tripplett 2007). In hybrid activities, as discussed earlier, this is an even bigger dilemma due to the fact that the systems of financial performance, or national accounting, do not systematically cover hybrid activities. In many measurement systems, they may be nonexistent.
- Ambiguities in *communicating for and about the performance of hybrids*. There are multiple audiences for the performance information of hybrid activities. These may include, for example, the management of hybrid organisations, the shareholders of a company operating in outsourced public activities, media using the performance reporting of hybridised social and health care systems, or citizens willing to express their voice concerning the caveats of service delivery. With such multiple audiences, there needs to be variation in the messages given and the ways in which performances are justified and reasoned among hybrid activities (Tilly 2006).

Measurees

As societal activities are transforming more and more into systems with several interdependencies between public and private forms of institutional action (Perry and Rainey 1988; Thynne and Wettenhall 2010), there is a need for novel theorisations of performance problems and their relevant solutions. Consider the impacts of the following institutional elements on the performance measurement of hybrid activities:

- Ownership and funding for public policies and public sector activities may come from both public and private sources. Financiers may include, for example, taxpayers, clients, venture capitalists, construction companies, and infrastructure providers. There may be extremely complicated multilayered systems for financing societal operations. Individuals may finance their services through insurance schemes (Ebrahim et al. 2014). Subsequently, we need to ask *if performance measurement is intended to provide evidence of 'the value for money.' Whose money are we actually talking about when referring to hybrid contexts?*
- Organising societal activities has become more hybrid, as we have described (Battilana and Lee 2014). The institutional rules of the game cannot be defined

as purely public or private (North 1990). Instead, hybrid activities need to cope with goal incongruences and multiple parallel institutional logics (Skelcher and Smith 2015). Therefore, organising some activities to pursue specific societal goals necessitates a regulatory toolbox that includes the use of political authority for some specific tasks. In contrast, for some other tasks, market-based action may result in the most efficient outcomes (Bozeman 1987). We have to ask this question: *If performance measurement is intended to demonstrate performance in organising and allocating resources in society, how do we deal with societal activities that cannot be reduced to 'public' or 'private' organisations but that need to deal with goal incongruences and parallel institutional logics*?

- Producers of services may be of different types: public, private, and hybrid (Hodge and Greve 2005). This introduces problems for performance metrics. It makes the measuree blurred, an entity with no clear-cut boundaries. In order to make the accountability system of service delivery work, output control and formal clear-cut boundaries between entities and their environments would be required. However, as this is not the case, impacts on the performance of public agencies and business firms may be unpredictable. Thus, we need to ask another question: *How should we deal with the attribution problem in the systems of service delivery; that is, how should we assign accountabilities like credit or blame for high or low performance among different producers of services?*

The problem is also associated with the level of hybrid activity we are referring to. First, we may deal with *hybrid systems*, defined as policy-level networks of institutions and actors pursuing societal macro-level goals but with different sets of institutional backgrounds, institutional logics, and decision-making rationales. Consider the example of the R&D system. As Nelson (1993) argued as early as the 1990s, it is not easy to refer to an R&D system as something that governments, firms, or other actors have consciously built. Rather, a set of institutional actors aims to contribute to innovations, employing their own decision-making rationalities. Second, we may be interested in *hybrid industries*, a cluster of public and private actors pursuing public goals but within a more specific institutional field of action (Padgett and Powell 2012). Consider our previous case of the cleantech industry, in which several actors – including public policy makers, business firms, and multiple associations – aim to contribute to the common good of clean air by producing environmentally friendly technologies and solutions to the global marketplace. Finally, we may be interested in *hybrid organisations* pursuing public goals by employing parallel institutional logics. It is obvious that the performance measurement of hybrid activities is dependent on the level of hybridity we are talking about.

For measurees, it is difficult to classify hybrids into a monolithic ideal of an entity, activity, or system. There are different types of hybrids, not merely with respect to their dimension, extent, or level of hybridity, but also with respect to the societal tasks they aim to accomplish and the functions that they aim to serve. Consider the higher education system, in which the source of ambiguity in performance measurement systems stems from (1) hybridity and (2) the complexity of valuing and weighing performance criteria that is assigned by institutions of external accountabilities and the academic oligarchy, the academic profession itself. There may be notable differences as to how performance measurement systems ought to be understood in the context of higher education: Are they systems of attention directing and learning, or are they performance measurements used to demonstrate accountability and control (Vakkuri 2003)? Moreover, as defined by the matrix of a scientific research system vis-à-vis a formal educational system, university organisations can be seen as a collection of invisible colleges in which the boundaries between different activities and institutional structures are decoupled, dispersed, and widely distributed (Crane 1972). Whose performance should we actually count, that of a formal 'university organisation' (a research organisation transcending the formal boundaries of universities), or, for instance, that of university-industry clusters constituting new types of hybrid logics of action or have and have-not universities (Powell and Owen-Smith 1998)?

Finally, objects of measurement are not static and passive. Instead, they are dynamic and reactive. As performance metrics systems are designed and used to assess distinct forms of value (Moore 1995; Stark 2009; Boltanski and Thévenot 2006) and to define the worth and accountabilities of actors (Hood 2011), they are subject to a sophisticated system of tactics and dynamic reactions by institutions and actors. Ultimately, performativity is defined in a reciprocal relationship between measurers, measurees, and the utilisers of performance information (Bevan et al. 2006). Hybrid organisations or systems do not live a static life with unadjusted interests of performance improvements (Roslender et al. 2015).

Measurement system

One of the prerequisites of institutional development in the market economy is that of being able to distinguish variability from alterability, to demonstrate what the contribution of 'nature' is and what the contribution of 'servant' is. In other words, there are mechanisms that influence organisational performance but that are not controllable, and there are factors influencing performance that organisations and decision-makers can control (Allen 2012). For the purposes of legitimacy, societies need ways to demonstrate what has been achieved (or not) and who is accountable for that.

The difference between variability and alterability is complicated to verify in any institutional context and may thus constitute, if not an illusion of control (Shapiro 1987), at least a desperate need for methods to seek for more certainty, clarity, and governability in public affairs. In performance measurement, rule systems are used for this purpose. They are utilised to select which construction of performance one should count on, to solve problems of assigning value to activities and organisations under measurement, to deal with conflicting political processes and relevant accountabilities, and to conduct experiential learning processes based on the processes of quantification (March et al. 2000).

In the recent history of public sector reforms, measurement rules have been influenced by practices adopted from the private sector. Rules diffuse, and they are transposed from one area of rules to another (Padgett and Powell 2012). This assumption maintains that more efficiency is achieved when practices are adopted from the private sector (Boyne 2003), which creates two problems. First, it is difficult to ascertain whether and to what extent measurement rules – such as the accrual-based accounting model, annual financial statements, or the productivity metrics of production processes – can be in general applied to public service systems. For instance, how do we compare financial performance and social performance (Lapsley 1988; Ebrahim et al. 2014)? Secondly, there is a problem of transposition and refunctionality (Padgett and Powell 2012). The measurement rules of public sector performance metrics are not just transposed from one area of activity to another; they are given new meanings and interpretations in the new context. As non-neutral instruments of order, the measurement rules drastically reshape the ways in which performance is evaluated and measured in new contexts (Vakkuri 2013).

Hodges (2012) discusses problems of valuing and measuring hybrid (joined-up) activities in the context of UK public sector reforms. His main argument proposes a shift from an entity-based metrics philosophy to a network-based evaluation. It is indeed true that the long-standing research tradition and the rule system for performance measurement has relied on an entity-based assumption of organisational systems, which has made it complicated to understand service delivery with networks, lateral accountabilities, and collaborative governance (Hopwood 1996a). The theoretical principles of this rule system originated from systems theory, with clear-cut boundaries for environment and other organisations and stakeholders.

This assumption of clear-cut boundaries of measurees holds in a stable environment, where the links between outputs and outcomes can be internalised into a system of individual and autonomous organisational hierarchies. However, the assumption does not hold too well in the contemporary context of society and public service delivery, in which achieving social impacts necessitates distributed intelligence and collaborative forms of governance among public, private, and non-profit organisations as well as the end users of public services. From the viewpoint of performance metrics, there seems to be significant, yet unrealised, potential in theorising the links between hybrid organisations and their performances (Stark 2009; Hodges 2012; Grossi et al., forthcoming).

Furthermore, Hodges (2012, 38) addresses an important question in the discussion about outcomes of public policy making: Does joining up deliver? In other words, can we expect to see positive impacts of hybrid activities on end users, customers, and citizens? The question of performance cannot only be reduced to the internal optimality of organisational forms (public, private, hybrids). Instead, performance should be assessed with respect to impacts on citizens and users. In fact, demonstrating public value through performance metrics is difficult due to the problems of effectiveness measurement. It is easier for public agencies and private firms to prove their efficiencies and procedural optimalities instead of the effects of services on users, citizens, and society at large.

Rule systems are not able to capture the global rationality of service systems. Instead, measurement rules are designed on the assumption that global rationality may be detected by adding up 'local' rationalities (individual entities) into a larger whole. Therefore, performance measurement rules reflect a sequential, linear process of valuing complicated societal activities. 'Organisational goods' become 'public' or 'common goods.' Such a rule system covers neither a plethora of action (and actor) interdependencies nor the understanding of the mechanisms of policy outcome design.

Kurunmäki and Miller (2006) succinctly discuss the limitations of modern accounting measurement in understanding economic transactions that take place on margins or boundaries. They refer to Hopwood's (1996b) editorial in *Accounting, Organizations and Society*, in which Hopwood emphasises the important role of further understanding lateral information flows and lateral or horizontal accountabilities within institutional settings. Indeed, a somewhat elusive intellectual commitment to a hierarchical organisation has limited understanding of the ways in which activities and other things are actually organised in organisations, between organisations, in networks, and in society at large. Research on budgeting, cost accounting, performance evaluation, and measurement as well as the uses of performance management techniques has consistently followed a pretty simple logic of hierarchical organisations. There, issues of decision-making, power structures, and assigning value to activities can be neatly distinguished from their environments. This does not mean that accounting disciplines or other fields of research have been successful in making a case for the performance measurement of hybrid activities. The assumption of hierarchical entities may only have been a safe choice to count on when researching complex environments and networks.

It could be argued that if the object of measurement becomes hybrid, the rule systems of quantification should be able to trace that hybridity (Stark 2009). Performance metrics ought to be hybrid as well. However, theoretical thinking in current performance measurement systems is too inflexible for that purpose. In terms of validity and relevance, measurements are at their best when they have stable measurement objects and institutional environments as well as easily verifiable processes, outputs, and outcomes (Golany and Roll 1989). Accordingly, many performance evaluation systems in hard-to-measure environments aim at balancing between contrasting expectations, conceptualisations, and measurement practices (Kelly and Swindell 2002). Of course, in some regards, rule systems for performance measurement are indeed hybrid. Consider the distinction between financial and nonfinancial performance measurement, in which the acknowledgment of the multidimensionality of performance is assumed to contribute to a more comprehensive understanding of performance and to more relevant uses of information (Richard et al. 2009). Nevertheless, even with this distinction, rule systems are limited by their focus on entities.

Measurement results

Performance measurement results are often a topic of vivacious debate, not merely because of their fundamental nature in public agencies, business firms, and political activities, but also because uses are complicated by who the factual user is (Van Helden et al. 2012).

The user may indicate different things in business firms, as in public policies. A common approach in research is to talk about external and internal uses and users. For instance, in a public agency, external users may include financiers, taxpayers, the media, and relevant stakeholders, whereas internal users would include agency management and personnel (Poister 2003). In a hybrid setting, external users in particular may vary. Modes of use are also often difficult to grasp in hybrid settings, whether we are talking about hard or soft use, formula-based use, or interpretative use (Van Dooren and Van de Walle 2008). As Behn (2003) argues, the answer to the question, 'Why measure performance?' is contextual; measurement results are usually useful for a specific institutional context and for a specific managerial purpose. Behn challenged the widely held assumption that performance measurement systems can be universally designed to simultaneously address different managerial purposes.

As March and Sutton (1997) note, the problems and limitations in contributing to functional explanations – that is, explaining variations in organisational performance – are not news. They are well known. Rather, the persistence of researchers in making judgments on performance variations that are known to be suspect remains a constant surprise. Such persistence is an important driver of thinking in the area of performance measurement design, especially uses of performance measurements. Performance metrics systems are assumed to be functional when they contribute to the goal attainment of organisations and dysfunctional when they inhibit an organisation from achieving its goals (March and Sutton 1997). For instance, Peter Smith (Smith 1995) referred to the impacts or potentially dysfunctional effects of performance measurement. Dysfunctionality is somewhat difficult, because it assumes a clear interpretation of organisational missions, goals, and the mechanisms through which the achievement of goals can be assessed. The implicit assumption, quite naturally, has to be that goals are taken as a given. This difficulty is reflected in a theoretically unbalanced discussion regarding the link between the functional and dysfunctional effects of using measurement results.

Despite all the known constraints and complications in measurement results, let alone in the uses and impacts of the results' uses (Van Helden et al. 2012), performance metrics are widely used. Why? A theoretical discussion provides interesting approaches as to why performance metrics are widely adopted and utilised. It may be in the interests of some actors or institutions to ensure that performance measurement innovations are diffused, or at least that they are not rejected. There are interesting justifications for not rejecting performance metrics systems that have important impacts on measuring hybrid activities:

- Performance metrics systems are considered justified because there is no unified agreement on the goals that public agencies, business firms, or hybrids should attain. The quest for a more rational order is strong (the uncertainty argument) (Weick 1976). *Therefore, performance metrics provide some form of 'rational order' for hybrid activities.*

- Performance metrics are justified because conceivably successful organisations have employed them (the mimetic isomorphism argument)(DiMaggio and Powell 1983; March and Sutton 1997; Abrahamson 1991). *Thus, performance metrics are an instrument to alleviate the obscurity and impurity of hybrid activities.*
- Performance metrics are justified because agencies with links to the environment cannot be totally distinct from their outside surroundings (the connectedness argument). *Performance metrics systems incentivise hybrid organisations to position themselves with other organisations. This may transform their behaviour towards the average* (Llewellyn and Northcott 2005).
- Performance metrics are adopted if there are no conspicuous 'counterbandwagons' to jump on (the absence of alternatives argument) (Staw and Epstein 2000). *Hence, performance metrics are used to make sense of the future of hybrid activities.* We extend this discussion next.

The world of performance measurement, in hybrid settings as well as in other institutional contexts, consists of knowing about performance but also about doing performance (Vakkuri 2010). Therefore, we need to understand both 'stories' and demonstrations of performance as well as the ways in which institutional action is influenced, enabled, constrained, and facilitated by actors' interpretations of performance.

These two aspects of performativity have important influences on how performance in hybrid settings may be understood. We can treat performances as deliberate and emergent (Mintzberg and Waters 1985). 'Deliberate' refers to institutional performance that comes with intentions and intentionality, and 'emergent' is associated with performance that is realised but not intended in the first place. Why is it important to understand performance that may be realised but was not intended? To discuss this, let us consider the following set of assumptions commonly referred to in research on performance measurement and the valuing of economic and social activities (Miller and Rose 2008; March 1987):

- More information is antecedent to more rational choice; that is, the most important problem in making intelligent choices is a paucity of information.
- In the context of performance measurement, the implication is that more high-quality measurements almost automatically result in performance improvements.
- In institutional practice, problems of performance measurement are those of design, not of the uses and users of the information. Accordingly, performance measurement problems may be solved through the introduction of more sophisticated performance measurement models and techniques.

However, what do our 'practice lenses' tell us about actual forms of design and the use of performance measurement in social activities (Orlikowski 2000)? First, these lenses tell us that performance measurement, albeit sophisticated, does not necessarily ensure its competent use, which is due, for instance, to institutional learning capacities, incomplete data systems, or complex links of causes and effects in performance (Vakkuri 2003). Therefore, it is indeed relevant to understand the actions and activities of performance – the methods through which institutions make sense of performances. Design is just not enough. Furthermore, as the solution turns into a problem, we actually come across a whole new dilemma. How do we understand such sense-making procedures among users of performance information? How do hybrids make sense of performance information?

In general, such reasoning provides a different emphasis on performance measurement. Hybrids are seen as platforms of conscious decision-making and choice, not as objects of external assessment or quantification. From this perspective, performance metrics ideology and systems may include several ways to legitimise activities in hybrid contexts. Let us consider one important argument intelligently raised by Van Dooren (forthcoming). In 'difficult-to-measure contexts' of institutional action (Ouchi 1979), the traditional doctrine of performance management does not usually suffice. In other words, an engineering-based logic imperative to (1) define objectives and choose indicators, (2) measure achievements, and (3) reward or punish is usually too straightforward to succeed in complicated contexts with ambiguous goals, multiple vertical and horizontal accountabilities, and collaborative action. The gap between the increasing complexity of service provision and delivery vis-à-vis the instruments of quantification and measurement seems to be widening (Virtanen and Vakkuri 2015).

This argument works only if we assume a linearly organised process of sense-making in hybrid contexts. Instead, we may assume that for hybrid settings there are actually several gains to be achieved using performance metrics. Van Dooren (forthcoming) provides three important arguments. First, performance metrics may provide a useful setting for the decoupling of goals from action. This may make sense, as many hybrid organisations are faced with parallel conflicting and contrasting expectations and demands. As the demands for demonstrating performances become more diverse in hybrid contexts, it becomes literally impossible to satisfy them all (Koppell 2005). The obscurity of performance reporting may thus become legitimate and acceptable in the eyes of stakeholders, financiers, and citizens. Legitimisation audiences increase as the level of complexity increases. For hybrid organisations, this may be a coping method, an instrument to muddle through. Second, in hybrid contexts, performance measurement may provide one way to standardise activities. In a more complex environment, there is a growing need for simplification. Often, this means simplification through standardisation. Actors and decision-makers need reference points and points for comparison that make sense. Performance metrics may serve this role as sense-making procedures, a method for constructing calculated order. Finally, in hybrid settings with a high level of complexity, performance metrics may be particularly useful because of the calculated order they are able to contribute. Measurements may provide an aura of perceived rationality, technology of distance, and illusion of control (Shapiro 1987), which is especially useful for those institutions and actors with great trust in numbers (Porter 1995; Porter 2008). In hybrid contexts, this may be an important resource. The case of universities (Case 5.2) shows the problems of performance measurement in practice.

CASE 5.2 PERFORMANCE MEASUREMENT PROBLEMS IN HYBRID UNIVERSITIES

Among hybrid organisations and activities, universities are a particular context. As we have discussed, it is not easy to characterise universities as purely public or private. In fact, they may be considered hybrids according to all four characteristics of hybrid activities: ownership, goal systems, resource base, and control practices. Universities' main activities are research, teaching, and the third mission. These activities are in many respects hybrid by their characteristics. Understood as 'goods,' they all include properties that justify their production in the marketplace. Just consider commissioned research projects, higher education degrees funded through student tuition fees, or university-related consultancy intended to support local business clusters or environments. In addition, the very same activities of higher education systems incorporate features of, for example, significant externalities and spillover effects, which constitute an important basis for long-term economic growth and development and which societies are, therefore, eager to control. We might assume that systems of coordination have become adjusted over time to such a plethora of complexities in institutional activities.

An additional distinctive feature of universities that sets the scene for performance measurement problems is known as the academic oligarchy (Clark 1983). Clark's characterisation of the triangle of coordination in higher education systems entails the control of government and markets as well as the self-control and peer pressure exerted by the academic profession itself. These control forces are understood as mutually exclusive with each other, implicating that for a given higher education system the decrease of state control would result in more control by the markets or by the academic oligarchy. This may implicate higher resource dependency on the markets (external sources of funding) and/or more locally determined forms of coordination and control. Although this may be a somewhat constraining assumption (i.e. many higher education systems of the world may be influenced by parallel and simultaneous changes of policy control), it gives us an understanding of the notion of hybridity in the context of higher education systems. Moreover, it should be recognised that, as general categories, markets, the state, and the academic oligarchy involve different types of organisations, institutions, and actors. Using our categorisation of the actors and determinants of performance measurement systems (i.e. measurer, measuree, measurement system, measurement results), we can understand some of the major problems in designing and using performance evaluation systems in universities.

Measurer

In the university context, measurers are numerous. They also explicate different accountability demands and interests directed to the performance measurement of universities. We could assume that the main categories of measurers fall into market measurers (e.g. students and companies collaborating with universities), state measurers (e.g. ministries and other levels of politico-administrative policy apparatus), and academic oligarchy measurers (e.g. peers, colleagues, and other university institutions). From this perspective, it is difficult to provide a coherent, unanimous notion of university performance because the interests for measurement vary.

Measuree

The assumptions as to how the performance of universities' activities should be understood may be distinct from different viewpoints of the triangle. For market measurers, performativity mainly concerns the interaction between universities and their external partners and constituencies. For state measurers, universities are successful in the extent to which they are able to contribute to the objectives of higher education policies. The academic oligarchy may emphasise more the uniqueness and novelty of scientific research and teaching.

Measurement system

The three performance measurement perspectives operate on different rule systems and conceptual bases. For instance, value creation and effectiveness may yield distinct representations depending on the measurement viewpoint and the ways in which value is determined and assessed. If universities are expected to provide positive impacts on society through science or higher education policies, measurers of effectiveness are of a particular type. However, if we make an assumption that the effectiveness of universities ought to be evaluated and measured by 'users,' 'customers,' or 'students,' we get different sets of measurements. It is no wonder that there is a tendency in the university context towards a balanced approach and multidimensional indices. These are efforts to balance the distinct rationales of measurement systems.

Measurement results

Uses of performance measurements are contingent upon the purposes of use (Behn 2003). In the university context, the three viewpoints have different sets of users and audiences with distinct purposes of use. Therefore, the three viewpoints include different legitimisation strategies for performance information uses. For instance, the perspective of the academic oligarchy emphasises variation, novelty, and uniqueness. Performance information is utilised to make a difference, to be differentiated from others by new and novel knowledge. In contrast, state measurers may emphasise conformity and convergence, in which different universities and departments are easily compared, and in which research and teaching outputs and outcomes can be compared across different units and institutions.

We can combine the perspectives to discuss the ambiguity of performance measurement in universities (see Table 5.2).

TABLE 5.2 Performance measurement problems and questions in hybrid organisations: the case of universities

Measurement/ measurement principles	Market	State	Academic oligarchy	Perspectives combined: the ambiguity of performance measurement
Measurer	Students, partners, constituencies	Science and higher education policy actors	Peers, colleagues, other universities, and academic institutions	Measurement interests vary, multiple accountabilities, 'Whose value should be increased?' Impacts on 'whom?'
Measuree	Universities as service providers	Universities as institutions contributing to the policy goals and intellectual capital of society	Universities as a scientific community, a collection of academic tribes	Assumptions on university behaviour and performance vary, 'What is a university? What kind of performance can we expect from them?'
Measurement system	Performance as meeting the needs and expectations of constituencies	Performance as the attainment of policy goals	Performance as novel research and high-quality teaching	Distinct rule systems of performance measurement, 'How is the relative importance of different rules and conceptualisations defined?' 'How is the performativity of universities produced?'

(Continued)

TABLE 5.2 (Continued)

Measurement/ measurement principles	Market	State	Academic oligarchy	Perspectives combined: the ambiguity of performance measurement
Measurement results	Legitimisation through satisfaction and choice	Legitimisation through the attainment of policy goals	Legitimisation through the reproduction and accumulation of scientific knowledge	Strategies and audiences of legitimisation vary, uses of performance information are contingent upon the rationales of legitimisation, 'Who should be convinced of university performance?'

As hybrids, higher education systems are indeed a special case. The role and importance of the academic oligarchy in research and teaching can be understood as another dimension of hybridity in universities. In higher education, the interaction between the public and the private is shaped by the self-coordination and control of an academic profession that in all circumstances seeks autonomy and independence from external bureaucratic, managerial, policy, and, in many cases, market influence. This may help us understand problems and limitations with respect to the implementation of whole-of-government policy reforms in universities or the restructuring of university organisations to meet the needs of local constituencies and stakeholders (Mouwen 2000). Furthermore, this discussion reflects an expectations gap between the presumption of university organisations promoting public, or common, goods in society vis-à-vis the de facto opportunities for mobilising resources to enable those wishes. In research literature, this gap is said to refer to complex work processes (Knorr-Cetina 1999); garbage-can type decision-making; the loosely coupled organisational structures of universities (Weick 1976); and unclear and incongruous, and, to some extent, ambivalent preferences and identities (Merton 1976). The higher education system epitomises an institutional context in which the performance evaluation of activities is enmeshed with distinct rationalities of accountabilities as well as the design and uses of performance information. Higher education policies and university organisations may be discussed as an important context for exploring ambiguities in the performance measurement of hybrid organisations.

6
CHARTERING THE TERRAIN OF MONSTERS

Exploring strategy-performance interfaces in hybrid activities

This chapter concludes the discussion of the two previous chapters by combining the goal-oriented actions of strategic thought with ideas from performance measurement literature. Our focus is solely on hybridity, without much reference to business enterprise or public agencies. First, the following discussion points to possible actions that hybrid organisations may take in following their strategic goals and performance measurement regimes in fulfilling dual expectations originating from public policies and business goals. By default, hybrids face the simultaneous demands of multiple audiences and environments. Second, this chapter deals with the macro-level consequences of hybrid activities in society. Here, the embeddedness of hybrid activity as well as the interplay between the top-down flow of dependencies and bottom-up mobility constitutes the basis of our discussion.

Any institutional action needs to balance strategies and performances, both in terms of doing institutional action and justifying it. Interdependent logics are numerous. Strategy may precede performance by providing a structure and system for goal achievement logics and demonstrations of performativity. Performance may precede strategy by instigating an understanding and interpretation of history, asking what is possible in terms of goal setting. It is often the case that links between strategies and performances are not temporally based. In fact, they are both part of the common system of sense making and legitimisation, in which institutions muddle through by exploring what has happened, what is possible, and how institutional activities are to be legitimised and justified in the eyes of relevant stakeholders.

We wish to provide conclusive thinking about the strategy-performance relationship in hybrid contexts. We see this as a method to explore the theoretical underpinnings of hybrid activities and organisations as an institutional space of their own by associating hybrids with two prominent perspectives. We acknowledge that this link between strategy and performance would be an important aspect to theorise as such, whether in business firms or public agencies. Nevertheless, we are eager to take this setting one step further by discussing such a dynamic interaction in hybrid contexts. Based on our reasoning in this book, our expectation is that societies in general and hybrid organisations in particular have to invest significant amounts of intellectual and financial resources for regulating, coordinating, evaluating, and legitimising hybrid activities. How do they do this? What forms of institutional action do we see as a result?

Case illustrations revisited: hybridity through its contexts

Before we proceed to our conclusive argument on strategy-performance interfaces, let us briefly emphasise the case illustrations of hybrid activities in this book and use them to discuss the link between strategy and performance. The case contexts of our book offer rich sources of inspiration for understanding hybridity in general. However, here we use them specifically to explore strategy-performance interfaces. The following illustrative contexts have been addressed in this book:

- Publicans in the Roman Empire
- Highway networks and road maintenance
- Health policy
- The cleantech industry
- National innovation systems
- Global air travel
- The System of National Accounts
- Energy policy
- Health care organisations
- Pension policy
- Universities

As we indicated in the beginning of the book, we are interested in hybrid contexts which serve some important functions and activities in society, things that have important value to citizens. Therefore, we have explored transportation, intellectual capital formation, social and health policy, and physical environment, all of which epitomise some of the institutional activities in societies for which the distinction between public and private becomes more obscure and fluid and through which it becomes more important to understand the rationales for hybrid activities (Simon 1998). The following discussion offers concluding insights on these contexts.

In general terms, transportation networks connect local communities to the global environment by different means, such as roads or air travel. One of the features of hybrids is that they are able to connect different levels of organisations together. The demands of the system-level networks may diverge from the subunit requirement. In our discussion, hybrids in the airline business might be instrumental in securing local connectivity with regional development aims. Similarly, China's local road network development through hybrid arrangement might be instrumental in amassing extra resources for subnational transport needs, which are not necessarily in the focus of central government agenda. These insights are important in terms of both strategy formation and performance measurement. Sometimes hybrids might be vehicles to serve local strategic aims, which can improve or decrease performance in comparison to purely public or private activity.

In intellectual capital formation, universities, as well as their connection to technology development firms and government units, have been one interesting focus of our examination. The variety of university organisation forms reflect universities' multiple client and stakeholder groups, such as governments, businesses, scholars, and students of higher education facilities. The formation of national innovation systems comprising hybrid arrangements between universities, governments, and technological firms gathers resources to achieve goals of product and service development for commercial purposes. Private enterprises benefit directly from such efforts, and governments are able to enjoy the fruits of private activities through an increased level of employment and tax revenues. At the same time, such a constellation might not as equally serve other purposes of knowledge formation, such as the general availability of scientific results and scientific progress through the open debate of scientific findings.

Social and health issues have appeared in our case descriptions of the micro-level development of Coxa Hospital, the meso-level formation of the public-private European pension construct, and system-level health policy. In all these cases, the goal was to secure the needs of the general population by combining public and private activity. In health and pension policy, hybridity does not originate from government privatisation or outsourcing efforts. In these cases, the mixing of public goals and the use of private resources have deep roots in the reliance on private insurance in service production in the US and the relatively strong position of social partners in public policy formation in Europe. Hybrids are not necessarily inventions but political and social solutions to previous political and social grievances in society. In social and health policy, hybridity also reflects the complicated properties of goods. In the world of uncertainty there are markets for insurance, yet there may also be wider policy rationales in providing insurance. Therefore, we could argue that there is a need and demand for insurance that is partly channelled through individual and market interests and partly channelled through political and societal activities. The whole system benefits from pooling resources from private and public activity in attempting to achieve a balance between individual and more collective goals. It would not make sense to reduce the system activities to either private or public efforts only, as there are important synergies and complementarities between the two.

Two of our case descriptions have concentrated on the environment. Environmental sustainability has been the focus of the development of the cleanteach industry, and the design to exploit natural resources for energy generation has been another environment-related theme. The cleantech industry is a showcase of hybridity in connecting public policy goals with business aims. In other words, the market mechanism is used to advance the sustainability of the environment. The blossoming of such an industry is dependent upon government regulation on standards of production and permitted levels of emissions. What makes the cleantech industry a fragile construct is that the development of green industries requires intergovernmental agreements not to allow unfair competitive advantage due to the lack of regulation in certain countries or regions. In the end, such agreements depend on mutual belief in the sources of climate change and the means to combat such change. Within the area of energy production, positive increase in economic activity easily results in the need of energy imports in developing countries. The lack of functional markets puts hybrid organisations in a difficult planning situation, which is characterised by parallel and possibly conflicting demands between the reliability of the long-term supply of energy and the use of price information in guiding energy procurement.

As always in researching institutions, organisations, and systems, we are faced with the problem of idiosyncrasy regarding the extent to which we are able to generalise institutional characteristics from different organisational populations. Discussion on the strategy-performance link in hybrid contexts is no exception. Upon reflection of our case illustrations, it would be tempting to propose that there may be different categories of hybrids: social and health hybrids, infrastructure hybrids, intellectual capital hybrids, and environmental hybrids. The link between strategy and performance would then vary depending on the specific characteristics of the hybrid in question. In fact, these categories are plausible and indeed a relevant topic for further theorisation and conceptualisation. However, at the risk of overgeneralising different types of hybrid contexts, we consider it important to discuss strategy-performance interfaces in hybrid activities through more general reasoning. We shall do that next.

Strategy-performance constellations in hybrid activities

Figure 6.1 provides one conclusive approach to thinking of strategy-performance interfaces. We use our earlier conceptualisations on strategy and performance and explore the interaction of these perspectives in hybrid contexts. What do these interactions tell us about hybrid activities? There are multiple ways to understand the boundary conceptualisations in the figure. On the one hand, the boundary conceptualisations could be understood as technocratic ideals of how hybrid activities should be controlled, coordinated, and measured. For societies, political systems, and policy makers, the wisdom could thus concern prescriptive policy rationales. On the other hand, these interactions may be understood as descriptive emblems of hybrid activities and systems 'in practice.' Then we would be dealing with the activities of hybrids in their pursuance of institutional survival: What may be the coping mechanisms of different types of hybrids when adapting to highly complicated environmental conditions and contrasting expectations of different audiences? Moreover, another interpretation could be that we are dealing with hybrids as a more general macro-level institutional solution in order to overcome some of the inherent problems of strategies and performances of societal action. In this regard, hybrids are not seen as problems that should be alleviated and overcome. Instead,

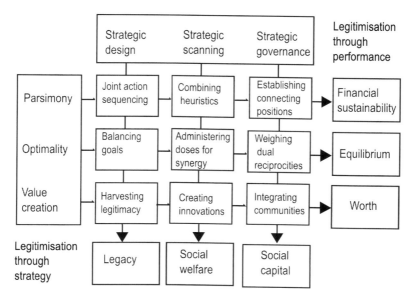

FIGURE 6.1 Strategy-performance link in hybrid activities

hybrids are seen as limitedly rational institutional solutions to decision-making problems that involve severe problems of complexity in goal incongruence in addition to problems of obscurity in demonstrating performance and accountability. Hybrids are not perfect; however, in some cases, they may work better than their public or private counterparts.

Joint action sequencing

The action sequences in the strategic design tradition include the separation of strategy formulation from its implementation, and such sequences often include hierarchical steps, from the most general formulation of goals to the minutest details of individual work tasks. The identification of value chain activities has been one device used to see how consecutive steps in the process advance value during the production. Hybrid organising involves two value chains that are operational at the same time: one to deal with profit generation and the other to take care of social and public policy goals. The integration of these production lines with a unified strategy process could be one option to formulate the parsimonious sequencing of organisational actions. In a more general sense, action sequencing deals with the formulation of predefined stages in organising the production of goods and services. Pettigrew (1992) assumes the existence of the following predefined stages to guide strategy process research: (1) embeddedness (the examination of processes in multiple levels of analysis); (2) temporality (the study of past, present, and future processes); (3) a role in the explanation of content and action; (4) a search for a holistic rather than a linear explanation of process; and (5) a need to link process analysis to the location and explanation of outcomes.

The development of the global airline industry is a good illustration of processual considerations. Basically, air travel is the quite straightforward endeavour of moving passengers and cargo from one place to another, but in practice it is entangled in complex government-business interactions. In the airline industry, both hybridity and processual thinking is present in multiple levels of analysis. Airlines sometimes have mixed ownership, which might result in providing service to some domestic destinations with little commercial gain. Air service agreements tie government and commercial airlines together. In other words, there is no way any commercial flight can take off without inclusion in a bilateral government contract. This signifies a threshold condition for entering the airline markets, which does not influence the actual value chain activities of the airline operators. The regulatory power of individual governments has impeded the formation of fully competitive markets by restricting foreign operators to flying between two places in domestic airspace. The establishment of global airline alliances is a response to such a restrictive regulatory framework. Membership in an alliance enables the scheduling of connecting flights between airlines. In practice, the organisation of global air travel into major airport hubs connecting regional airports not only makes such arrangement possible but also minimises the number of empty seats in aircrafts and gives traditional airlines a competitive edge over their low-cost carrier rivals. But, at the same time, airlines face the problem of acquiring landing rights in congested airports owned predominantly by public authorities. To put it otherwise, the landing of an aircraft depends on complicated contracts between airlines and government authorities. This is a type of business-government interaction which affects the internal processes of airline operators. Consequently, the seemingly straightforward practice of taking off and landing is not possible without public-private interactions. These developments do not originate from any grand overall design but from piecemeal deregulation and consequent adaptation to new circumstances.

Heuristics in combining public and private resources

Institutional action is based on bounded rationality and the use of simple heuristics fulfilling the demands of the task at hand. These heuristics include simple rules of thumb, such as 'increase advertisement if sales decrease,' or 'minimise costs to produce services.' When should specific rules or heuristics be employed? The explanation may be the individual history of a decision-maker. For example, as previously discussed, if a manager learns to use a rule when there is little time to make a decision, the use of such a rule is more likely used in choice situations with time pressures. Such a situation makes it obvious that it is possible to influence judgments and choices by designing situations in which tasks incorporate or simulate initial learning conditions (Einhorn 1982). Therefore, things like the amount and schedules of reinforcements and the number of trials should be considered in understanding modelling behaviour. Another explanation is outcome feedback.

Since outcome feedback is the main source of information for evaluating the quality of judgment rules, a critical part of explaining heuristics becomes the knowledge of how task variables both affect outcomes and influence the way outcomes are coded and stored in memory. This makes it important to understand the perceived causalities of managers in their decision-making (Weiner 1986). In other words, decision-makers using the clear-cut distinction between public and private need to be convinced of the assumed cause-effect relationships between decisions made and outcomes produced. Decision-makers ask themselves: How can I determine the relationship between the distinction and the outcome achieved? Where can I see the benefit? How do I value them?

The role of heuristics can be both positive and negative. Heuristics can be seen as an irrational aspect of organisations which leads to strategic failure, but heuristics are also a positive learning tool to achieve more accurate evaluation and improve the processes of an organisation (Bingham and Eisenhardt 2011). An important feature of hybrids' behaviour is related to how they combine public and private resources in ways that help save those resources. How to define the resource combinations between public and private resources in an intelligent way, or how to compile a minimum set of means to attain both public and private goals at the same time, is a question for heuristics in the hybrid context. The case of Chinese state-owned enterprises (SOEs) shows a clever way of increasing efficiency and decreasing corruption in a hybrid setting. The Communist Party indoctrinates the management of SOEs with political education to decrease corruption, and the SOEs try to increase efficiency by motivating the employees with market-oriented financial rewards. In such a way, the public and private realms simultaneously operate at the same organisation.

Establishing connecting positions

The relational task of the hybrid organisation is seemingly simple. Active brokering between public and private sectors is the essence of such activity. Whether these positions are instrumental in achieving some specific goal is not an issue here. The connections might have multiple purposes, but in hybrid contexts, governments and businesses represent important stakeholders that cannot be ignored. However, due to the multiplicity of purposes for connections, it is difficult for organisations and institutions to know which of those connections they should focus their attention on. One decision-making criterion may be the parsimony principle of finding the minimum set of means to create a justifiable set of connections. In organisational hierarchies, one way of economising external interactions is centralising interorganisational interactions with top management. In such a constellation, hybrids are able to maintain connectivity with their external private stakeholders and public constituencies with a minimal number of ties. Naturally, this choice is shaped by perceptions of what is considered justified and legitimate. In society, hybrid activities are one important instrument for minimising costs for such collaborative action. Hybrid contexts may vary significantly with respect to their ability to practice the parsimony principle. Therefore, hybrids are not a perfect solution to the parsimony problem, but they may be seen as representations of such an effort.

Balancing goals

What are the most important goals of an organisation? We know that there is not a universal or ubiquitous answer to this question. This is because organisations constitute a bundle of activities that are guided by different preferences for action. Different people have different stakes in the organisation. The idea that goals are defined exogenously and externally may be in concert with the long historical tradition of consequentialist thinking in the area of rational choice. According to this thinking, human ends are taken as given, but not necessarily in hybrid activities and contexts, in which institutional action is also about creating new goals, not only acting upon prestated goals.

However, the nature of many institutional processes is to attempt to solve the problem of incongruent, ambiguous, and ambivalent goals of action. This explains processes of politics, in which the 'important' objectives are determined by different ideological underpinnings; processes of competition in the marketplace, in which 'important' objectives are defined by the competitive dynamics of industries; and, interestingly enough, some important properties of hybrid contexts and activities. Hybrid organisations may be seen as an institutional arena, a forum for interacting and balancing incongruent goals, the origin of which may be public or private. The interests of business in contrast to public or social goals does not need to be equally represented in the goal setting of a hybrid organisation, as the system of goals is usually not a case of balanced goal setting. The unbalanced, unequal distribution of distinct goals is more a starting point, not a deviation from a perceived optimum of goal setting. The performance of hybrid systems in their attempts to balance different levels and different types of goals is contingent upon the optimality of making incongruent goals more sensible, transparent, and legitimate. Consider cleantech companies as systems with a balance between economic development and growth, on the one hand, and ecological sustainability and eco-efficiency on the other. Sometimes it may be the case that the balancing process provides public goods and important lucrative business opportunities at the same time. Or consider universities as hybrid organisations attempting to find an optimal balance between organisational goals (public or private) and wider social goals of higher education and science policies in society. In this process, universities may explicate some problems and dilemmas for governance and regulation, yet they may be fit for carrying out the aim of balancing the goals of different levels.

Administering doses for synergy

The idea of synergy in biochemistry refers to the cooperative action of two or more stimuli or drugs. In organisational contexts, synergy usually refers to the positive outcomes of combining entities (employees, technologies, units) together. The optimisation of resources requires the assessment of the proper dosage of public and private resources to produce unique new forms of action. In European pension provision, there are many schemes that are mandated by public bodies but run by private institutions – often with some constraints in comparison to typical business enterprises – and financed by employers and employees. It is quite easy to see that those who pay the piper call the tune. In other words, those paying the largest part of the expenses are entitled to make decisive choices. Of course, this is not based on egalitarian democratic principles. Limited public funding in public-private pension schemes puts public bodies in the role of supervisor with respect to providing a regulative framework for such activity. However, the accountability mechanism in the management of these schemes is such that private providers are made accountable to employers rather than employees. Yet again, the accountability mechanism follows, to a large extent, the funding structures that tend to put more of a burden on the employers rather than employees. Consequently, changing the accountability mechanism or, more generally, the balance of power between the most important stakeholders probably requires a change in funding structures as well.

Weighing dual reciprocities

How reciprocal are the contacts between the public and private spheres? Basically, the norms of reciprocity are important devices for upholding social intercourse in the long run. These norms might originate from societal norms or a proximate community group, but their role is always the same – to provide some guarantee for the continuation of interaction. A basic idea within social capital literature is that social closure is a determinant of the building of trust and the obligation to cooperate. The formation of trust enables the circulation of favours (credit slips) among the members of a community. Both of these features lower the transaction cost in economic intercourse (Coleman 1988). The problem of hybrids is that the formation of tightly knit communities requires social closure in making a distinction between insiders and outsiders. This is an evident problem for hybrid organisations and activities which should, according to this logic, find membership in multiple communities. It is also the case that sometimes the genuine presence of multiple spheres makes the participants true members of multiple worlds at the same time. Stark (2009) gives a useful description of factory workers in a socialist country who perform their duties as civil servants during the daytime and their duties as employees of a private business in the evenings. The facilities and work processes remain the same, but the clients and the compensation for the work are different. In this case, the change in institutional context fundamentally alters the role of the employees, although the actual work tasks remain the same. The point here is that, within hybrid settings, an evaluation of reciprocities includes hybrid-private reciprocities and hybrid-public reciprocities. In a temporal examination, it is easy to see that changes in connections are also evolving over time according to patronage and the availability of resources. The different developments of social enterprises in the US and Europe are examples of such evolution. Declining government funding has meant that nonprofits in the US turn to markets for funding their social missions, whereas in Europe national and supranational institutions are active in boosting social enterprise activities to decrease unemployment in particular. Developments in the US have increased the reliance of nonprofits on their private market activity while they retain the variety of their missions, whereas developments in Europe have made nonprofits become more reliant on public funding and specific public policy goals.

Harvesting legitimacy

As we have noted, hybrid activities require constant legitimation for their existence. However, it is important to ask whether there is something institutionally mysterious in hybrid organisations that would call for special needs for legitimisation, or whether some of the institutional activities that societies pursue incorporate characteristics that need to be justified. In other words, maintaining infrastructure in society, for instance, may require special forms and systems of legitimisation that have been used to evidence the performance and endurance of those systems for centuries. Therefore, legitimisation needs to be harvested in one way or the other. Hybrid institutions are just one form of doing that in society. In a structural sense, universities are well equipped to cater to the legitimation demands of a variety of audiences. Students add value to the human capital of nations (Becker 1993), but they are also important devices to lower youth unemployment, both of which are good legitimation tools for the government. Research engagement with private enterprises enables the emergence of commercialised products and services and lends credibility in business environments. The fact that universities are not extensions of public agencies (which they can formally be) or subsidiaries of business enterprises rests on the rule of academic oligarchy, which defines the standards for high-quality research and performance metrics for the evaluation of research effort.

Creating innovations

One of the key ingredients of resource-based thinking is that a combination of capabilities creates something new. Following this thought, one of the valuation principles of hybrid activity is its ability to formulate new ideas. However, in a hybrid context, the type of innovation need not be connected to the product, process, position, and paradigm innovation types formulated in business environments (Bessant and Tidd 2011). However, a hybrid could cover public innovations, such as strategic innovations in formulating new goals or arguments for further action, governance innovations in establishing new forms of civic engagement, democratic forums, and positional innovations by creating new user groups (Moore and Hartley 2008). The level of analysis issue is also important here. If hybridity is seen as a meso-level concept, it comprises a variety of public and private actors, which, as a whole, form the hybrid. National innovation systems connecting governments, universities, and private businesses are an evident example of such meso-level constructs, which also bears some of the deficiencies of such an approach. First, the national innovation system is a theoretical construct, a human artefact that does not require that its participants share the same goals or purposes. The participants could even be unaware of their membership in such a constellation. There is no ready-made performance management system able to grasp the internal functioning of such constructs consisting of multiple institutions in both public and private contexts. Output measures, such as the number of patents or commercialised products, can be extracted, but the internal action of hybrid arrangements in national innovation systems cannot be well understood with such measures. Moreover, national innovation systems are geared more towards commercialised products and services, and this practice does not give credit to the public nature of possible innovations.

Integrating communities

The most obvious role for hybrids is to connect civil society to political decision-making through participation in voluntary organisations. The idea is that membership in voluntary organisations provides additional links between otherwise unconnected groups and thus helps in solving possible conflicts between them. Putnam et al. (1993), Putnam 2000) has stressed the importance of the egalitarian nature of participation in voluntary organisations as a condition for improved political decision-making. As hybrid organisations represent a larger part of social and economic action than voluntary organisations, individuals participate in hybrid activity in many cases as paid labour, such as in SOEs and in PPP arrangements, which to some extent requires subordination to the hierarchical order of organisations. Even so, hybrids offer a connecting device to integrate public and private spheres together due to the dual interest of hybrids in public policies and business activity. In this sense, hybrids shorten the social distances between politics and business, which lubricates the circulation of information even if it does not necessarily result in conflict resolution (Putnam et al. 1993).

Hybrid organisations function as integrating devices connecting businesses and the political elite. In the pyramidal structure of society, there is always a small number of elites and a large number of people at lower levels of status and hierarchy. In social intercourse, there is also a tendency of people to bond with those who are similar to them (Blau 1977). Therefore, there is a need to establish arenas for the interaction of the numerically small elite, which is often geographically dispersed (Granovetter 1985). SOEs offer suitable forums for the joint presence of business and political communities. There is a genuine need for political wisdom in fulfilling public policy goals and a demand for business knowledge to survive in market competition. Engagement in nonprofit activity and participation in management boards provide additional forums for the joint presence of the business and political elite. The result of mixing different elite groups based on the different goals and resource needs of hybrid organisations is that the social distance between government and private enterprises gets smaller.

Why and how do hybrids justify their actions? Strategy-performance interfaces as a problem in the justification of hybrid activities

Justification to multiple audiences

One characteristic feature of hybrid activities is their 'impurity' as organisational or institutional forms (Ménard 2004; Powell 1987). There are several mechanisms that we have addressed in this book explaining the nature of that impurity and the reasons why activities located in between the pure types of organising would easily be called the monsters and weirdos of institutional and political life. However, it is still worth asking why. Why does it appear to make sense for human beings and institutions to avoid the space in between the pure types? Could we not assume that the rich, lengthy evolution of institutional life may have created more than two 'pure' types of organisations? In other words, perhaps the problem is associated more with categorisations, taxonomies, control, policies of social order, or forms of administrative pragmatism than with our fundamental systems of understanding institutional life. We think that we are not influenced by institutional naïvety, that we are actually rational when delimiting the possible forms of organising into controllable and governable categories of institutional action (see Chapter 3). In order to understand hybrid activities in such a constellation, we are interested in looking for approaches and concepts that would combine our two perspectives of the purposive action of hybrid activities: strategy and performance. It is important to discuss the legitimisation and justification of hybrid activities.

A simple logical argument would be the following: If you are a manager in a hybrid organisation that is regarded as a residual deviation from the average, or as excessively different from others, you need to invest a considerable amount of attention on proving to your relevant audiences that your activities are legitimate both in terms of the aims of your organisation and in terms of past records and accountabilities. In hybrid contexts, the fundamental question is, who are these audiences? They are numerous (DiMaggio and Powell 1983; Llewellyn and Northcott 2005; Meyer and Rowan 1977).

Multiple audiences create a particular environment for legitimisation processes. Goal incongruence may be both a problem and a blessing. It is a problem because it is difficult to set goals that meet the expectations of all the different audiences. There is always room for critical remarks on why certain goals are not addressed, or why the system of goals may include inherent contradictions and ambivalences. Thus, different audiences may have different levels of trust in the legitimacy of hybrid activities. Furthermore, as we have discussed, demonstrating performance may involve significant ambiguities due to the multifaceted set of interests among measurers. Different audiences wish to hold hybrids accountable for different issues. Given the lack of consistent and clear performance measurement rule systems, there is no common and uniform interpretation of how different criteria of performance should contribute to the overall performance of hybrids. In practice, expectations for performance are indeed polysemic (Stark 2009). However, the problem of multiple audiences may also be a window of opportunity for hybrid organisations. It is easier for hybrids to make loose promises and set multiple goals for multiple audiences, as hybrids are aware that it is much more difficult to be held accountable for these promises afterwards (Brunsson 2006). In a similar fashion, it is easier to game different performance criteria and metrics without being subject to strict accountability and control procedures (Koppell 2005). The multiple audience problem instigates some fundamental problems in terms of goal setting and performance demonstrations, but the problem also incentivises the behaviour of blame games and blame avoidance (Hood 2011).

Justification of the future, justification of the past

While, as forums for the justification of hybrid activities, strategy and performance may incorporate similar characteristics, problems, and opportunities, they have slightly different perspectives when it comes to temporality. As justification mechanisms, strategies are needed to justify future activities, and performances are utilised to justify the past. We can think of a time continuum in which hybrids, with an aim to maintain their legitimacy, over time employ performance demonstrations to convince different audiences of their past achievements and create visions and goals to justify their future actions. This is partly explained by the fact that constructions of performance are based on historical data, and strategy making may also involve using historical records in order to explore the future, though devising strategy is not limited to this practice alone.

We should not understand the time perspective too much as a constraining argument. Quite naturally, strategy and performance interact over time. In other words, the ways in which past activities are justified have an important bearing on the methods of justifying future goals. It is complicated to set future goals without an understanding of the past. Reasonable goals are thus influenced by an historical understanding of institutional performance that indicates what is possible, feasible, and attainable. This process is also true vice versa: Performance evaluation is closely linked to the goals that have been set for hybrid activities. In this regard, it may be difficult to chronologically delineate the past from the future, or performance from strategy. They may be seen as two sides of the same coin in hybrids' system of purposive action (Allen 2012).

Interaction between strategies and performance in the justification of hybrid activities is emblematic of some performance management paradoxes that are known to all organisations, be they business firms, public agencies, or hybrid organisations (De Bruijn 2002; Van Dooren and Van de Walle 2008). In general, the basic statement of these paradoxes is that the link between goals and performance may often be a dysfunctional one. Knowing that their performance will be measured and monitored and that measured performance has important effects on their legitimacy, organisations act on that understanding in two ways. First, organisations put special emphasis on giving an optimal account of their activities from the viewpoint of legitimacy. They have to emphasise performativity. Second, organisations adjust their behaviour according to the performance criteria in use (Vakkuri and Meklin 2006).

Discussing these paradoxes helps us explore particularities as regards the multiple audience problem in hybrids. Let us consider three important arguments (Koppell 2005, 2006). First, the presence of multiple audiences is a complicated case for attention allocation in the managing of hybrid activities. Therefore, solutions to management problems sometimes necessitate simplification and concentration of focus. The paradox lies in the tension between multiple audiences and the imperative to narrow focus for managing hybrid activities. In hybrids, given the starting point that there are more audiences than in other institutional contexts, the paradox appears more vivid and tangible. Second, coping with the management problem in hybrid settings may require the standardisation and convergence of activities. Performance metrics systems may be of enormous help in this regard (Van Dooren, forthcoming). However, for multiple audiences, standardisation – although it makes sense for managing activities and organisations – gives the impression of a poor understanding of different voices, and it may create different types of legitimisation problems. Third, from the legitimacy viewpoint, gaming strategies and performances is a persistent feature of all institutional life (Smith 1995). However, hybrid contexts may be subject to specific forms of gaming. With multiple audiences, it is tempting for hybrid organisations to make loose promises, as it is highly unlikely that the accountability system would be able to grasp all the broken promises or even attribute credit or blame in evaluating whether the broken promises are due to the success or failure of hybrid activities.

Legitimisation through strategy

Legacy

The long-term orientation of strategic goals includes the aspect of intergenerational justice. In essence, there is a fundamental asymmetry of the present population with past and future generations. Those present at the moment cannot influence the choices of those already dead, nor do those members of unborn generations have any say in the choices made by those who are presently alive (Barry 1989). Concern for intergenerational justice is connected to the usage of natural resources and the sustainability of the environment, but hybrid arrangements add some additional features to such considerations. What is the significance of dual goal setting in the long run? Some PPP arrangements are explicitly based on rolling the cost to the future and selecting discount rates determined by the expected future cost of operations, whether related to the building of hospitals or motorways or the provision of pensions. Evaluation of effectiveness is dependent upon not only the performance of the hybrid organisation but also on the judgment of future populations who will use the facilities and services created through hybrid activity. The evident problem in long-lasting contracts is that they tie up the decision-making options of future populations for which we cannot have proper measurement tools. The legacies of public-private activity can, however, be examined using past developments as anchor points. The legacy left by the public-private arrangement of the ancient Roman Republic is neither particularly great nor flattering. A few notes in the Bible as a stereotype of despised persons (Luke 18:10–11, Luke 18:13, Matthew 10:3) and their reputation as ruthless tax farmers is the basic information we are given about the *publicani* for their operation in the public administration of a large premodern state.

Legacy also refers to generational succession, family trees, and intergenerational evolution. Hybridity is also a dynamic process. It may originate from a variety of sources: citizen assemblies, voluntary self-help cooperatives, corporate social responsibility, government outsourcing, and the building of quasi-markets in areas where they were previously unrepresented. In this sense, hybrids can be seen as a compilation of novel activities, governance structures, organisational forms, and networks of organisations that have not yet attracted the full attention of government regulation. Following this line of thought, the expansion of hybrid activities will gradually incite more government attention and new forms of regulation. Taking the idea even further, the hybrid constellation is a product of government-economy dynamics, which follow evolutionary development rather than rational planning.

Social welfare

The well-being of an entire society is hardly solely dependent upon hybrid organisations or hybrid arrangements. The previous discussion has pointed out difficulties in defining clear uniform goals or accurate performance metrics for hybrid activity. It is likely that the legitimation of hybrid activity requires promotion of their fulfilment of both public policy goals and their business objectives.

Hybrid arrangements are part of the economic and social regime of societies. An examination of the role of government in providing services for its citizens (Esping-Andersen 1990) and an examination of the institutional structures of economic activities within societies (Hall and Soskice 2001) give basically similar results, despite the fact that the most extensive social democratic welfare does not have a corresponding capitalist form in comparative capitalism literature (see, however, Thelen 2012). Nations do not only differ from one another in terms of welfare spending or labour market bargaining; they compose qualitatively different types of market societies that have their own advantages and disadvantages. Liberal societies provide meagre public services for their citizens but aim at maintaining fluid markets, which are able to accommodate changing economic circumstances with innovation and offer new employment opportunities to workforces with general skills. Coordinated or corporatist societies offer more public services and build upon the coordination of economic activity through labour market bargaining, interfirm cooperation, and the application of employee skills to the use of individual firms in order to induce piecemeal improvements in existing technologies. In this case, the enlarged role of the public sector is meant to guarantee a safety net for those who have invested their skills in a specific use that might become obsolete due to a competitive environment and changes in technology.

The difference between social and economic constellations of societies results in different roles for resource acquisition and hybrid arrangements in those societies. Within market-reliant liberal societies, the diversity of market activities offers hybrids a solid resource base. In terms of social policy, there is an evident need for social activity to fill the gaps of limited public service provision. As for economic activity, the value of hybrid activity might be in its ability to induce innovations and new economic activity due to its position in connecting separate spheres of public and private activity. Within coordinated economies, resources for hybrid activities are more likely to be found in public sources due to governments' greater role in society. In this context, social policy aims for hybrids are not as apparent as in liberal societies, but the maintenance of specific skills of the workforce for the use of individual firms offers plenty of work for hybrids.

Social capital

In the most general sense, social capital refers to the integration of society as a whole. Hybrid organisations provide links between private enterprises and government, and, by doing so, they bridge connections between separate realms of society. Bridging in social capital comprises social networks between socially heterogeneous groups. Bridging allows different groups to share and exchange information, ideas, and innovation, and it builds consensus among groups representing diverse interests (Putnam 2000). Linking social capital refers to the extent to which individuals build relationships between layers of hierarchy with those who have relative power over them (Woolcock 2001). The grassroots activities of social enterprises are tools for connecting the needs of members with the providers of those needs, and hybridity might equally include a strong top-down character.

Hybrids are part of highly different communities. They might be partners in alliances, clientelist communities, triple helix innovation systems, and mixed public-private governance forms. Alliances involve inherently voluntary and relationally egalitarian forms of network formation, which resembles hybrid contracting between hierarchically organised firms and unrestricted market transactions proposed by transaction cost theory (Williamson 1999b). An additional feature of alliances is that they can incorporate both private and public actors. Clientelist communities build upon hierarchical differences between levels of society. Hybrid organisations may represent but one level in command chains, which originate from the nexus of political decision-making and extend to the governance of individual organisations. More often than not, national governments are interested in securing the strategic assets of their countries. The organisation of these assets under the control of SOEs is one way of guaranteeing state involvement in controlling these assets. The fact that SOEs are most prominent in developing countries that do not always have functional markets or political institutions points to the possibility that hybrids may function as devices to connect vertical levels of society with the control of the ruling political elite. Still, there are also multiple levels of dependence. On one end of the continuum, there are mutual adjustment mechanisms transmitting information from one level to another. On the other end of the continuum lies parasitic communities totally dependent upon the patronage of higher level authorities. Triple helix communities composed of governments, universities, and business enterprises signify how developed societies exploit the possibilities of their advanced levels of human capital in the form of the education, skills, and capabilities of their population. In one sense, it is a human-made construct, an artefact of our imagination that is used to better guide the innovation production process, and it also has a bottom-up character by putting forward the importance of regional interaction in the vicinity of higher education facilities. As for other public-private governance forms, road construction and public-private pension provision have served, among others, as case examples of these forms' variety. Road construction in China signifies the reciprocity involved in the use of private initiative and resources to achieve public goals, which in the end turns out to be a lucrative instrument for a variety of public purposes, such as collecting resources or easing traffic congestion.

Legitimisation through performance

Financial sustainability

It is one of the axiomatic principles of hybrid activities that, in the long run, they need to be able to make ends meet. This founding principle does not differ from that of any other form of institution or organisation. Financial sustainability, and the ways in which it can be achieved, is one important criterion for the emergence and long-term survival of hybrid activities and organisations. For this purpose, hybrids may practice distinct forms of organisational solutions, decision-making heuristics, and legitimisation strategies. Therefore, instead of asking what the problems are in hybrid organisations as they demonstrate their strategies and performances, we should ask what the advantages and disadvantages are among hybrid forms of governance as they pursue long-term financial sustainability. We are not necessarily looking for deviations from an abstract efficiency principle. Instead, we are exploring the possible intelligence and hidden rationalities of hybrid arrangements and solutions.

In order to survive, hybrid activities have to create sensible cost-minimisation strategies for coping with goal incongruence. They need to operate on principles of parsimony when combining public and private resources to produce goods and commodities with hybrid properties. Moreover, hybrids have to practice sound economic reasoning when taking part in collaborative action, or when finding useful locations in the network of actors. One aspect of studies on hybrid governance should concern the parsimony of hybrid solutions in the context of complicated goals, resource pooling, and network relations. Can we discover some intelligent solutions in minimising the costs of collaborative action, and is there some important potential in the parsimony of joint productions through hybrids?

Equilibrium

Hybrid activities and organisations search for equilibrium in many respects. For hybrids, equilibrium is about finding the optimal balance between contrasting expectations, goals, resource pools, and actor networks. While it is important to aim to use minimal means to achieve such ends, it is also extremely relevant for hybrids to be able to understand the relative-value orderings of things. Therefore, equilibrium is mainly only about discerning what the proper combination of goals, resources, and systems of relationships is when that combination needs to be justified to multiple owners and funders, or to users and stakeholders of different kinds. Furthermore, something is usually to be given up for the sake of reaching a reasonably legitimate equilibrium. To understand hybrid activities, we need to comprehend the institutional mechanisms through which hybrids aim to reach for such equilibrium, how hybrids value the expected costs and benefits of the equilibrium, and what the impacts of the equilibrium are on societal activities.

It is obvious that any equilibrium is hardly a perfect one. Equilibrium is the compromise of compromises, in which choices are justified through a complex web of interactions between institutions, stakeholders, and society as a whole. Any equilibrium may violate several criteria for a perfect equilibrium, for instance, criteria for the political status quo, existing regulation systems of society, parsimony and cost control, or distinct forms of value creation. However, as indicated earlier, we should not only focus our attention on equilibrium as on outcome; it is also a process. We should look closely at the activities and choices of hybrid organisations when they try to reach the equilibrium that they see fit.

Worth

The survival of any institutional activity is dependent upon its ability to create value for society as well as for important stakeholders and customers. Thus, it is indeed important how the notion of value is perceived, how it is demonstrated and measured in different contexts, and how different actors are made accountable whether or not value has been produced. Hybrid organisations aim to create value by sustaining a long-term legacy of societal activities, enhancing welfare through social innovations, and developing social capital and coherence by building bridges between communities that may remain separate without hybrid activities. The extent to which hybrids succeed in creating such forms of value determines their actual worth in society. Worth is not an easy concept. It includes different systems, levels, and actors of value creation. Worth transcends public and private value creation processes. Moreover, worth can mean different things in different contexts of hybrid activities. It is polysemic by definition. Stark (2009) talks about the problem of understanding dissonance; that is, diverse criteria for demonstrating worth in societal activities. For researchers of hybrid governance, this leaves us with two important and interesting thoughts. First, it makes sense to explore hybrid organisations as institutional systems that aim to find their institutional niche through specific systems and accounts of worth. An important characteristic of those accounts is that they are not separately organised pieces of value creation. Instead, they are aggregates of distinct forms of value that constitute compromises of performance criteria, incongruences of goals, and, to some extent, paradoxical means of accountabilities and strategies of legitimisation. Worth is something that epitomises value creation initiatives among hybrid organisations. Second, it may be easier to understand hybrid activities and organisations when such a broad concept of worth is systematically addressed. Many of the mysteriously appearing activities and dilemmas may be more comprehensible when such theoretical principles are considered. The limitations of hybrid activities, the bounded rationalities of their goals, and their performances make more sense when the ambiguity of measuring, demonstrating, and legitimising worth in hybrid activities is seriously acknowledged.

7
ARE THEY MONSTERS AFTER ALL?

Understanding the governance of hybrid organisations

Where have we come?

This book has discussed the multifaceted nature of hybridity in social life and institutional organising. The focus of examination in this book has been on the area between the public and private sectors, between government agencies and private enterprises. The simple starting point of the book was to find out what the space is in between private enterprise and government action, which is signified by the notion of hybrids, hybridity, hybrid action, and hybrid governance. These notions cannot easily be reduced to the existing categorisations of the public and private sectors.

On the one hand, this book has introduced analytical distinctions defining features and properties of hybridity in regard to public and private sector organisations and activities. On the other hand, this book has played with the important dualism of purposive institutional action by discussing the links between strategy and performance in the context of hybrid organisations. Strategies search for the legitimation of the future, whereas performance measurement aims to legitimise past actions and accountabilities. The demarcation line between private and public strategies lies in the difference between adaptation and change. Private enterprise aims at adapting to its environment, while government has the ability to change the features of its environment. Within the realm of performance measurement, the difference between profit seeking and effectiveness in striving for public policy goals separates private and public activities from one another. Hybrids combine public policy goals for change and private goals for adaptation in their strategy formation. Hybrids are able to resort to both public and private resources, and they are able to connect to both businesses and government circles. Within the performance regime, hybridity signifies focus on the economy, efficiency, and effectiveness of actions; that is, cost awareness, balancing mechanisms, and anticipation of future benefits when striving for multiple goals, combining a variety of resources, and connecting with various stakeholder groups.

From a bird's-eye view, hybrid arrangements may seem to be a messy activity that does not constitute a unified whole. This activity also does not belong to a proper industry sector, nor is it an identifiable government activity. The possibility to serve multiple masters may bring about benefits not shared by other types of actors. Nonprofits that are able to acquire funding from market transactions to fund their social missions, state-owned enterprises (SOEs) that are able to resort to government funding for their investment needs, or hospitals that are able to reinvest profits in the improvement of their own services exemplify the different benefits of being a hybrid. The performance measurement regime is inherently ambiguous for hybrid activity. This measurement system should ideally track both the business and public policy benefits that hybrids are supposed to produce. In practice, there are hardly any such systems. Consequently, there are always two separate, nonoverlapping yardsticks for the evaluation of hybrids' goal attainment. To put it differently, hybrids do not have a clear super-goal that can capture its activity uniformly, let alone a clear performance measurement regime. Furthermore, the duality of performance measurement opens up possibilities of gaming profit generation and the production of public value. The achievements of public policy goals can forgive the lack of business results and vice versa.

For this book, we have employed a working definition of hybridity based on previous research, according to which institutional action may be hybrid in terms of ownership, institutional logics, goal incongruences, funding mechanisms, resource bases, and forms and systems of control. We may deal with hybridity of different extents and criteria. For instance, we may talk about hybrid organisations through ownership schemes, about hybrid systems through combinations of public and private goals, and about PPP arrangements through modes and models of combined public and private funding mechanisms. Hybrids have mixed ownership arrangements that connect public and private owners. They are steered by multiple principles, they strive for goals that cannot always be easily matched together, and their institutional logics embody practices that signify features of both public bureaucracies and private enterprises.

Organisations are the most obvious subject for the examination of hybridity. The fact that organisations striving for unified goals or performing the same types of duties, such as hospitals or universities, can be arranged as private enterprises, public bureaucracies, or hybrid forms signifies the equifinality of their organising principles. In other words, there are multiple ways to reach the objective of organising. SOEs and social enterprises signify organisational forms that cannot easily be reduced to purely public or private action. In this book, the variety of organisational forms between public and private actions is not seen only as a result of the market emulating the reforms of governments in recent decades; it is also a result of compilations of government-induced business activity for the use of government aims in diverse areas. Just consider supplying equipment for the military or finding business opportunities for clean-energy solutions, civic engagement in advocacy, and self-help and community production efforts.

Moreover, it has been our deliberate intention to move beyond hybridity as hybrid organisations. Being fully aware of the importance of organisational thinking, we have introduced some difficulties in understanding hybridity merely through organisational foci. To us, the seemingly straightforward view of hybridity as organisations is deceptive, as the organisation-based view cannot take into account the nature of multiple hybrid arrangements in societies. In many cases, hybridity is in fact a versatile compilation of institutional levels and structures. Hybridity can be investigated through a macro perspective; a system-level perspective; a meso perspective (constituting new forms of industrial fields that mix public and private features); and a micro perspective (in which the traditional idea of hybrid organisations operating under parallel and somewhat contrasting logics, objectives, and ownership schemes holds). Moreover, the notion of hybridity invites theoretical scrutiny of the structures of social organising. Governance of hybrids may include singular modes by which individual entities operate in their institutional environment, dyadic modes of transactional and reciprocal relationships between two entities, and triadic modes of multilateral governance composed of three participants. Based on our book, it seems fair to conclude that we may learn more about hybridity by loosening the primacy of organisational thinking in this area of research. We argue that this approach would significantly benefit not only other levels of hybridity but also research on hybrid organisations.

The relevance of hybridity varies in different parts of the market economy. This book has demonstrated that hybridity becomes more important when dealing with the governance of important societal activities and functions, such as infrastructure, energy, health, education, and the well-being of our physical environment. If the nature of goods is taken as a starting point, hybrid governance would be best, but not solely, oriented to the production of public or common pool goods, such as fisheries or forestries, in which there is difficulty excluding potential beneficiaries, and the use of one consumer diminishes the options for the use of other consumers. These same difficulties are also evidenced by toll goods, such as private clubs or theatres. Both of these categories represent deviations from purely public or private goods. In measurement practice, however, calculations represented in systems of national accounting do not take into account these theoretical principles. The standards of national accounting acknowledge the existence of two basic types of hybrid activity: (1) public-private partnerships (PPPs) and (2) nonprofit institutions. For the purposes of classification, PPPs are forced to be either public or private via rules of thumb for assessing bearers of economic risk, and the substance of PPP activities is not given any importance in the categorisation. As for the second type of hybrid activity, nonprofit activity is defined as organisations with voluntary membership, independence from government, and lack of profit generation, which puts nonprofit organisations outside of the economic activity of those identified in the System of National Accounts. Neither of these activity types follow the categorisations of the production of goods in economic theory.

The evolution of economy-government relationships offers one view of hybrid arrangements. The building of nation states has involved the formation of government bureaucracies and the building of infrastructure for economic activity, including securing property rights, setting a legal framework for dispute settlements, and building a stable financial system for economic actors to operate. The division of labour between government and the economy is not fixed in any particular pattern or form of interaction. Increased reliance on the market provision of public services does not liberate the producers from government control, nor does the market activity escape government regulation if the activity is deemed to serve the strategic interests of the state. Waves of nationalisation and privatisation in industrialised countries exemplify historical changes in government-business interfaces. The recent government bailout of private enterprises that were too big to fail in the aftermath of the financial crisis of 2008 signifies another development in mixing public and private activity. In the evolutionary view, the hybrid space in between public and private spheres is a product of the double movement between government and the economy. Hybridity is often an administrative solution to practical problems in securing the functioning of societies. Another option is to see hybridity as a coincidental result of institutional movements between government and the economy. In this sense, hybridity is the gravel left behind in the constant grinding of the public-private dichotomy.

Governing hybrid organisations revisited

If you have a hammer, all you see is nails: the external and internal approaches to hybrids and hybridity

It indeed matters whether hybrid activities and organisations are seen as objects of regulation and control or whether they are perceived as an institutional space of their own, incorporating their own institutional logics, goals, and ambitions as well as distinct legitimisation strategies. The problem of governing hybrid organisations seems different depending on the perspective.

If you take an external perspective on hybrids, it is tempting to search for anomalies and paradoxes among hybrid organisations. Due to the impurity of institutional design and the complexity of categorising hybridity by characteristics of the public and private sectors, the task of controlling hybrid organisations is not an easy one. This task is filled with complicated contractual arrangements, rule systems mixing public policy goals and profit-seeking motives, and limited possibilities to demonstrate accountabilities among hybrid systems and organisations. For government systems and societies applying administrative pragmatism, in which something that is perceived to work is considered a more enduring decision-making imperative than something that may be an accurate and detailed illumination of institutional reality, the control problem is solved by introducing clarity, structure, path dependency, and known histories. In such a setting, the successful control and regulation of hybrid organisations may incentivise regulators to emphasise clear-cut distinctions between the public and private sectors, in which hybridity as an institutional feature constitutes a 'regulatory problem,' not an institutional modus operandi. If you are looking for anomalies in the existing categorisations, you are bound to find conceptual cracks in them. Still, it seems evident that the private and public sectors are themselves fragile constructs that do not have clear-cut lines of demarcation.

If you adopt an internal approach, the world of hybrids looks different. The idea of seeing hybrids and hybridity as having an institutional space of their own determines the ways in which institutional action is assumed to behave. Therefore, hybrid organisations are seen as a complex system of parallel institutional logics, goal setting, and cultural identities, which have a fundamental and persistent motive to survive and thrive. From the internal perspective, we have been more interested in exploring the process of survival among hybrids – their survival methods of coping with goal incongruences and sometimes perverse and pathological accountability structures. From such a perspective, the question to be asked is not what type of institutional complexities are created through hybrid organisations and organising, but instead how do hybrid organisations aim to survive despite institutional complexities in place.

Being fully aware of the relevance of both perspectives, we are not claiming the supremacy of either approach. In order to organise and provide important services, processes need to be controlled from outside and managed from within. Furthermore, it is also obvious that, in order to execute successful forms of regulation and control of hybrid organisations, a comprehensive understanding of their institutional mechanisms and logics is required. More intelligent control is probably needed, and to execute more intelligent control requires a more multifaceted understanding of hybrid logics. Perhaps the major problem for scientific research concerns understanding the relationships between external and internal approaches to hybrids. Looking at hybrids from the outside, you end up pounding nails to pinpoint the anomalies of hybrids in comparison with the public and private sectors. Looking at hybrids from the inside, one tends to find plausible excuses for being 'different' by emphasising the legitimate forms of hybrid activities and organisations. Maybe we should better understand both sides of the coin.

Hollow politics or lousy business? Hybrids as deviations from a perceived optimum

Human beings are almost fixated on finding rationality and irrationality in organisations and institutional activities. The world of hybrids is indeed no exception. The role and position of hybrids and hybridity in institutional life is significantly determined by the extent to which their action and behaviour is perceived as rational. Most often, rationality is then understood through consequentialist logic; that is, the value and worth of hybrid actions are primarily determined by their consequences, which sometimes leads to excessive simplifications of causal inferences regarding hybrid activities (March and Sutton 1997). It may even be too easy to give credit or blame to hybrid organisations without truly understanding them.

However, our book has indicated that there is something inherent in the logics of hybrid governance that makes it complicated to discuss in the traditional vocabulary of rational action. With respect to rationality, hybrid systems and organisations may indeed appear as institutional weirdos (Ménard 2004), a system of hollow politics in which important strategic choices have been made through somewhat obscure and nontransparent processes and mechanisms of decision-making, or a system of lousy business practices in which, in terms of performance, bureaucratic red tape and the pursuit of a common good prevent the pursuit of sensible profit maximisation. Just consider health care firms providing public health care service and simultaneously seeking profits, or consider state-owned corporations carrying out other public policy goals while creating value for shareholders (including government shareholders). Are we then dealing with important and significant limitations to the rationality of hybrid activities and organisations?

Probably not, unless we are able to specify our notion of rationality. In fact, both positions are limited in their own ways. Hybrid organisations do not constitute a monolithic system, as they consist of a loosely coupled network of organisations and institutions with ambiguous and sometimes sporadic connections to political objectives, business interests, and the needs of the general public. Therefore, we are not able to provide an exclusive notion of rationality, or an intellectual idea that would be able to capture different dimensions of rationality, or an idea that would be universally applicable to the distinct contexts of institutions, human decision-making, and choice (Gigerenzer 2000; Audi 2001). In fact, as this book has demonstrated, the search for rational ideas is significantly limited in every sphere of institutional life. The problem with understanding the rationalities of hybridity and hybrid organisations may actually be very simple. The intellectual systems of rationality we employ in hybrid activities are similar to those we use to understand other forms of organisations and organising. The limitations of that intellectual design become significantly more prominent in hybrid contexts. We are not able to fully understand the performance evaluation and measurement of hybrid activities, which is why we may be searching for rationality in the wrong environments. We may give credit for no particular reason, and we may also assign blame to hybrid organisations with insufficient causal reasoning and improper evidence. In allocating and organising resources for society and individuals, hybrid organisations are responsible for creating space and opportunities for both profit-seeking activities and the pursuit of common public policy goals, but the overall bottom line in achieving joint goal achievement is often lacking. As we indeed already have important problems and limitations in assessing value in the public sector or in business, this problem becomes significantly more complex in hybrid contexts.

Our book makes a specific suggestion regarding the notion of rationality in hybrid contexts. We have always maintained the position that it makes little sense to commit oneself to one universal notion of rationality to understand organisations or institutional action, and we have instead suggested exploring organisational life through the lens of multiple rationalities. This book has made us even more aware of the importance of the lens of multiple rationalities in the context of hybrid organising. There is no uniform notion of rationality applicable to distinct contexts of social organising, but, multiple rationalities are applicable in different ways in different contexts. Our discussion in this book regarding two important emblems of modern forms of rationality, strategy and performance, as well as the associations between them, teaches us something about the theoretical roots of rationality in hybrid constellations (Figure 6.1). Fundamental virtues of economic reasoning and goal setting need to be combined with the idea of hybrid action, which involves a multiplicity of goals, audiences, accountabilities, and performances. The problem of understanding rationality in hybrid contexts lies in the difficulties of dealing with such multiplicity. This limitation should be considered in attempts to comprehend rationalities in hybrid organising and in the diffusion and transposition of rationality ideals from one institutional space to another.

Strategies for muddling through

How can we explain why hybrids and hybridity survive in institutional life? An obvious explanation would be the traditional adaptation argument, which proposes that there must be something inherently efficient in hybrid forms of organising that keeps them in the apparatus of institutional design over time. But what would that be?

Our book has approached this question from the viewpoint of survival strategies, including muddling through conflicting interests of action. Let us consider two levels in this discussion. First, we can think of the survival strategies of hybridity and hybrid organisations as a society-level construct, in which hybridity constitutes a solution to governance problems of societal functions. Then we would be dealing with hybrids as a general macro-level institutional solution to overcome some of the fundamental governance dilemmas of societal action. In this regard, hybrids are not seen as problems that should be alleviated. Instead, they are seen as (limitedly rational) solutions to decision-making problems that involve severe, complex problems in goal incongruence and obscurity in demonstrating performances and accountability. As stated earlier, hybrids are not perfect; however, they may work better than their public or private counterparts. Sometimes the choice may be between the lesser of two (or three) evils.

Second, we may think of strategies of muddling through as initiated by hybrid organisations themselves. From this perspective, we can think of hybridity as a window of opportunity for institutional actors to survive. The complexity and ambiguity of goals and performances are considered a means of survival. Obscurity and fuzziness are not necessarily something to get rid of. They may constitute a venue of institutional action by taking advantage of the dilemma between hollow politics and lousy business.

Hybrids are not expected to be legitimate in all aspects of their activities, which gives leeway for them to make choices about which legitimisation for specific audiences is the most important. This may explain problems in goal setting and performance evaluation and also some regulatory problems. Hybrid organisations may wish to remain hidden just because it is possible for them. Consider the following forms:

1. As agents, hybrids are not expected to demonstrate accountabilities in all directions or to be loyal to all principals. Different stakeholders and audiences are more permissive of the ambiguity of accountabilities, which gives opportunities for hybrids to select those accountability structures they wish to be evaluated against.
2. One important characteristic of hybrid activities is that, despite high expectations, hybrids are not able to produce all kinds of value. Stakeholders recognise the dissonance of value creation mechanisms and also forms of demonstrating value and worth. Hybrids may have an option to choose the modes of value they wish to demonstrate and to not disclose those forms of value they wish to hide.
3. Hybrids may be able to benefit from the problem of multiple decision-making heuristics and institutional logics. This may be an excuse for hybrids to justify their decision-making procedures by selecting the forums in which they wish to be present.

These muddling-through strategies may vary significantly in different institutional contexts. While in some cases such windows of opportunity may provide relevant strategies and courses of action, in other contexts possibilities are extremely limited, and there may be important limitations of resource dependency. We want to emphasise here that we are making a theoretical argument, not an empirical argument. However, in a more general fashion, it is also important to recognise that, while the ambiguity of hybrid activities may sometimes be a problem to be solved, sometimes ambiguity may be a solution. Ambiguity then is not something to be controlled and diminished; instead, it is something to be managed and used for deliberate institutional purposes.

Hybridity by design and by default

In this book, we have aimed to provide a temporally rich interpretation of hybridity. We have associated hybridity with the fundamental mechanisms of societal activities, in which interfaces between the public and private sectors evolve over time. Therefore, we have maintained that hybridity should not merely be considered an invention of contemporary organisational life. There have always been societal functions and activities for which the task of organising is not easy to categorise into public or private forms of organising. This links the *publicani* of the Roman Republic to modern day public sector contractors or PPP arrangements. The governments of antiquity and of the modern age have been eager to practice administrative pragmatism to carry out societal activities.

However, the idea of hybrids travelling through time provides an important aspect of understanding hybridity in a more general fashion. Hybridity may have served distinct purposes at different times. Hybridity may be an artefact of deliberate institutional design, or it may be an outcome of an institutional process that has produced unintended, unexpected, unanticipated, and perhaps also undesired consequences. Thus, we may see hybridity as having evolved both by design and by default. This distinction between hybridity as 'by design' and as 'by default' reminds us of the importance of societal and governmental processes in regulating and controlling hybridity, eliminating and alleviating hybridity, and also facilitating and even instigating hybridity. In many cases, hybrid structures and organisations may be the unintended consequences of transforming 'public hierarchies' into 'markets.' This process of transformation does not create markets but instead aims to keep most public policy goals in the policy apparatus while trying to introduce competitive dynamics (markets) to the public sector (Hood and Dixon 2015). In contrast, many PPP arrangements are a conscious effort by governments to create hybrid contracting arrangements, in which the network of actors includes cities, government, and business firms.

If hybrid organisations are not perceived as a sector of society, or as conceptual and institutional compromises of markets and hierarchies, or as public and private forms of action, we are left with questions about what moves social and institutional action and what kinds of institutional processes produce hybrid forms of governance. If you posed these questions to institutional theorists and students of decision-making, their answer would most probably include at least two important aspects. First, decision-makers and decision-making are heavily moved by uncertainty, particularly the avoidance of uncertainty in choice and policy making. Second, institutional change is facilitated by complicated mechanisms of learning, imitation, and peer pressure.

Hybrid forms of governance are a way to understand attempts by organisations and regulators to avoid uncertainty in their fundamental choices. Different institutional forces incentivise actors to model their actions according to their peers (DiMaggio and Powell 1983). The actual sources of these incentives may be perceived as 'best' practices, mimetic practices, legal rules and standards, professional and ethical codes, or other relevant value systems of society. However, the different methods of modelling actions in relation to others are far from clear and self-evident. On the contrary, they are excessively complicated and subject to contrasting interpretations of what is useful and feasible and what makes sense to organisations and policy makers (Noordegraaf and Abma 2003; Vakkuri 2010). Thus, the modelling process is driven by simplicity. Administrative pragmatism involves heuristics for avoiding complicated structures and for sticking to practices that already have a history of use, which is available and thus constitutes a system of prior experience. It makes sense not to consciously build unclear structures. However, it is obvious that the outcomes of institutional modelling do not equate with the perceived aims of imitation. The dissonance of imitation processes increases the likelihood for policy reforms to yield different outcomes from those that are used to model practices. Thus, rational intentions for imitating your peers may in fact result in, to a certain degree, dissimilar practices among actors. Even with the aim of imitating the best characteristics of market mechanisms, government activities do not become market-based action. These activities transform into something that is not markets. However, they are not purely public anymore. They are something in between.

An interesting underlying mechanism is the perception of the pure form of institutional action that decision-makers search for. With all its limitations and caveats of understanding, the black-and-white distinction between the public and private may serve as a reasonable point of reference, but not in the descriptive sense. Much of the discussion in this book has pointed out that in the 'real world' there are no pure forms of public or private systems and agencies. Instead, the distinction may work in a prescriptive sense. Perceived 'pure' forms of institutional action provide an important leverage point for muddling through (Lindblom 1959), modelling the world (Padgett and Powell 2012), dreaming of a (more) rational organisation (Brunsson 2006), or just plainly and simply surviving (North 1990). There may be several hidden rationalities in hybridisation that have evolved by default.

Hybrids as institutional solutions to governance problems

What kind of a solution does hybridity actually provide? The globalisation of trade and the economic growth of developing countries make it more difficult to see hybridity as a feature of industrialised countries alone. This book has illustrated this point through many examples. From the perspective of market-based societies in North America and Europe, the value of hybridity can be found in its ability to provide bottom-up integration with society as a whole by encouraging voluntary civic engagement in leisure, advocacy, and the production of services. Within developing countries, the lack of capital or functional markets implies that hybrid arrangements mixing public and private ownership, as well as control and institutional logics, could be the only viable option to organise any large-scale economic activity. Here, hybridity can be seen as a transitory phase of the eventual separation of the economy and government. Yet, there is a fair chance that some state-centric countries, such as Russia or China, use hybrids in a top-down fashion to integrate all levels of society and economic activity with the central influence of the government. In these settings, there is no need to see hybridity as a transitory phase. Instead, hybridity can be seen as a device to retain continuous top-down government control of market transactions.

In a more general sense, hybridity is connected to the nature of economic and social environments. Hybrids are reflections of their surrounding environments. Therefore, not all problems and ambiguities are necessarily the limitations of hybrids and hybridity; instead, they are more general problems of institutional environments. From the viewpoint of liberal market-based economies, it is easier to see hybrid activity as an extension of market activity with a social twist. When considering the highly coordinated market economies in Nordic countries, hybridity easily appears to be a government-driven system with a market twist. These ideas do not contradict the ambiguities related to hybrid activity, but they emphasise the different perspectives on hybridity in industrialised countries. If hybrid arrangements are the only option to organise large-scale economic activity in the developing world, hybridity is not an extension of the existing categories but instead an anchor point for organising economic structures and government activity in the future. This reflection lends a special perspective on the public and private spheres. Hybridity is not a question of the extension of business or government but instead a way of organising functional society in the first place. Therefore, in addition to our question of whether hybrids are monsters after all, we may ask how modern monsters might be turned into something more comprehensible, more governable, and perhaps even more beautiful.

REFERENCES

Aberbach, J., Putnam, R. and Rockman, B., 1981. *Bureaucrats and politicians in Western democracies.* Cambridge, MA; London: Harvard University Press.

Abrahamson, E., 1991. Managerial fads and fashions: The diffusion and rejection of innovations. *The Academy of Management Review*, **16**(3), pp. 586–612.

Adler, P. and Kwon, S., 2002. Social capital: Prospects for a new concept. *The Academy of Management Review*, **27**(1), pp. 17–40.

Alexius, S. and Cisneros Örnberg, J., 2015. Mission(s) impossible? Configuring values in the governance of state-owned enterprises. *Public Sector Management*, **28**(4), pp. 286–306.

Allen, D., 2012. *The institutional revolution: measurement and the economic emergence of the modern world.* Chicago: University of Chicago Press.

Audi, R., 2001. *The architecture of reason: the structure and substance of rationality.* New York; Oxford: Oxford University Press.

Badian, E., 1983. *Publicans and sinners: private enterprise in the service of the Roman republic, with a critical bibliography.* Ithaca: Cornell University Press.

Bain, J., 1968. *Industrial organization.* New York: Wiley.

Barney, J., 1991. Firm resources and sustained competitive advantage. *Journal of Management*, **17**(1), pp. 99–120.

Barney, J. and Hesterly, W., 1999. Organizational economies, understanding the relationship between organizations and economic analysis. In: S. Clegg and C. Hardy, eds, *Studying organization: theory and method.* London: Sage, pp. 109–141.

Barney, J., Wright, M. and Ketchen, D., 2001. The resource-based view of the firm: Ten years after 1991. *Journal of Management*, **27**(6), pp. 625–641.

Barrow, J., 1991. *Theories of everything: the quest for ultimate explanation.* Oxford; New York: Clarendon Press; Oxford University Press.

Barry, B., 1989. *A treatise on social justice.* London: Harvester-Wheatsheaf.

Bartlett, W., Propper, C., Wilson, D., Legrand, J. and May, M., eds, 1994. *Quasi-markets in the welfare state: the emerging findings.* Bristol: Saus.

Bartunek, J., 1984. Changing interpretive schemes and organizational restructuring: The example of a religious order. *Administrative Science Quarterly*, **29**(3), pp. 355–372.

Battershell, A., 1999. *The DOD C-17 versus the Boeing 777: a comparison of acquisition and development.* Washington, DC: National Defense University.

Battilana, J. and Lee, M., 2014. Advancing research on hybrid organizing – Insights from the study of social enterprises. *The Academy of Management Annals*, **8**(1), pp. 397–441.

Becker, G., 1993. *Human capital: a theoretical and empirical analysis, with special reference to education.* Chicago: The University of Chicago Press.

Behn, R., 2003. Why measure performance? Different purposes require different measures. *Public Administration Review*, **63**(5), pp. 586–606.

Berger, P. and Luckman, T., 1967. *The social construction of reality.* London: Penguin Books.

Bessant, J. and Tidd, J., 2011. *Innovation and entrepreneurship.* Chichester, West Sussex, UK: Wiley.

Bevan, G., Hood, C. and Dixon, R., 2006. What's measured is what matters: Targets and gaming in the English public health care system. *Public Administration*, **84**(3), pp. 517–538.

Billis, D., 2010. *Hybrid organizations and the third sector: challenges for practice, theory and policy.* Basingstoke, Hampshire, UK; New York: Palgrave Macmillan.

Bingham, C. and Eisenhardt, K., 2011. Rational heuristics: The 'simple rules' that strategists learn from process experience. *Strategic Management Journal*, **32**(13), pp. 1437–1464.

Blau, P., 1977. *Inequality and heterogeneity: a primitive theory of social structure.* New York: Free Press.

Bó, E.D., 2006. Regulatory capture: A review. *Oxford Review of Economic Policy*, **22**(2), pp. 203–225.

Boltanski, L., Chiapello, E. and Elliott, G., 2005. *The new spirit of capitalism.* London: New York: Verso.

Boltanski, L. and Thévenot, L., 1999. The sociology of critical capacity. *European Journal of Social Theory*, **2**(3), pp. 359–377.

Boltanski, L. and Thévenot, L., 2006. *On justification: economies of worth.* Princeton: Princeton University Press.

Borgatti, S. and Foster, P., 2003. The network paradigm in organizational research: A review and typology. *Journal of Management*, **29**(6), pp. 991–1013.

Borges, J., 1966. *Other inquisitions 1937–1952.* New York: Washington Square Press.

Bowker, G. and Star, S.L., 2000. *Sorting things out: classification and its consequences.* Cambridge, MA: Massachusetts Institute of Technology.

Boyne, G., 2002. Public and private management: What's the difference? *Journal of Management Studies*, **39**(1), pp. 97–122.

Boyne, G., 2003. Sources of public service improvement: A critical review and research agenda. *Journal of Public Administration Research and Theory*, **13**(3), pp. 367–394.

Bozeman, B., 1987. *All organizations are public: bridging public and private organizational theories.* San Francisco: Jossey-Bass.

Bozeman, B., 2013. What organization theorists and public policy researchers can learn from one another: Publicness theory as a case-in-point. *Organization Studies*, **34**(2), pp. 169–188.

Bozeman, B. and Moulton, S., 2011. Integrative publicness: A framework for public management strategy and performance. *Journal of Public Administration Research and Theory*, **21**(Supplement 3), pp. i363–i380.

Brandsma, G. and Schillemans, T., 2013. The accountability cube: Measuring accountability. *Journal of Public Administration Research and Theory*, **23**(4), pp. 953–975.

Bremmer, I., 2010. *The end of the free market: who wins the war between states and corporations?* New York: Portfolio.

Brunsson, N., 1989. *The organization of hypocrisy: talk, decisions, and actions in organizations.* Chichester; New York: Wiley.

Brunsson, N., 2006. *Mechanisms of hope: maintaining the dream of the rational organization.* Copenhagen: Copenhagen Business School Press.

Bruton, G.D., Peng, M., Ahlstrom, D., Stan, C. and Xu, K., 2015. State-owned enterprises around the world as hybrid organizations. *Academy of Management Perspectives*, **29**(1), pp. 92–114.

Bryson, J., 1995. *Strategic planning for public and nonprofit organizations: a guide to strengthening and sustaining organizational achievement*. San Francisco: Jossey-Bass Publishers.

Buchanan, J., 1965. An economic theory of clubs. *Economica*, **32**(125), pp. 1–14.

Burt, R., 1992. *Structural holes: the social structure of competition*. Cambridge, MA: Harvard University Press.

Caldwell, B., 1984. *Beyond positivism: economic methodology in the twentieth century*. London; Boston: G. Allen & Unwin.

Calhoun, C., 1998. The public good as a social and cultural project. In: W. Powell and E. Clemens, eds, *Private action and the public good*. New Haven: Yale University Press, pp. 20–35.

Callinicos, A., 2006. *The resources of critique*. Cambridge; Malden, MA: Polity.

Cameron, K., 1984. The effectiveness of ineffectiveness. *Research in Organizational Behavior*, **6**, pp. 235–285.

Cameron, K., 1986. Effectiveness as paradox: Consensus and conflict in conceptions of organizational effectiveness. *Management Science*, **32**(5), pp. 539–553.

Castellacci, F. and Natera, J.M., 2013. The dynamics of national innovation systems: A panel cointegration analysis of the coevolution between innovative capability and absorptive capacity. *Research Policy*, **42**(3), pp. 579–594.

Castells, M., 1996. *The rise of the network society*. Malden, MA: Blackwell Publishers.

Cento, A., 2009. *The airline industry: challenges in the 21st century*. Heidelberg: Physica-Verlag.

Chaffee, E., 1985. Three models of strategy. *The Academy of Management Review*, **10**(1), pp. 89–98.

Chaiklin, S. and Lave, J., 1993. *Understanding practice: perspectives on activity and context*. Cambridge; New York: Cambridge University Press.

Chan, D., 2000. The development of the airline industry from 1978 to 1998 – A strategic global overview. *Journal of Management Development*, **19**(6), pp. 489–514.

Charnes, A., Cooper, W. and Lewin, A., 1994. *Data envelopment analysis: theory, methodology and applications*. Boston: Kluwer.

Christensen, T. and Lægreid, P., 2007. The whole-of-government approach to public sector reform. *Public Administration Review*, **67**(6), pp. 1059–1066.

Clark, B., 1983. *The higher education system: academic organization in cross-national perspective*. Berkeley: University of California Press.

Clegg, S., Courpasson, D. and Phillips, N., 2006. *Power and organizations*. London: Sage.

Cochran, C., 1974. Political science and 'the public interest'. *The Journal of Politics*, **36**(2), pp. 327–355.

Coleman, J., 1988. *Social capital in the creation of human capital*. Chicago: University of Chicago Press.

Cooke, P., 2008. Cleantech and an analysis of the platform nature of life sciences: Further reflections upon platform policies. *European Planning Studies*, **16**(3), pp. 375–393.

Cooper, R. and Kaplan, R., 1991. *Design of cost management systems*. Englewood Cliffs: Prentice-Hall.

Crane, D., 1972. *Invisible colleges; diffusion of knowledge in scientific communities*. Chicago: University of Chicago Press.

Das, T. and Teng, B., 2000. A resource-based theory of strategic alliances. *Journal of Management*, **26**(1), pp. 31–61.

Davies, H., Nutley, S. and Smith, P., 1999. What works? The role of evidence in public sector policy and practice. *Public Money & Management*, **19**(1), pp. 3–5.

Davis, J., Schoorman, F. and Donaldson, L., 1997. Toward a stewardship theory of management. *The Academy of Management Review*, **22**(1), pp. 20–47.

Davis, P. and Hersh, R., 1981. *The mathematical experience.* Boston: Birkhäuser.

De Bruijn, J., 2002. *Managing performance in the public sector.* London: Routledge.

Defourny, J. and Nyssens, M., 2008. *Social enterprise in Europe: recent trends and developments.* Bingley: Emerald Group Publishing.

Defourny, J. and Nyssens, M., 2010. Conceptions of social enterprise and social entrepreneurship in Europe and the United States: Convergences and divergences. *Journal of Social Entrepreneurship*, **1**(1), pp. 32–53.

Defourny, J. and Nyssens, M., 2014. The EMES approach of social enterprise in a comparative perspective. In: J. Defourny, L. Hulgård and V. Pestoff, eds, *Social enterprise and the third sector: changing European landscapes in a comparative perspective.* London: Routledge, pp. 42–65.

Denhardt, J. and Denhardt, R., 2007. *The new public service: serving, not steering.* Armonk: M.E. Sharpe.

Dewey, J., 1939. *Freedom and culture.* New York: G.P. Putnam's Sons.

Dimaggio, P. and Powell, W., 1983. The iron cage revisited: Institutional isomorphism and collective rationality in organizational fields. *American Sociological Review*, **48**(2), pp. 147–160.

Dimaggio, P. and Powell, W., 1991. The iron cage revisited: institutional isomorphism and collective rationality in organization fields. In: W. Powell and P. Dimaggio, eds, *The new institutionalism in organizational analysis.* Chicago: The University of Chicago Press, pp. 63–82.

Donaldson, T. and Preston, L., 1995. *The stakeholder theory of the corporation: concepts, evidence, and implications.* Emmitsburg: National Emergency Training Center.

Dopfer, K., 2013. *Evolutionary economics.* 1308. Jena: Max-Planck-Institut für Ökonomik.

Dopfer, K., Foster, J. and Potts, J., 2004. Micro-meso-macro. *Journal of Evolutionary Economics*, **14**(3), pp. 263–279.

Dowdeswell, B. and Vauramo, E., 2009. Coxa hospital, Tampere, Finland. In: B. Rechel, J. Erskine, B. Dowdeswell, S. Wright and M. Mckee, eds, *Capital investment for health: case studies from Europe.* Observatory Studies Series, No. 18 edn. Copenhagen: World Health Organization, European Observatory on Health Systems and Policies, pp. 27–40.

Dunleavy, P., 1991. *Democracy, bureaucracy and public choice: economic explanations in political science.* New York; London: Harvester.

Dyer, J. and Singh, H., 1998. The relational view: Cooperative strategy and sources of interorganizational competitive advantage. *The Academy of Management Review*, **23**(4), pp. 660–679.

Ebrahim, A., Battilana, J. and Mair, J., 2014. The governance of social enterprises: Mission drift and accountability challenges in hybrid organizations. *Research in Organizational Behavior*, **34**, pp. 81–100.

Einhorn, H., 1982. Learning from experience and suboptimal rules in decision-making. In: D. Kahneman, P. Slovic and A. Tversky, eds, *Judgment under uncertainty: heuristics and biases.* Cambridge; New York: Cambridge University Press, pp. 268–284.

Eisenhardt, K., 1989. Agency theory: An assessment and review. *Academy of Management Review*, **14**(1), pp. 57–74.

Ellison, B., 2006. Bureaucratic politics as agency competition: A comparative perspective. *International Journal of Public Administration*, **29**(13), pp. 1259–1283.

Emery, F. and Trist, E., 1965. The causal texture of organizational environments. *Human Relations*, **18**(1), pp. 21–32.

Esping-Andersen, G., 1990. *The three worlds of welfare capitalism.* Princeton: Princeton University Press.

Etzioni, A., 1986. Mixed scanning revisited. *Public Administration Review*, **46**(1), pp. 8–14.

References

European Commission, 2014. *State aid for airline restructuring: Does it give you wings?* Issue 10. Competition Directorate – General of the European Commission.

Fernandez, R. and Gould, R., 1994. A dilemma of state power: Brokerage and influence in the national health policy domain. *American Journal of Sociology*, **99**(6), pp. 1455–1491.

Fountain, J., 2001. Paradoxes of public sector customer service. *Governance*, **14**(1), pp. 55–73.

Freeland, R., 1996. The myth of the M-form? Governance, consent, and organizational change. *American Journal of Sociology*, **102**(2), pp. 483–526.

Freeman, C., 1987. *Technology, policy, and economic performance: lessons from Japan*. London; New York: Pinter Publishers.

Freeman, C., 1995. The national system of innovation in historical perspective. *Cambridge Journal of Economics*, **19**(1), pp. 5–24.

Friedman, M., 1997. *Capitalism and freedom*. Washington, DC: Heritage Foundation.

Giddens, A., 1979. *Central problems in social theory: action, structure, and contradiction in social analysis*. Berkeley: University of California Press.

Gigerenzer, G., 2000. *Adaptive thinking: rationality in the real world*. New York; Oxford: Oxford University Press.

Godin, B., 2009. National innovation system. *Science, Technology & Human Values*, **34**(4), pp. 476–501.

Golany, B. and Roll, Y., 1989. An application procedure for DEA. *Omega*, **17**(3), pp. 237–250.

Goold, M., Pettifer, D. and Young, D., 2001. Redesigning the corporate centre. *European Management Journal*, **19**(1), pp. 83–91.

Gortner, H., Mahler, J. and Nicholson, J.B., 1997. *Organization theory: a public perspective*. Fort Worth: Harcourt Brace College.

Grandori, A. and Soda, G., 1995. Inter-firm networks: Antecedents, mechanisms and forms. *Organization Studies*, **16**(2), pp. 183–214.

Granovetter, M., 1985. Economic action and social structure: The problem of embeddedness. *American Journal of Sociology*, **91**(3), pp. 481–510.

Grant, R., 1991. *Contemporary strategy analysis: concepts, techniques, applications*. Cambridge, MA: Blackwell.

Greve, C. and Hodge, G., 2007. *The challenge of public-private partnerships: learning from international experience*. Cheltenham: Edward Elgar.

Griliches, Z., 1994. Productivity, R&D, and the date constraint. *American Economic Review*, **84**(1), pp. 1–23.

Grossi, G., Hansen, M.B., Johanson, J., Vakkuri, J. and Moon, M., 2016. Introduction: Comparative performance management and accountability in the age of austerity. *Public Performance & Management Review*, **39**(3), pp. 499–505.

Grossi, G., Reichard, C., Thomasson, A. and Vakkuri, J., Forthcoming. Performance measurement of hybrid organizations. *Public Money & Management*.

Guan, J. and Chen, K., 2012. Modeling the relative efficiency of national innovation systems. *Research Policy*, **41**(1), pp. 102–115.

Guriev, S., 2010. Business groups in Russia. In: A. Colpan, H. Takashi and J. Lincoln, eds, *The Oxford handbook of business groups*. New York: Oxford University Press, pp. 526–546.

Hall, P. and Soskice, D., 2001. *Varieties of capitalism: the institutional foundations of comparative advantage*. Oxford; New York: Oxford University Press.

Hampson, N. and Shamsad, A., 2013. *Aviation finance: Fasten your seatbelts*. London: Price Waterhouse Cooper's.

Hanlon, J., 2007. *Global airlines: competition in a transnational industry*. Oxford: Elsevier.

Hansmann, H., 1996. *The ownership of enterprise*. Cambridge, MA: Belknap Press of Harvard University Press.

Hared, B., Abdullah, Z. and Huque, S., 2013. Management control systems: A review of literature and a theoretical framework for future researches. *European Journal of Business Management* **5**(26), pp. 1–14.

Harlow, C., 2006. Global administrative law: The quest for principles and values. *European Journal of International Law*, **17**(1), pp. 187–214.

Harris, G., 2016. Transforming health through multisector partnerships. *North Carolina Medical Journal*, **77**(4), pp. 286–289.

Hey, J., 1982. Search for rules for search. *Journal of Economic Behavior and Organization*, **3**(1), pp. 65–81.

Heywood, A., 2002. *Politics*. New York: Palgrave.

Hjern, B. and Porter, D., 1981. Implementation structures: A new unit of administrative analysis. *Organization Studies*, **2**(3), pp. 211–227.

Hodge, G. and Greve, C., 2005. *The challenge of public private partnerships: learning from international experience*. Cheltenham: E. Elgar.

Hodge, G. and Greve, C., 2009. Public-private partnerships: PPPs: The passage of time permits a sober reflection. *Economic Affairs*, **29**(1), pp. 33–39.

Hodges, R., 2012. Joined up government and the challenges to accounting and accountability researchers. *Financial Accountability & Management*, **28**(1), pp. 26–51.

Hogwood, B. and Gunn, L., 1984. *Policy analysis for the real world*. Oxford; New York: Oxford University Press.

Hood, C., 1991. A public management for all seasons? *Public Administration*, **69**(1), pp. 3–19.

Hood, C., 1995. The "new public management" in the 1980s: Variations on a theme. *Accounting, Organizations and Society Accounting, Organizations and Society*, **20**(2–3), pp. 93–109.

Hood, C., 2011. *The blame game: spin, bureaucracy, and self-preservation in government*. Princeton: Princeton University Press.

Hood, C. and Dixon, R., 2015. *A government that worked better and cost less?: evaluating three decades of reform and change in UK central government*. Oxford: Oxford University Press.

Hopwood, A., 1996a. Looking across rather than up and down: On the need to explore the lateral processing of information. *Accounting, Organizations and Society*, **21**(6), pp. 589–590.

Hopwood, A., 1996b. Editorial. *Accounting, Organizations and Society Accounting, Organizations and Society*, **21**(7–8), pp. 627–627.

Horwitz, A., 1990. *The logic of social control*. New York: Plenum Press.

Hua, J., Miesing, P. and Li, M., 2006. An empirical taxonomy of SOE governance in transitional China. *Journal of Management & Governance*, **10**(4), pp. 401–433.

Hudson, J. and Jones, P., 2005. "Public goods": An exercise in calibration. *Public Choice*, **124**(3–4), pp. 267–282.

IATA, 2011. *Vision 2050*. Singapore: IATA.

Ijiri, Y., 1967. *The foundations of accounting measurement; a mathematical, economic, and behavioral inquiry*. Englewood Cliffs: Prentice-Hall.

Ijiri, Y., 1975. *Theory of accounting measurement*. Sarasota: American Accounting Association.

Jacobs, J., 1992. *Systems of survival: a dialogue on the moral foundations of commerce and politics*. New York: Random House.

Jagd, S., 2007. Economics of convention and new economic sociology: Mutual inspiration and dialogue. *Current Sociology*, **55**(1), pp. 75–91.

Johanson, J., 2009. Strategy formation in public agencies. *Public Administration*, **87**(4), pp. 872–891.

Johanson, J., 2014. Strategic governance in public agencies. In: P. Joyce, J. Bryson and M. Holzer, eds, *Developments in strategic and public management: studies in the US and Europe*. Basingstoke, Hampshire, UK: Palgrave Macmillan, pp. 268–284.

Johnson, H. and Kaplan, R., 1987. *Relevance lost: the rise and fall of management accounting.* Boston: Harvard Business School Press.

Jordana, J. and Levi-Faur, D., 2004. *The politics of regulation: institutions and regulatory reforms for the age of governance.* Cheltenham, UK; Northampton: E. Elgar.

Jorgensen, T. and Bozeman, B., 2007. Public values: An inventory. *Administration & Society*, **39**(3), pp. 354–381.

Joyce, P., 1999. *Strategic management for the public services.* Buckingham; Philadelphia: Open University Press.

Kahneman, D., 2003. *Choices, values, and frames.* New York: Russell Sage Foundation.

Kahneman, D., 2012. *Thinking, fast and slow.* London: Penguin Books.

Kale, P., Singh, H. and Perlmutter, H., 2000. Learning and protection of proprietary assets in strategic alliances: Building relational capital. *Strategic Management Journal*, **21**(3), pp. 217–237.

Kaplan, R. and Norton, D., 1996. *The balanced scorecard: translating strategy into action.* Boston: Harvard Business Press.

Kaufmann, F., Majone, G. and Ostrom, V., 1986. *Guidance, control, and evaluation in the public sector: the Bielefeld interdisciplinary project.* Berlin; New York: W. de Gruyter.

Kelly, J., 2005. The dilemma of the unsatisfied customer in a market model of public administration. *Public Administration Review*, **65**(1), pp. 76–84.

Kelly, J. and Swindell, D., 2002. A multiple-indicator approach to municipal service evaluation: Correlating performance measurement and citizen satisfaction across jurisdictions. *Public Administration Review*, **62**(5), pp. 610–621.

Kendrick, J., 1996. *The new system of national accounts.* Boston: Kluwer Academic Publishers.

Kerlin, J., 2006. Social enterprise in the United States and Europe: Understanding and learning from the differences. *Voluntas*, **17**(3), pp. 247–263.

Kersbergen, K.V. and Waarden, F.V., 2004. "Governance" as a bridge between disciplines: Cross-disciplinary inspiration regarding shifts in governance and problems of governability, accountability and legitimacy. *European Journal of Political Research*, **43**(2), pp. 143–171.

Kickert, W., 2001. *Public management and administrative reform in Western Europe.* Cheltenham: Elgar.

King, L., 2007. Central European capitalism in comparative perspective. In: B. Hancké, M. Rhodes and M. Thatcher, eds, *Beyond varieties of capitalism: conflict, contradictions, and complementarities in the European economy.* Oxford: University Press Oxford, pp. 307–327.

Kissick, W.L., 1994. *Medicine's dilemmas: infinite needs versus finite resources.* New Haven, CT: Yale University Press.

Knorr-Cetina, K., 1999. *Epistemic cultures: how the sciences make knowledge.* Cambridge, MA: Harvard University Press.

Koopmans, T., 1957. *Three essays on the state of economic science.* New York: McGraw-Hill.

Koopmans, T., 1977. Concepts of optimality and their uses. *The American Economic Review*, **67**(3), pp. 261–274.

Koppell, J., 2005. Pathologies of accountability: ICANN and the challenge of "multiple accountabilities disorder". *Public Administration Review*, **65**(1), pp. 94–108.

Koppell, J., 2006. *The politics of quasi-government: hybrid organizations and the dynamics of bureaucratic control.* Cambridge: Cambridge University Press.

Kork, A. and Vakkuri, J., 2016. Improving access and managing healthcare demand with walk-in clinic: Convenient, but at what cost? *International Journal of Public Sector Management*, **29**(2), pp. 148–163.

Koteen, J., 1997. *Strategic management in public and nonprofit organizations: managing public concerns in an era of limits.* Westport: Praeger.

Koza, M., 1988. Regulation and organization: Environmental niche structure and administrative organization. *Research in the Sociology of Organizations*, **6**, pp. 183–201.

Krackhardt, D., 1999. The ties that torture: Simmelian tie analysis in organizations. *Research in the Sociology of Organizations*, **16**(1), pp. 183–210.

Kreps, T. and Monin, B., 2011. "Doing well by doing good"? Ambivalent moral framing in organizations. *Research in Organizational Behavior Research in Organizational Behavior*, **31**(2), pp. 99–123.

Kurunmäki, L. and Miller, P., 2006. Modernising government: The calculating self, hybridisation and performance measurement. *Financial Accountability & Management*, **22**(1), pp. 87–106.

Lancaster, K., 1979. *Variety, equity, and efficiency: product variety in an industrial society*. New York: Columbia University Press.

Lane, J., 1993. *The public sector: concepts, models and approaches*. London: Sage.

Lapsley, I., 1988. Research in public sector accounting: An appraisal. *Accounting, Auditing & Accountability Journal*, **1**(1), pp. 21–33.

Lapsley, I. and Mitchell, F., 1996. *Accounting and performance measurement: issues in the private and public sectors*. London: Paul Chapman Pub.

Larson, A., 1992. Network dyads in entrepreneurial settings: A study of the governance of exchange relationships. *Administrative Science Quarterly*, **37**(1), pp. 76–104.

Lave, J., 1988. *Cognition in practice: mind, mathematics, and culture in everyday life*. Cambridge; New York: Cambridge University Press.

Le Grand, J. and Bartlett, W., 1993. *Quasi-markets and social policy*. Houndmills, Basingstoke, Hampshire, UK: Macmillan Press.

Lebas, M. and Euske, K., 2007. A conceptual and operational delineation of performance. In: A. Neely, ed, *Business performance measurement – unifying theory and integrating practice*. Cambridge: Cambridge University Press, pp. 125–139.

Lee, K. and Raadschelders, J., 2008. Political-administrative relations: Impact of and puzzles in Aberbach, Putnam, and Rockman, 1981. *Governance*, **21**(3), pp. 419–438.

Leigh Star, S. and Griesemer, J., 1989. Institutional ecology, 'translations' and boundary objects: Amateurs and professionals in Berkeley's Museum of Vertebrate Zoology, 1907–39. *Social Studies of Science*, **19**(3), pp. 387–420.

Lincoln, J. and Gerlach, M., 2004. *Japan's network economy: a structure, persistence, and change*. Cambridge; New York: Cambridge University Press.

Lindblom, C., 1959. The science of "muddling through". *Public Administration Review*, **19**, pp. 79–88.

Lindblom, C., 1977. *Politics and markets: the world's political economic systems*. New York: Basic Books.

Lindblom, C., 1979. Still muddling, not yet through. *Public Administration Review*, **39**(6), pp. 517–526.

Lipsky, M., 1971. Street-level bureaucracy and the analysis of urban reform. *Urban Affairs Review Urban Affairs Review*, **6**(4), pp. 391–409.

Llewellyn, S. and Northcott, D., 2005. The average hospital. *Accounting, Organizations and Society*, **30**(6), pp. 555–583.

Lockett, A. and Thompson, S., 2004. Edith Penrose's contributions to the resource-based view: An alternative perspective. *Journal of Management Studies*, **41**(1), pp. 193–203.

Luhmann, N., 1995. *Social systems*. Stanford: Stanford University Press.

Lundvall, B., 1992. *National systems of innovation: towards a theory of innovation and interactive learning*. London; New York: Pinter Publishers, St. Martin's Press.

Mahoney, J., 2005. *Economic foundations of strategy*. Thousand Oaks: Sage.

Mahoney, J., Mcgahan, A. and Pitelis, C., 2009. The interdependence of private and public interests. *Organization Science*, **20**(6), pp. 1034–1052.

Mahoney, J. and Pandian, J., 1992. The resource-based view within the conversation of strategic management. *Strategic Management Journal*, **13**(5), pp. 363–380.

Malmendier, U., 2009. Law and finance "at the origin". *Journal of Economic Literature*, **47**(4), pp. 1076–1108.

Mansbridge, J., 1998. Starting with nothing: on the impossibility of grounding norms solely in self-interest. In: A. Ben-Ner and L. Putterman, eds, *Economics, values, and organization*. Cambridge: Cambridge University Press, pp. 151–168.

March, J., 1978. Bounded rationality, ambiguity, and the engineering of choice. *The Bell Journal of Economics*, **9**, pp. 587–608.

March, J., 1987. Ambiguity and accounting: The elusive link between information and decision making. *Accounting, Organizations and Society*, **12**(2), pp. 153–168.

March, J., 1988a. *Decisions and organizations*. New York: Blackwell.

March, J., 1988b. The technology of foolishness. In: J. March, ed, *Decisions and organizations*. New York: Blackwell, pp. 253–265.

March, J. and Heath, C., 1994. *A primer on decision making: how decisions happen*. New York: Free Press.

March, J. and Olsen, J., 1999. *The institutional dynamics of international orders*. Oslo: Arena.

March, J., Schulz, M. and Zhou, X., 2000. *The dynamics of rules: change in written organizational codes*. Stanford: Stanford University Press.

March, J. and Sutton, R., 1997. Organizational performance as a dependent variable. *Organization Science*, **8**(6), pp. 698–706.

Margolis, J., 1955. A comment on the pure theory of public expenditure. *The Review of Economics and Statistics*, **37**(4), pp. 347–349.

Marquand, D., 2004. *Decline of the public: the hollowing-out of citizenship*. Cambridge; Malden, MA: Polity Press.

Mayston, D., 1993. Principals, agents and the economics of accountability in the new public sector. *Accounting, Auditing & Accountability Journal*, **6**(3), 68–96.

McCloskey, D., 1983. The rhetoric of economics. *Journal of Economic Literature*, **21**(2), pp. 481–517.

Megginson, W. and Netter, J., 2001. From state to market: A survey of empirical studies on privatization. *Journal of Economic Literature*, **39**(2), pp. 321–389.

Ménard, C., 2004. The economics of hybrid organizations. *Journal of Institutional and Theoretical Economics/Zeitschrift für die gesamte Staatswissenschaft*, **160**(3), pp. 345–376.

Merton, R., 1976. *Sociological ambivalence and other essays*. New York: Free Press.

Metcalfe, J., 1995. The design of order: Notes on evolutionary principles and the dynamics of innovation. *Revue économique*, **46**(6), pp. 1561–1583.

Meyer, J. and Rowan, B., 1977. Institutionalized organizations: Formal structure as myth and ceremony. *American Journal of Sociology*, **83**(2), pp. 340–363.

Meyer, M., 2002. *Rethinking performance measurement: beyond the balanced scorecard*. Cambridge: Cambridge University Press.

Meyer, M., 2007. Finding performance: the new discipline in management. In: A. Neely, ed, *Business performance measurement: unifying theory and integrating practice*. Cambridge: Cambridge University Press, pp. 113–124.

Miller, P., Kurunmäki, L. and O'Leary, T., 2008. Accounting, hybrids and the management of risk. *Accounting, Organizations and Society*, **33**(7–8), pp. 942–967.

Miller, P. and Rose, N., 2008. *Governing the present: administering economic, social and personal life*. Cambridge: Polity.

Mintzberg, H., 1994. *The rise and fall of strategic planning: reconceiving roles for planning, plans, planners*. New York; Toronto: Free Press; Maxwell Macmillan Canada.

Mintzberg, H., Ahlstrand, B. and Lampel, J., 1998. *Strategy safari: a guided tour through the wilds of strategic management*. New York: Free Press.

Mintzberg, H. and Waters, J., 1985. Of strategies, deliberate and emergent. *Strategic Management Journal*, **6**(3), pp. 257–272.

Modell, S., 2001. Performance measurement and institutional processes: A study of managerial responses to public sector reform. *Management Accounting Research*, **12**(4), pp. 437–464.

Moore, M., 1995. *Creating public value: strategic management in government*. Cambridge, MA: Harvard University Press.

Moore, M., 2013. *Recognizing public value*. Cambridge, MA: Harvard University Press.

Moore, M. and Hartley, J., 2008. Innovations in governance. *Public Management Review*, **10**(1), pp. 3–20.

Moran, M., 2002. Review article: Understanding the regulatory state. *British Journal of Political Science*, **32**(02), pp. 391–413.

Morrell, K., 2009. Governance and the public good. *Public Administration*, **87**(3), pp. 538–556.

Morrell, K. and Harrington-Buhay, N., 2012. What is governance in the 'public interest'? The case of the 1995 property forum in post-conflict Nicaragua. *Public Administration*, **90**(2), pp. 412–428.

Mouwen, K., 2000. Strategy, structure and culture of the hybrid university: Towards the university of the 21st century. *Tertiary Education and Management*, **6**(1), pp. 47–56.

Muller, P., 2003. A history of national accounting. *Courrier de statistiques, English Series*, (9), pp. 35–50.

Musgrave, R., 1959. *The theory of public finance; a study in public economy*. New York: McGraw-Hill.

Nahapiet, J. and Ghoshal, S., 1998. Social capital, intellectual capital, and the organizational advantage. *The Academy of Management Review*, **23**(2), pp. 242–266.

Neave, G., 2002. *Research and research-training systems: towards a typology*. Paris: UNESCO.

Neely, A., 2007. *Business performance measurement: unifying theories and integrating practice*. Cambridge; New York: Cambridge University Press.

Nelson, R., 1992. National innovation systems: A retrospective on a study. *Industrial and Corporate Change*, **1**(2), pp. 347–374.

Nelson, R., 1993. *National innovation systems: a comparative analysis*. New York: Oxford University Press.

Nelson, R., 2005. *The limits of market organization*. New York: Russell Sage foundation.

Nelson, R. and Winter, S., 2002. Evolutionary theorizing in economics. *The Journal of Economic Perspectives*, **16**(02), pp. 23–46.

Niskanen, W., 1971. *Bureaucracy and representative government*. Chicago: Aldine, Atherton.

Nonaka, I. and Takeuchi, H., 1995. *The knowledge-creating company: how Japanese companies create the dynamics of innovation*. New York: Oxford University Press.

Noordegraaf, M., 2008. Meanings of measurement: The real story behind the Rotterdam safety index. *Public Management Review*, **10**(2), pp. 221–239.

Noordegraaf, M. and Abma, T., 2003. Management by measurement? Public management practices amidst ambiguity. *Public Administration*, **81**(4), pp. 853–871.

Norreklit, H., Norreklit, L. and Melander, P., 2006. US 'fair contract' based performance management models in a Danish environment. *Financial Accountability and Management*, **22**(3), pp. 213–233.

North, D., 1990. *Institutions, institutional change, and economic performance*. Cambridge; New York: Cambridge University Press.

Nutt, P. and Backoff, R., 1992. *Strategic management of public and third sector organizations: a handbook for leaders*. San Francisco: Jossey-Bass Publishers.

Oates, W., 2005. Toward a second-generation theory of fiscal federalism. *International Tax and Public Finance*, **12**(4), pp. 349–373.

OECD, 1997. *National innovation systems*. Paris: OECD Publishing.

OECD, 2001. *Financial management and control of public agencies*. Paris: OECD Publishing.

OECD, 2014. *Air service agreement liberalisation and airline alliances*. Paris: International Transport Forum.

OECD, 2015a. *Health at a glance 2015: OECD indicators*. Paris: OECD Publishing.

OECD, 2015b. *OECD guidelines on corporate governance of state-owned enterprises*. Paris: OECD Publishing.

Okhmatovskiy, I., 2010. Performance implications of ties to the government and SOEs: A political embeddedness perspective. *Journal of Management Studies*, **47**(6), pp. 1020–1047.

Orlikowski, W., 1992. The duality of technology: Rethinking the concept of technology in organizations. *Organization Science*, **3**(3), pp. 398–427.

Orlikowski, W., 2000. Using technology and constituting structures: A practice lens for studying technology in organizations. *Organization Science*, **11**(4), pp. 404–428.

Orlikowski, W., 2002. Knowing in practice: Enacting a collective capability in distributed organizing. *Organization Science*, **13**(3), pp. 249–273.

O'Rourke, A., 2009. *The emergence of cleantech*. New Haven: Yale University.

Ostrom, E., 1990. *Governing the commons: the evolution of institutions for collective action*. New York: Cambridge University Press.

Ostrom, E., 2010. Beyond markets and states: Polycentric governance of complex economic systems. *Transnational Corporations Review*, **2**(2), pp. 1–12.

Otley, D., 2007. Accounting performance measurement: a review of its purposes and practices. In: A. Neely, ed, *Business performance measurement: unifying theory and integrating practice*. Cambridge: Cambridge University Press, pp. 11–35.

Ouchi, W., 1979. A conceptual framework for the design of organizational control mechanisms. *Management Science*, **25**(9), pp. 833–848.

Pache, A. and Santos, F., 2013. Inside the hybrid organization: Selective coupling as a response to competing institutional logics. *Academy of Management Journal*, **56**(4), pp. 972–1001.

Padgett, J. and Powell, W., 2012. *Emergence of organizations and markets*. Princeton: Princeton University Press.

Panzar, J. and Willig, R., 1981. *Economies of scope*. Princeton: Woodrow Wilson School of Public and International Affairs, Princeton University.

Patel, P. and Pavitt, K., 1994. The nature and economic importance of national innovations systems. *STI Review*, (14), pp. 9–32.

Penrose, E.T., 1952. Biological analogies in the theory of the firm. *The American Economic Review*, **42**(5), pp. 804–819.

Penrose, E.T., 1960. The growth of the firm a case study; The Hercules powder company. *Business History Review*, **34**(1), pp. 1–23.

Perry, J. and Rainey, H., 1988. The public-private distinction in organization theory: A critique and research strategy. *The Academy of Management Review*, **13**(2), pp. 182–201.

Pettigrew, A., 1992. *Fundamental themes in strategy process research*. Chichester; New York: Wiley.

Petty, R. and Guthrie, J., 2000. Intellectual capital literature review measurement, reporting and management. *Journal of Intellectual Capital*, **1**(2), pp. 155–176.

Pierson, P., 2000. Increasing returns, path dependence, and the study of politics. *American Political Science Review*, **94**, pp. 251–268.

Poister, T., 2003. *Measuring performance in public and nonprofit organizations*. San Francisco: Jossey-Bass.

Poister, T.H., Pitts, D.W. and Edwards, L.H., 2010. Strategic management research in the public sector: A review, synthesis, and future directions. *American Review of Public Administration*, **40**(5), pp. 522–545.

Polanyi, K., 1944. *The great transformation*. Boston: Beacon Press.

Pollitt, C., 1986. Beyond the managerial model: The case for broadening performance assessment in government and the public services. *Financial Accountability and Management*, **2**(3), pp. 155–170.

Pollitt, C., 2001. Clarifying convergence. Striking similarities and durable differences in public management reform. *Public Management Review*, **3**(4), pp. 471–492.

Pollitt, C. and Hupe, P., 2011. The role of magic concepts. *Public Management Review*, **13**(5), pp. 641–658.

Porter, M., 1980. *Competitive strategy: techniques for analyzing industries and competitors*. New York: Free Press.

Porter, M., 1990. *The competitive advantage of nations*. New York: Free Press.

Porter, T., 1995. *Trust in numbers: the pursuit of objectivity in science and public life*. Princeton: Princeton University Press.

Porter, T., 2008. Locating the domain of calculation. *Journal of Cultural Economy*, **1**(1), pp. 39–50.

Porter, T.M., 2006. Speaking precision to power: The modern political role of social science. *Social Research: An International Quarterly*, **73**(4), pp. 1273–1294.

Powell, W., 1987. *The nonprofit sector: a research handbook*. New Haven: Yale University Press.

Powell, W., 1990. Neither market nor hierarchy. In: B. Staw and L. Cummings, eds, *Research in organizational behavior 12*. Greenwich: JAI Press, pp. 295–336.

Powell, W. and Dimaggio, P., 1991. *The new institutionalism in organizational analysis*. Chicago: University of Chicago Press.

Powell, W., Koput, K. and Smith-Doerr, L., 1996. Interorganizational collaboration and the locus of innovation: Networks of learning in biotechnology. *Administrative Science Quarterly*, **41**(1), pp. 116–145.

Powell, W. and Owen-Smith, J., 1998. Universities as creators and retailers of intellectual property: life-sciences research and commercial development. In: B. Weisbrod, ed, *To profit or not to profit: the commercial transformation of the nonprofit sector*. Cambridge: Cambridge University Press, pp. 168–185.

Powell, W. and Sandholtz, K., 2012. Amphibious entrepreneurs and the emergence of organizational forms. *Strategic Entrepreneurship Journal*, **6**(2), pp. 94–115.

Power, M., 1997. *The audit society: rituals of verification*. Oxford; New York: Oxford University Press.

Power, M., 2000. The audit society – Second thoughts. *International Journal of Auditing International Journal of Auditing*, **4**(1), pp. 111–119.

Prahalad, C. and Hamel, G., 1990. *The core competence of corporation*. Canada: Harvard Business School Reprint.

Prokop, D., 2014. Government regulation of international air transportation. In: J. Peoples, ed, *The economics of international airline transport*. Bingley, UK: Emerald, pp. 45–60.

Provan, K.G. and Kenis, P., 2008. Modes of network governance: Structure, management, and effectiveness. *Journal of Public Administration Research and Theory*, **18**(2), pp. 229–252.

Putnam, R., 2000. *Bowling alone: the collapse and revival of American community*. New York: Simon & Schuster.

Putnam, R., Leonardi, R. and Nanetti, R., 1993. *Making democracy work: civic traditions in modern Italy*. Princeton: Princeton University Press.

References

Rabin, J., Miller, G. and Hildreth, W., 2000. *Handbook of strategic management.* New York: M. Dekker.

Radner, R. and Rothschild, M., 1975. On the allocation of effort. *Journal of Economic Theory*, 10(3), pp. 358–376.

Ranga, M. and Etzkowitz, H., 2013. Triple helix systems: An analytical framework for innovation policy and practice in the knowledge society. *Industry and Higher Education*, 27(4), pp. 237–262.

Ranson, S., Hinings, B. and Greenwood, R., 1980. The structuring of organizational structures. *Administrative Science Quarterly*, 25(1), pp. 1–17.

Reay, T. and Hinings, C., 2009. Managing the rivalry of competing institutional logics. *Organization Studies*, 30(6), pp. 629–652.

Rich, P., 1992. The organizational taxonomy: Definition and design. *Academy of Management Review*, 17(4), pp. 758–781.

Richard, P., Devinney, T., Yip, G. and Johnson, G., 2009. Measuring organizational performance: Towards methodological best practice. *Journal of Management*, 35(3), pp. 718–804.

Richards, J., 2001. Institutions for flying: How states built a market in international aviation services. *International Organization*, 55(4), pp. 993–1017.

Ritzer, G., 1993. *The McDonaldization of society: an investigation into the changing character of contemporary social life.* Newbury Park: Pine Forge Press.

Roslender, R., Marks, A. and Stevenson, J., 2015. Damned if you do, damned if you don't: Conflicting perspectives on the virtues of accounting for people. *Critical Perspectives on Accounting*, 27, pp. 43–55.

Rumelt, R., 1991. How much does industry matter? *Strategic Management Journal*, 12(3), pp. 167–185.

Samuelson, P., 1954. The pure theory of public expenditure. *The Review of Economics and Statistics*, 36(4), pp. 387–389.

Sanchez, R. and Heene, A., 1997. Reinventing strategic management: New theory and practice for competence-based competition. *European Management Journal*, 15(3), pp. 303–317.

Schillemans, T., 2011. Does horizontal accountability work?: Evaluating potential remedies for the accountability deficit of agencies. *Administration & Society*, 43(4), pp. 387–416.

Scholes, K. and Johnson, G., 2001. *Exploring public sector strategy.* Harlow, UK; New York: Financial Times; Prentice Hall.

Scott, R., 1991. Unpacking institutional arguments. In: W. Powell and P. Dimaggio, eds, *The new institutionalism and organizational analysis.* Chicago: The University of Chicago Press, pp. 164–182.

Scott, W., 2000. *Institutional change and healthcare organizations: from professional dominance to managed care.* Chicago: University of Chicago Press.

Sekhri, N., Feachem, R. and Ni, A., 2011. Public-private integrated partnerships demonstrate the potential to improve health care access, quality, and efficiency. *Health Affairs*, 30(8), pp. 1498–1507.

Shapiro, S., 1987. The social control of impersonal trust. *American Journal of Sociology*, 93(3), pp. 623–658.

Silver, M., 2007. Fiscalism in the emergence and extinction of societates publicanorum. *Pomoerium*, 6, pp. 47–71.

Simmel, G. and Wolff, K., 1964. *The sociology of Georg Simmel.* New York: The Free Press.

Simon, H., 1955. A behavioral model of rational choice. *The Quarterly Journal of Economics*, 69(1), pp. 99–118.

Simon, H., 1979a. *Models of thought.* New Haven: Yale University Press.

Simon, H., 1979b. Rational decision making in business organizations. *The American Economic Review*, **69**(4), pp. 493–513.

Simon, H., 1991. *Models of my life*. New York: Basic Books.

Simon, H., 1998. Why public administration? *Journal of Public Administration Research and Theory*, **8**(1), pp. 1–11.

Simon, H. and Barnard, C., 1947. *Administrative behavior: a study of decision-making processes in administrative organization*. New York: Macmillan Co.

Skelcher, C., 2005. Public-private partnerships. In: E. Ferlie, L. Lynn and C. Pollitt, eds, *The Oxford handbook of public management*. New York: Oxford University Press, pp. 347–370.

Skelcher, C. and Smith, S., 2015. Theorizing hybridity: Institutional logics, complex organizations, and actor identities: The case of nonprofits. *Public Administration*, **93**(2), pp. 433–448.

Smith, P., 1995. On the unintended consequences of publishing performance data in the public sector. *International Journal of Public Administration*, **18**(2–3), pp. 277–310.

Sokal, A., 1996. Transgressing the boundaries: An afterword. *Dissent*, **43**(4), pp. 93–99.

Sorsa, V., 2016. Public-private partnerships in European old-age pension provision: An accountability perspective. *Social Policy & Administration*, **50**(7), pp. 846–874.

Sorsa, V. and Johanson, J., 2014. Institutional work and accountability in public-private partnerships. *International Review of Public Administration*, **19**(2), pp. 193–205.

Sprenger, C., 2010. State ownership in the Russian economy: Its magnitude, structure and governance problems. *The Journal of Institute of Public Enterprise*, **33**(1&2), pp. 63–110.

Stark, D., 2009. *The sense of dissonance: accounts of worth in economic life*. Princeton: Princeton University Press.

Staw, B. and Epstein, L., 2000. What bandwagons bring: Effects of popular management techniques on corporate performance, reputation, and CEO pay. *Administrative Science Quarterly*, **45**(3), pp. 523–556.

Stern, J., 2000. Electricity and telecommunications regulatory institutions in small and developing countries. *Utilities Policy*, **9**(3), pp. 131–157.

Streeck, W., 2014. *Buying time: the delayed crisis of democratic capitalism*. London: Verso.

Swoyer, C., 1987. The metaphysics of measurement. In: J. Forge, ed, *Measurement, realism and objectivity*. Dordrecht: Springer, pp. 235–290.

Taro, K., 2016. *The attribution problem in performance measurement in the public sector: lessons from performance audits in Estonia*. Tallinn: Tallinn University of Technology.

Thelen, K., 2012. Varieties of capitalism: Trajectories of liberalization and the new politics of social solidarity. *Annual Review of Political Science*, **15**, pp. 137–159.

Thévenot, L., Moody, M. and Lafaye, C., 2000. Forms of valuing nature: Arguments and modes of justification in French and American environmental disputes. In: M. Lamont and L. Thévenot, eds, *Rethinking comparative cultural sociology: repertoires of evaluation in France and the United States*. Cambridge: Cambridge University Press, pp. 229–272.

Thomas, W. and Janowitz, M., 1966. *On social organization and social personality: selected papers*. Chicago: University of Chicago Press.

Thompson, G., 2003. *Between hierarchies and markets: the logic and limits of network forms of organization*. Oxford; New York: Oxford University Press.

Thynne, I., 2011. Ownership as an instrument of policy and understanding in the public sphere: Trends and research agenda. *Policy Studies*, **32**(3), pp. 183–197.

Thynne, I. and Wettenhall, R., 2010. Symposium on ownership in the public sphere. *International Journal of Public Policy*, **5**(1), pp. 1–102.

Tilly, C., 2006. *Regimes and repertoires*. Chicago: University of Chicago Press.

Toninelli, P., 2008. *The rise and fall of state-owned enterprise in the Western world*. Cambridge: Cambridge University Press.

Tripplett, J., 2007. Zvi Griliche's contributions to economic measurement. In: E. Berndt and C. Hulten, eds, *Hard-to-measure goods and services: essays in honour of Svi Griliches*. Chicago: University of Chicago Press, pp. 573–590.

Tugores-García, A., 2013. *Analysis of global airline alliances as a strategy for international network development*. Cambridge, MA: Massachusetts Institute of Technology.

Tversky, A. and Kahneman, D., 1974. Judgment under uncertainty: Heuristics and biases. *Science*, **185**(4157), pp. 1124–1131.

UNESCO, 2009–last update. Introduction to satellite accounts. Training course material for e-library on system of national accounts [Homepage of United Nations] [Online]. Available: http://dqaf.uis.unesco.org/images/1/13/SIAP-Introduction_to_Satellite_Accounts.pdf; [01/18/2017].

United Nations, 2003. *Handbook on non-profit institutions in the system of national accounts*. New York: United Nations.

United Nations, 2009. *System of national accounts 2008*. New York: European Communities, International Monetary Fund, Organisation for Economic Co-operation and Development.

Vakkuri, J., 2003. Research techniques and their use in managing non-profit organisations – An illustration of DEA analysis in NPO environments. *Financial Accountability & Management*, **19**(3), pp. 243–263.

Vakkuri, J., 2010. Struggling with ambiguity: Public managers as users of NPM-oriented management instruments. *Public Administration*, **88**(4), pp. 999–1024.

Vakkuri, J., 2013. Interpretive schemes in public sector performance: Measurements creating managerial problems in local government. *International Journal of Public Sector Performance Management*, **2**(2), pp. 156–174.

Vakkuri, J. and Meklin, P., 2006. Ambiguity in performance measurement: A theoretical approach to organisational uses of performance measurement. *Financial Accountability and Management*, **22**(3), pp. 235–250.

Vakkuri, J., Meklin, P. and Oulasvirta, L., 2006. Emergence of markets – Institutional change of municipal auditing in Finland. *Nordic Organization Studies*, **8**, pp. 1–31.

Van der Wal, Z., Graaf, G.D. and Lasthuizen, K., 2008. What's valued most? Similarities and differences between the organizational values of the public and private sector. *Public Administration*, **86**(2), pp. 465–482.

Van Dooren, W., 2005. What makes organisations measure? Hypotheses on the causes and conditions for performance measurement. *Financial Accountability & Management*, **21**(3), pp. 363–383.

Van Dooren, W., Forthcoming. A bull in a China shop? How performance targets confront complexity and survive. *Public Money & Management*,.

Van Dooren, W., Bouckaert, G. and Halligan, J., 2015. *Performance management in the public sector*. Milton Park: Routledge.

Van Dooren, W. and Van de Walle, S., 2008. *Performance information in the public sector: how it is used*. Basingstoke, Hampshire, UK; New York: Palgrave Macmillan.

Van Helden, J., Johnsen, Å. and Vakkuri, J., 2008. Distinctive research patterns on public sector performance measurement of public administration and accounting disciplines. *Public Management Review*, **10**(5), pp. 641–651.

Van Helden, J., Johnsen, Å. and Vakkuri, J., 2012. The life-cycle approach to performance management: Implications for public management and evaluation. *Evaluation*, **18**(2), pp. 159–175.

Vanoli, A., 2005. *A history of national accounting*. Washington, DC: IOS Press.

Vedung, E., 2010. Four waves of evaluation diffusion. *Evaluation*, **16**(3), pp. 263–277.

Vickers, D., 1997. *Economics and ethics: an introduction to theory, institutions, and policy.* Westport: Praeger.
Vining, A. and Globerman, S., 1999. A conceptual framework for understanding the outsourcing decision. *European Management Journal*, **17**(6), pp. 645–654.
Virtanen, P. and Vakkuri, J., 2015. Searching for organizational intelligence in the evolution of public-sector performance management. *Journal of Public Administration and Policy*, **8**(2), pp. 89–99.
Vries, P.D. and Yehoue, E.B., 2013. *The Routledge companion to public-private partnerships.* Abingdon, Oxon, UK; New York: Routledge.
Ward, M., 2006. An intellectual history of national accounting. *Review of Income and Wealth*, **52**(2), pp. 327–340.
Wasserman, S. and Faust, K., 1994. *Social network analysis: methods and applications.* Cambridge; New York: Cambridge University Press.
Weber, M. and Winckelmann, J., 1985. *Gesammelte Aufsätze zur Wissenschaftslehre.* Tübingen: J.C.B. Mohr.
Weick, K.E., 1976. Educational organizations as loosely coupled systems. *Administrative Science Quarterly*, **21**(1), pp. 1–19.
Weick, K.E., 1995. *Sensemaking in organizations.* Thousand Oaks: Sage Publications.
Weiner, B., 1986. *An attributional theory of motivation and emotion.* New York: Springer-Verlag.
Wenger, E., 1998. *Communities of practice: learning, meaning, and identity.* Cambridge: Cambridge University Press.
Whitley, R., 2000. *Divergent capitalisms: the social structuring and change of business systems.* Oxford; New York: Oxford University Press.
Whittington, R., 1993. *What is strategy, and does it matter?* London; New York: Routledge.
Wildavsky, A.B., 1986. *Budgeting: a comparative theory of the budgeting process.* Oxford: Transaction Publishers.
Williamson, O.E., 1985. *The economic institutions of capitalism: firms, markets, relational contracting.* New York: Free Press.
Williamson, O.E., 1999a. *The economic institutions of capitalism: firms, markets, relational contracting.* Beijing: China Social Sciences Publishing House.
Williamson, O.E., 1999b. *The mechanisms of governance.* New York: Oxford University Press.
Williamson, O., 2000. The new institutional economics: Taking stock, looking ahead. *Journal of Economic Literature*, **38**(3), pp. 595–613.
Wilson, J.Q., 1989. *Bureaucracy: what government agencies do and why they do it.* New York: Basic Books.
Woolcock, M., 2001. Microenterprise and social capital: A framework for theory, research, and policy. *Journal of Socio-Economics*, **30**(2), pp. 193–198.
World Bank, 2014. *Corporate governance of state-owned enterprises: a toolkit.* Washington, DC: World Bank Group.
Xu, G.J. and Wu, Y., 2015. A study on collaboration between the government and enterprises in the construction and operation of China's highway. In: Y. Jing, ed, *The road to collaborative governance in China.* New York: Palgrave Macmillan, pp. 171–184.
Zuidberg, J. and Veldhuis, J., 2012. *The role of regional airports in a future transportation system.* Amsterdam: SEO Economisch Onderzoek.

INDEX

accountability in public-private partnerships 123–6
Accounting, Organizations and Society 131
administrative pragmatism 69–73
agency theory 22
Airbus A380 aircraft 4
airlines 61–3, 140–1; dyadic nature of 66; as singular entities 64–5; triadic governance 66–7
Allen, D. 32
All Organizations Are Public 24
ambiguity 109–10, 126–7
American Society for Public Administration 22
audiences, multiple 139, 150–1, 152
authority 25

balancing of goals 146
Behn, R. 114, 132
Beijing-Shanghai High-Speed Railway 4
blood donation 35–6
Boltanski, L. 33
Borges, J. 12
bounded rationality 76–7
Boyne, George 25–7
Bozeman, Barry 24–5
Bremmer, I. 82
bureaucracy 90

Calhoun, C. 30
capitalism 20
Celestial Emporium of Benevolent Knowledge 12

Channel Tunnel 4
characteristics of hybrids 2–4
China highway network 28–9
classification principles 12–13, 160; making sense of public-private distinctions 67–73
cleantech industry 49–51, 141–2
clientelist communities 154
Cochran, C. 38
collusion 90
commercial moral syndrome 2
common pool goods 30
competing institutional logics 3–4
connecting positions 145–6
consequentialist logic 115
contracting out 41
control, managerial 86–7
control systems, public and private forms of 4
Cooke, P. 50
Coxa Hospital 96–7, 141

decision-making in distinguishing public from private 76–8
Denhardt, J. 37
Denhardt, R. 37
design, strategic 9, 88–93, 164–5; in hybrid organisations 90–1; in private enterprises 88–9; in public agencies 89–90
distinctions, public-private 67–73
Dixon, R. 42
Dopfer, K. 51, 52
dual reciprocities 147–8
dyadic nature of air travel 66

economic sociology 32–3
economy 11, 113, *118,* 119, 120–1
effectiveness 11–12, 114, *118,* 119–20, 121
efficiency 11, 114, *118,* 119, 121
Emery, F. 85
Etzioni, A. 89
external and internal approaches to hybridity 161–2
externalities 19

feedback, outcome 145
Friedman, Milton 40
funding, multiplicity of arrangements for 4
future, justification of the 151–2

global air travel *See* airlines
goals: balancing 146; incongruence 3–4; reasonable 151
Goldman Sachs 38
governance, hybrid: adaptation and change in strategy formation for 8–10; external and internal approaches to 161–2; in global air travel 61–3; national innovation systems as 53–7; over time 17–22, 140; public policy considerations 57–9; as solution to governance problems 167–8; for solving tricky problems of health policy 46–7; in state-owned enterprises 91–3; triadic 66–7; tricky problems of 4–8
governance, strategic 10, 98–103; in hybrid organisations 101–3; in private enterprises 99–100; in public agencies 100–1
grammar 34
Greve, C. 41–2
grey area entities 75–6
Griliches, Z. 127
guardian moral syndrome 2
Guthrie, J. 95

Harrington-Buhay, N. 39
health policy, hybrid governance for solving problems of 46–7
Heene, A. 89
heuristics in combining public and private resources 144–5
history of hybrid governance 17–22, 140
Hodge, G. 41–2
Hodges, R. 130
Hood, C. 42
Hopwood, A. 131
hospital development in Finland 96–7
Hudson, J. 27, 28

human capital 86
hybrid industries 48, 49–50
hybridity 158–9; concept of 1–2, 159–60; contexts of 140–2; by design and by default 165–7; different forms of 13–14, 160; different perspectives of 43–4; empirical categorisations used to classify 5–6; and hybrids in context of government reforms 39–42, 160; as institutional solution to governance problems 167–8; levels of 45–51; as levels of societal activities 44–5
hybrid organisations 1–2, 158–9; characteristics of 2–4; classification of 13; design in 90–1; as deviations from a perceived optimum 162–4; goal incongruence and competing institutional logics 3–4; and hybridity in context of government reforms 39–42; legitimacy of activities 6; mixed ownership 3; multiple audiences and environments faced by 139, 150–1, 152; multiplicity of funding arrangements 4; performance measurement 10–12, 116–17, 121–38; public agencies 81; public and private forms of financial and social control over 4; public policy considerations with 57–9; scanning in 96; as singular, dyadic, and multilateral structures 59–67; state-owned enterprises 81–3; strategic governance in 101–3; strategies for muddling through with 164–5; theoretical underpinnings of 139–40; *See also* governance, hybrid
hybrid systems 48
hybrid universities 135–8, 141

imitation 166–7
industries, hybridization of 48, 49–50
innovations, creation of 148–9
institutional logics, competing 3–4
internal and external approaches to hybridity 161–2
International Space Station 4

Jacobs, Jane 2
joint action sequencing 143–4
Jones, P. 27, 28
justification of hybrid activities 150–2

Kahneman, Daniel 76, 77
Koopmans, T. 11
Koppell, J. 126
Kurunmäki, L. 131

Lane 30
legacy 152–3
legitimacy: harvesting of 148; through performance 155–7; through strategy 152–5
levels of hybridity 45–51
Lindblom, C. 25, 89
Linnaeus, Carl 68

macro level of societal analysis 51–7, 142
Mahoney, J. 37–8
managerial control 86–7
Mansbridge, J. 30
March, J. 132
Margolis, J. 28
Ménard, C. 3
meso as constitutive level of analysis 51–7, 141
Meyer, M. 110, 111
micro level of societal analysis 51–7
Miller, P. 131
mixed ownership in hybridity 3
Morrell, K. 30, 39
motto *118*
muddling-through strategies 164–5
multiplicity of funding arrangements 4

national innovation systems 53–7
Nelson, R. 128
New Public Management (NPM) 24, 39–40
nonprofit institutions (NPIs) 74–5; social enterprises 84

Occam's Razor 11, 119
OECD countries 39–40; national innovation systems 54–6
order of worth 33–7
organisational logics 44–5
organisational reasoning 22–7
O'Rourke, A. 49
Ostrom, E. 31
Otley, D. 110–11
outcome feedback 145
outsourcing 100
ownership: mixed 3; optimal structure 22

Padgett, J. 51
Panzar, J. 119
past, justification of the 151–2
pension provision, European 123–6
performance: dimensions in three contexts of institutional action 117–21; legitimisation through 155–7; metrics 132–3; performance, performativity, and quantification of 106–9; polysemic 109–10; *See also* strategy-performance interfaces
performance measurement 10–12, 109; elements of 121–2; measurees 127–9; measurer and problem of accountability in hybrid settings 122–7; principles applied to hybrid settings 121–38; in private enterprises 110–12; problems in hybrid organisations 116–17; problems in hybrid universities 135–8; in the public sector 112–16, 120; results 131–8; system 129–31
performativity 106–9, 133
Petro Vietnam Power Corporation 91–3
Pettigrew, A. 143
Petty, R. 95
Pierson, P. 77
Polanyi, Karl 20
polities 33–4
polysemic performance 109–10
Porter, T. 115
Powell, W. 51
private enterprises: design in 88–9; in history 17–22; organisational reasoning and 22–7; performance measurement in 110–12; scanning in 94–5; strategic governance in 99–100; strategy formation in 103–5
private goods 31
privatisation 41
profit seeking 10–12
property rights 25, 31
public agencies 81; performance 112–16, 120; scanning in 95–6; state-owned enterprises 81–3; strategic governance in 100–1; strategy formation in 103–5
public and private interests 37–9
public goods 27–8; classification of 30; properties of 31
public organisations: in history 17–22; organisational reasoning and 22–7
public policy considerations with hybrid governance 57–9
public-private interaction 5; beauty of simplification in distinguishing public from private and 76–8; dealing with 73–4; in hospital development in Finland 96–7; making sense of distinctions in 67–73; organisational reasoning and 22–3
public-private partnerships (PPPs) 41–2, 73–4, 100, 160; accountability in 123–5
Putnam, R. 149

quantification of performance 106–9, 121

Ranson, S. 67
rationality 162–4
reciprocities, dual 147–8
reforms, hybrids and hybridity in context of government 39–42
Richard, P. 111–12
rivalry of consumption 31
Roman Republic 17–19, 140, 165
rule systems 130–1

Samuelson, Paul 27, 28, 31, 32
Sanchez, R. 89
scanning, strategic 9–10, 94–8; in hybrid organisations 96; in private enterprises 94–5; in public agencies 95–6
Schillemans, T. 122–3
Scott, R. 45
Simon, Herbert 22–3
simplification 76–8, 166
singular entities 64–5
social capital 86, 154–5
social enterprises 84
social networks 33; analysis 99–100
social welfare 153–4
societal activities: hybridity as levels of 44–5; meso as constitutive level of analysis of 51–7
societal value 27–37; hybrid activities 6–7; public goods 27–8
space between public and private 5
Stark, D. 116, 147
state-owned enterprises (SOEs) 81–3, 149, 154; design in hybrid 90–1; hybrid governance in 91–3; scanning in 97–8; strategic governance in 102
strategic design 9, 88–93, 164–5; in hybrid organisations 90–1; in private enterprises 88–9; in public agencies 89–90
strategic governance 10, 98–103; in hybrid organisations 101–3; in private enterprises 99–100; in public agencies 100–1
strategic scanning 9–10, 94–8; in hybrid organisations 96; in private enterprises 94–5; in public agencies 95–6
strategy, legitimisation through 152–5
strategy formation 8–10, 79–81; analytic dimensions of 85–7; assumptions about environment in 85–6; in business, public, and hybrid contexts 103–5; managerial control and 86–7; in public agencies 81; role of strategy and 85; in state-owned enterprises and social enterprises 81–4; strategic design mode in 88–93; strategic governance mode in 98–103; strategic scanning mode in 94–8; types of capital and 86; *See also* strategy-performance interfaces
strategy-performance interfaces 139–40; administering doses for synergy at 146–7; balancing goals at 146; creating innovations at 148–9; establishing connecting positions at 145–6; harvesting legitimacy at 148; heuristics in combining public and private resources 144–5; in hybrid activities 142–9; hybridity contexts and 140–2; integrating communities and 149; joint action sequencing 143–4; as problem in the justification of hybrid activities 150–2; weighing dual reciprocities at 147–8
subtractability of use 31
Sutton, R. 132
synergy 146–7
System of National Accounts (SNA) 69–73, 160; dealing with entities in the grey area and 75–6; dealing with nonprofits and 74–5; dealing with public-private interaction and 73–4

Thévenot, L. 33, 116
toll goods 30
transaction cost framework 99–100
triadic governance 66–7
triple helix communities 155
Trist, E. 85
Tversky, A. 77

United Nations 75
universities, hybrid 135–8

valuation of activities in society *See* societal value
value creation 11–12, 119–20
Van der Wal, Z. 23, 24
Van Dooren, W. 134
venture capitalists 49
vouchers 40–1

Wertfreiheit principle 115
Whitley, R. 45
Willig, R. 119
worth, order of 33–7